Behavior modification is one of the newest approaches to correctional rehabilitation and management, challenging traditional thinking about the classification and remediation of the problems experienced by criminals, delinquents, and disturbed persons. How does behavior modification compare with established psychological methods? What principles are followed, and what techniques are used? Have favorable results been achieved by institutions adopting a behavior modification program?

This major study answers all these questions and more, concluding that behavior modification has considerable promise as an effective and ethical approach to rehabilitation and management. After first exploring current diagnostic procedures and finding little evidence that they improve rehabilitation and management practices, the authors then investigate the behavioral approach to problem behavior in detail, including a thorough discussion of specific techniques employed. This is supplemented by a description of program evaluation procedures and a discussion of ethical issues. The final section contains case studies of two behaviorally-based rehabilitation programs in maximum-security institutions. Here, behavior modification encouraged inmates to participate in rehabilitation programs and achieve stated objectives, offering them a means of preserving and enhancing their dignity and individuality while at the same time providing them with remedial education and vocational training.

Psychologists, sociologists, and everyone involved in the criminal justice system will discover through this illuminating work a psychological approach to rehabilitation and management that already gives evidence of being a highly effective method for the successful treatment of criminal offenders and the mentally ill.

791

CORRECTIONAL REHABILITATION AND MANAGEMENT

WILEY SERIES IN BEHAVIOR

KENNETH MacCORQUODALE, Editor

University of Minnesota

CORRECTIONAL REHABILITATION AND MANAGEMENT: A Psychological Approach

TEODORO AYLLON
Georgia State University

and

MICHAEL A. MILAN
Georgia State University

with the assistance of

MICHAEL D. ROBERTS
Columbus Mental Health Complex

and

JOHN M. McKEE
Rehabilitation Research Foundation

A WILEY-INTERSCIENCE PUBLICATION

JOHN WILEY & SONS, New York • Chichester • Brisbane • Toronto

Library of Congress Cataloging in Publication Data:

Ayllon, Teodoro, 1929—
   Correctional rehabilitation and management.

   (Wiley series in behavior)
   "A Wiley-Interscience publication."
   Includes index.
   1.   Correctional psychology.   2.   Rehabilitation
of criminals.   3.   Behavior modification.
I.   Milan, Michael A., joint author.   II.   Title.
HV9275.A94   365'.7   78-21703
ISBN 0-471-03843-1

Printed in the United States of America

10 9 8 7 6 5 4 3 2 1

FOREWORD

In 1976 we celebrated our nation's two-hundredth anniversary. During those years the American people have overcome almost every hardship, and have come to lead the world in almost every field. Yet the perplexing phenomena of crime and the criminal remain. The plain fact is that we have made significantly less progress toward solving the problems of crime and delinquency than have many of the other nations of this world. Why? Can we move to a position of leadership here as we have in so many other areas? How?

There are many reasons one could assign to the increasingly frightening and costly dilemma in which we now find ourselves regarding the treatment of those we call delinquent and criminal: feelings we harbor toward those so labelled; lack of interest and involvement by members of the scientific and intellectual communities; failure of the criminal justice system to demonstrate that an investment of financial and human resources can and will help to alleviate at least some of the problems that confront us. Perhaps a more accurate reason, despite claims to the contrary by the many voices now clamoring for easy administrative or political solutions, is that this nation has not yet really tried to correct the criminal offender.

Many will argue that the system called *corrections* does not and cannot work—that we should scrap it along with any notions we might have of the possibility of one person's influencing the conduct of another in a positive way if that other person has been convicted of a criminal act. They will argue that we should return to a criminal justice system that exists to mete out retribution and to punish those who, for whatever reason, have violated the laws of society—despite the fact that such a model has never discouraged criminal behavior in our culture.

The prospects of what we must become if the punishment model is

v

adopted and actively pursued is both frightening and dehumanizing. If Americans continue to cherish the liberties they hold dear, stand up for and defend their constitutional rights, and appreciate the complexities and apparent inconsistencies involved in defending their freedoms, I predict that the punishment model will never gain prominence in this country. I pray that I am right.

This is a book about corrections—about the rehabilitation and management of the imprisoned public offender. Its authors eschew the punishment model and with it the nostrums and pat solutions about which we hear and read daily. They set forth in a comprehensive and systematic manner a refreshingly new approach to dealing directly and effectively with the very behaviors it appears so essential to modify or to develop. Yet, the emphasis is on a positive and humane strategy that permits choices for the prisoner and encourages his learning of adjustive skills in an environment fostering responsibility and maximizing self-management—the meaning of real freedom.

The studies described in this book were conducted, interestingly enough, within the confines of two correctional institutions—one in Alabama, and the other in Georgia. Where custom and practices have not become too rigidly and bureaucratically entrenched, it is actually easier to introduce change, which more than any other single factor may account for the existence of these two projects. But to make any significant and permanent change, especially toward the goal of rehabilitation, such projects must be institutionalized. If this is to be done, the system of corrections must be understood, and its "politics" dealt with, and its leaders must create an environment that encourages positive innovation.

With few exceptions, correctional institutions have not been designed with a philosophy or goal in mind. Primarily the prison exists or is built prior to the development of an organization or program. The average prison in the United States was built prior to 1930. Seventy-seven of the 113 listed in the 1971 American Correctional Association Directory were built prior to 1930, and six prior to 1830. Further, prisons historically have been constructed far from the major population centers from which their inmates have come. This factor alone precludes the ability of the institution to keep the offender in touch with his or her family and community, raising the degree of institutionalization and thereby diminishing the possible impact of reform programs.

Historically, the building of institutions has been based, not on quality of impact on the offender, but instead on low cost construction. The average prison has been a large institution—so large as to be inoperable, and the offender becomes a number rather than an individual. The men who have tried to operate those institutions and the men who have had to live in them deserve an extra star in their crowns by the higher powers when they leave this earth for having had to live with and in them. I could here then condemn the men who designed them, but there was little if any research data available to help them. They were responding to the hue and cry of the politicians for cheap construction and the attitude of their time regarding the offender.

As we look at most correctional institutions of even recent construction, however, we find that they were designed for three purposes: to house the offender, to feed the offender, and to work the offender. Whereas these are necessary elements of an institution, the architects of many of these facilities did not include areas for recreation, libraries, educational facilities, and the many other activities that every community includes in its planning. Sometimes these amenities were added as afterthoughts if the correctional authority could get funds for construction, and they added to the hodgepodge of the institution, increased the confusion, and complicated the organization of the institutional program. The staffing of these monstrosities have further ensured their failure. Often even the security forces were either too understaffed or too underorganized to achieve their objectives, and, where there were treatment staffs, case loads and teaching loads were so large that they too were doomed to failure.

The goals of a correctional institution should be to safely house offenders sent by the court and to offer them an opportunity to retain their individuality and improve their abilities to live and deal with their environments, both within the institution and in the outside world. As we move toward these goals we must constantly evaluate our progress. Our society, with the economic crunch of the recent years, is now looking to government for accountability. The taxpayers are not allowing public administration to spend their funds without wanting some measure of return on their investment. Corrections should be prepared to demonstrate its worth.

Another function vital to the success of the corrections agency—to which we have failed to devote the proper amount of resources, in time, funds, or planning—is the training of personnel. We need to invest in people. Studies have shown that line-level people have the most effective impact on our offenders, yet we consistently fail to train them. It is my feeling that this function should receive all the sophisticated supervision an agency can generate. I fear that agencies in which training is supervised by institution or agency middle management tend to lack knowledge of learning theory. Further, they teach the new employee the bad habits and platitudes of the past. The supervising authority of training should be thoroughly versed in learning theory, new teaching equipment, and methods; should be committed to innovative directions; and should be instructing toward new horizons, not into the darkness of the past.

Corrections is an emerging profession. It is only in recent years that programs have reached maturity. It is my opinion that the field of corrections can make a meaningful contribution to criminal justice. We must be allowed to try. I have outlined practical ways in which the corrections system can be changed to become an effective tool of dealing with the offender. The professionals who now lead correctional systems, institutions, and agencies in many states, those who work in the ranks, and the many young people now pursuing education in the field of criminal justice in the colleges and universities of our states can and will impact the future of the field and lead toward change. Efforts such as those described in this book are prototypic of the ways correctional research and application can and should be combined to produce a better correctional system for both those who live in it and those who work in it.

ELLIS C. MACDOUGALL

About the authors

TEODORO AYLLON, Professor of Psychology and Special Education at Georgia State University, was Research Professor of the University of Pennsylvania and Director of Clinical Research at Anna State Hospital in Illinois. He is co-author, with Dr. Nathan Azrin, of THE TOKEN ECONOMY: A MOTIVATIONAL SYSTEM FOR THERAPY AND REHABILITATION. Dr. Ayllon received his Ph.D in Clinical Psychology from the University of Houston. He is a Diplomate in Clinical Psychology from the American Board of Professional Psychology, a Fellow of the American Psychological Association, and a member of the Inter-American Society for Psychology. He is on the Editorial Boards of the *Journal of Behavior Therapy and Experimental Psychiatry* and the *International Journal of Behavior Research and Therapy.*

MICHAEL A. MILAN is Assistant Professor of Clinical and Community Psychology at Georgia State University and a Consultant to the Ohio Division of Forensic Psychiatry. Previously he was a Psychologist at the Experimental Manpower Laboratory for Corrections in Alabama. A member of the Editorial Board of *Criminal Justice and Behavior* and the Executive Committee of the Southeastern Association for Behavior Therapy, Dr. Milan holds a Ph.D. in Psychology from the University of Florida.

MICHAEL D. ROBERTS is Clinical Director of the Regional Mental Health Complex in Columbus, Mississippi. He received his Ph.D. in Psychology from Georgia State University.

JOHN M. McKEE, Executive Director of the Rehabilitation Research Foundation in Alabama and Consultant to the Human Rights Committee of Bryce Hospital in Alabama, is a former Director of the Alabama Division of Mental Hygiene. Dr. McKee is a past president of the Alabama Psychological Association and a recipient of the Alabama Psychological Association's Distinguished Service Award and of the National Society of Performance and Instruction's Award for Outstanding Long-Term Contribution to Educational Technology. He holds a Ph.D in Clinical Psychology from the University of Tennessee.

SERIES PREFACE

Psychology is one of the lively sciences. Its foci of research and theoretical concentration are diverse among us, and always on the move, sometimes into unexploited areas of scholarship, sometimes back for second thoughts about familiar problems, often into other disciplines for problems and for problem-solving techniques. We are always trying to apply what we have learned, and we have had some great successes at it. The Wiley Series in Behavior reflects this liveliness.

The series can accommodate monographic publication of purely theoretical advances, purely empirical ones, or any mixture in between. It welcomes books that span the interfaces within the behavioral sciences and between the behavioral sciences and their neighboring disciplines. The series is, then, a forum for the discussion of those advanced, technical, and innovative developments in the behavior sciences that keep its frontiers flexible and expanding.

KENNETH MACCORQUODALE

Minneapolis, Minnesota

PREFACE

In the past decade there has occurred in applied psychology a veritable revolution in the manner in which seriously disturbing human behavior is examined, understood, and remediated. This new approach is the result of a rapprochement between psychology as a basic science and psychology as an applied science. It represents the first attempt to develop a viable science of human behavior that allows the practitioner to implement experimentally derived and validated principles in an applied setting. These principles are stated in clear and unambiguous terms, thereby permitting their easy communication to students and line workers and providing them the tools they so desperately need to become effective change agents. The theory from which these principles arise eschews the use of internal entities or processes inferred from the behavior they pretend to explain. It deals, instead, with specifiable relationships between acts and their antecedents and consequences through which the causes of behavior may be understood.

Unlike the more traditional approach, the hallmarks of this new approach are empiricism and objectivity. The new practitioner recognizes the importance of constantly monitoring and evaluating progress in an empirical manner. The statement of goals and desired outcomes in objective terms is an accepted practice. Only by so doing can the effectiveness of the procedures that have been implemented be determined and these, if found lacking, be replaced by alternative procedures. The adherents of this approach—variously labeled *operant conditioning, behavior modification, contingency management, applied behavior analysis,* and *behavior therapy*—see behavior as lawful. That is, behavior is viewed as a natural result of the learning history of the individual acts, and the regular consequences of the behavior. This book describes two projects that demonstrate how this new approach may be used to encourage prison inmates to participate and achieve in prison rehabilitation programs while at the same time preserving and enhancing their dignity and individuality.

T. Ayllon and M. Roberts acknowledge the contribution of Henry Kandel, Kathleen C. Kelly, Janet Volkman, Bob Dobes, and Rhonda Traylor to several of the studies in the Motivating Offender Rehabilitation Environment (MORE) project. The staff of the Program Development section of the Georgia Department of Offender Rehabilitation, in particular Richard E. Longfellow, William E. Baughman, and Margaret Veal, lent great support to the project. The MORE project owes its greatest debt to David E. England, Superintendent of the Georgia Training and Development Center, and to Paul De Francis, his successor as superintendent, for their interest, encouragement, and assistance.

Michael A. Milan and John M. McKee express their appreciation to Warden John C. Watkins, Classification Officer Wayne Booker, and Correctional Officer W. O. Brown of the Draper Correctional Center, and to staff members Robert R. Smith, Larry F. Wood, Robert L. Williams, Jerry G. Rogers, Lee R. Hampton, Michael Murphy, and Charles M. Petko of the Experimental Manpower Laboratory for Corrections (EMLC), who contributed greatly to the success of the EMLC projects described herein.

The authors also express special thanks and appreciation to the inmates of Buford Prison and Draper Correctional Center whose participation in the rehabilitative efforts described herein made the programs both possible and worthwhile, as well as to Steven Simon and Maurie Freed for their careful reading of this manuscript, to Michael Cole and Jeff Kresch for assistance in proofing and indexing the text, and to Deanna Hellman and Lindsay Davis for the typing of the final draft. The studies reported here were supported in part by the Georgia Department of Offender Rehabilitation Grant No. 433 and by the Georgia Bureau of State Planning and Community Affairs, Grant No. 72E−0006, and Grant No. 21−01−73−38 with the Manpower Administration of the U.S. Department of Labor. Organizations undertaking such projects under Federal Government sponsorship are encouraged to express their own judgment freely. Therefore, points of view or opinions stated in this document do not necessarily represent the official position or policy of the Department of Labor or other federal agencies mentioned herein.

TEODORO AYLLON
MICHAEL A. MILAN
MICHAEL D. ROBERTS
JOHN M. MCKEE

Atlanta, Georgia
February 1979

CONTENTS

CORRECTIONAL REHABILITATION AND MANAGEMENT

CHAPTER

$$\boxed{1}$$

INTRODUCTION

In order to monitor the incidence of adult and juvenile crime in the United States, the Federal Bureau of Investigation (FBI) operates the Uniform Crime Reporting Program (UCRP). The FBI's UCRP is a clearinghouse for the crime statistics of over 13,000 law enforcement agencies. As of 1976, the last year for which complete data of the incidence of crime is available at this writing, UCRP represented 98 percent of the country's population living in the U.S. Bureau of The Census' Standard Metropolitan Statistical Areas, 94 percent of the population in other cities, and 89 percent of the rural population. This coverage represents 96 percent of the total national population as estimated by the Bureau of the Census (U.S. Department of Justice, 1976). Accordingly, the UCRP provides a periodic, nationwide assessment of crime not available elsewhere in the criminal justice system. It provides the workers in the area of crime and delinquency a data base which is not available to most professionals working in other human service delivery systems.

Two types of data are maintained. The first is a record of all complaints of crimes received by law enforcement agencies from victims, other sources, and those that are discovered by police officers. The second is a record of the characteristics of individuals who have been arrested by law enforcement agencies. The record of offenses committed is broken down into two parts: Part I offenses are serious "index"

1

crimes and Part II offenses represent the remainder of the crimes recorded. Part I, or index crimes are offenses which fall into the following seven categories: (1) criminal homicide; (2) aggravated assault; (3) forcible rape; (4) robbery; (5) burglary; (6) larceny and theft; and (7) motor vehicle theft. The first three categories are considered "crimes of violence" while the last three are considered "crimes against property." Traffic violations are not included in this reporting system.

In the UCRP, the classification of offenses is based entirely upon police investigation as opposed to the determination of a court, medical examiner, coroner, etc. Criminal homicide (murder and non-negligent manslaughter) is defined as the willful killing of another. Aggravated assault is the unlawful attack by one person upon another for the purpose of inflicting severe bodily injury usually accompanied by the use of a weapon. Attempted murder is included in this second category.

Forcible rape is defined as the carnal knowledge of a female through the use of force or threat of force. Forcible attempts to commit rape are also included here but statutory rape without force is not. Robbery is the stealing or taking of anything of value from a person in his presence by force or by the threat of force. Attempted robbery is also reported here. Burglary is defined as the unlawful entry of a structure to commit a theft or other felony. The use of force to gain entry is not required to classify a crime as a burglary. Larceny and theft are defined as the unlawful taking or stealing of property or articles without the use of force, violence, or fraud. This category includes such crimes as shoplifting, pocket-picking, and purse-snatching while excluding such offenses as embezzlement, con games, and forgery. The last index crime, motor vehicle theft, is the unlawful taking or stealing of a motor vehicle.

Part II offenses consist of (1) simple assaults; (2) arson; (3) forgery and counterfeiting; (4) fraud; (5) buying, receiving, or possessing stolen property; (6) vandalism; (7) carrying, possessing, furnishing, manufacturing, etc. of deadly weapons; (8) prostitution and commercial vice; (9) sex offenses excepting forcible rape, prostitution, and commercial vice; (10) violation of narcotic drug laws; (11) gambling; (12) offenses against the family and children; (13) driving under the influence; (14) violation of liquor laws; (15) drunkenness; (16) disorderly conduct; (17) vagrancy; (18) juveniles' violatin of curfew and loitering laws; (19) juvenile runaways; (20) all other arrests excepting traffic laws; and (21) suspicion.

During our bicentennial year, one index crime was reported as having been committed every three seconds; this represented one violent crime every 32 seconds and one property crime every three seconds. Of the violent crimes, aggravated assault was the most common, followed by robbery, forcible rape, and murder. Of the property crimes, larceny and theft were the most common, followed by burglary and motor vehicle theft. A total of 18,780 murders were reported (representing a rate of 8.8 murders per 100,000 inhabitants). This was a decrease of approximately eight percent from the previous year. The typical murderer was a male between 18 and 22 years of age. A firearm was used in 64 percent of these killings. There were 490,850 aggravated assaults committed (228.7 per 100,000 inhabitants), an increase of approximately one percent over the previous year. The typical assaulter was a 19 year old male who used either his hands, fists, or feet in the assault. A total of 56,730 forcible rapes were reported (26.4 per 100,000 inhabitants). This represents an increase of approximately one percent over the previous year. The typical rapist was between 16 and 20 years of age. There were 420,210 robberies committed (196.8 per 100,000 inhabitants), a decrease of approximately 10 percent from the previous year. The typical offender was a male between 15 and 19 years of age.

For the crimes against property, there were 3,089,800 burglaries reported (1,439.4 per 100,000 inhabitants). This represents a decrease of approximately five percent from the previous year. The typical burglar was a male between 13 and 17 years of age. A total of 6,270,800 larcenies and thefts were committed (2,921.3 per 100,000 inhabitants), an increase of approximately four percent over the previous year. The typical thief was also a male between 13 and 17 years of age. Finally, there were 957,600 motor vehicle thefts (446.1 per 100,000 inhabitants). This represents a decrease of approximately five percent from the previous year. Again, the typical offender was a male between 13 and 17 years of age. Although the incidence of index crimes during 1976 is little changed from that of 1975, the figures reported represent an overall increase during the preceding five years of 37 percent in the absolute number of crimes reported and of 33 percent in the crime rate (number of crimes per 100,000 inhabitants). During this same five year period the population of the United States increased only three percent.

As would be expected, the number of reported arrests for index crimes for 1976 was slightly lower than during 1975, representing a seven percent decrease. However, the number of arrests for index crimes during the past five years increased by 44 percent. Arrests of persons under 18 years of age increased 23 percent while arrests of persons over 18 increased 51 percent during the past five years. Nationally, during 1976, persons under 15 years of age represented eight percent of the total arrests reported; persons under 18 accounted for 25 percent of all arrests; persons under 21 accounted for 41 percent of all arrests; and persons under 25 accounted for 57 percent of all arrests.

In real numbers, there was a total of 665,781 children below the age of

15 arrested; 1,307,473 adolescents between 15 and 18 arrested; 1,285,920 young adults between 18 and 21 arrested; and 1,230,865 adults between 21 and 25 arrested. The number of males arrested outnumber the number of females arrested by five to one. However, the number of males arrested during 1976 decreased by six percent while the number of females arrested increased by seven percent. Females accounted for 10 percent of the arrests in the four categories of violent crimes and 22 percent of the arrests in the three categories of property crimes.

A reported crime is said to be "cleared" when a law enforcement agency indicates it has identified the offender, has sufficient evidence to make a charge, and has actually taken that suspect into custody. The arrest of one person can clear several crimes, and conversely, several persons may be arrested in the clearing of one crime. A total of 21 percent of the index crimes committed during 1976 were cleared in this manner. Of the crimes of violence, law enforcement agencies cleared 79 percent of the criminal homicides, 52 percent of the forcible rapes, 63 percent of the aggravated assaults, and 27 percent of the robberies. Of the crimes against property, law enforcement agencies reported they cleared 17 percent of the burglaries, 19 percent of the larcenies and thefts, and 14 percent of the motor vehicle thefts.

Of those persons arrested and charged, 13 percent were acquitted, 18 percent had charges pending at the end of the reporting period, 33 percent were referred to juvenile court, and 36 percent were found guilty (33 percent of the offense with which they were charged and three percent of a lesser charge).

Of those charged with criminal homicide, 57.8 percent were convicted of that offense or of a lesser charge; 52.3 percent of those charged with aggravated assault were convicted; 40.4 percent of those charged with rape were convicted; 44.5 percent of those charged with robbery were convicted; 32.7 percent of those charged with burglary were convicted; 49.1 percent of those charged with larceny and theft were convicted; and 23.6 percent of those charged with motor vehicle thefts were convicted.

As can be seen from the preceeding data, juvenile and adult crime is a national problem of immense proportion, both in terms of absolute amount and the characteristics of the perpetrators. Most crimes are crimes against property (sometimes termed "economic" crimes), and those who commit these crimes are disproportionately young, with more than half those arrested being under 25 years of age. The gravity of the problem is most clearly seen when the number of juvenile and adult offenders in custody is compared to the number of hospitalized mental patients and institutionalized mental retardates (U.S. Department of

Commerce, 1977). At the end of 1975, 202,971 persons were patients in public and private psychiatric hospitals; 159,041 persons were residents of institutions for the mentally retarded. At the same time, 218,619 adults were confined in state and federal correctional facilities; 141,600 persons were held in jails; and 74,270 juveniles were residents of detention homes and training schools. In actual fact, then, there were more juvenile and adult offenders in custody (434,489) than there were institutionalized psychiatric patients and mental retardates (362,012).

A comparison of the average daily expenditures per person is equally revealing: The average daily expenditure for a person in a psychiatric facility was approximately $41; for a person in an institution for the mentally retarded it was $31; for an imprisoned adult it was $26; for a person detained in a jail it was $19; and for a juvenile in a detention home or training school it was $10. In summary, those professionals working in the criminal justice system are faced with problems which, although qualitatively different, are quantitatively greater than those of their peers in the mental health and mental retardation systems, but they have available to them far fewer financial resources than do their peers in terms of per-client expenditures.

During recent years, increased public concern over what appears to be a steadily rising crime rate and the apparent inability of existing legal, judicial, and correctional procedures to serve as either deterrents to or modifiers of criminal and delinquent behavior has been reflected in widespread demands for reform of the criminal justice system and in an intensive search for effective crime control procedures. Numerous commissions, panels, study groups, committees, conferences, symposiums, and so on, consisting primarily of professionals in the areas of government, law, political science, sociology, criminology, psychiatry, welfare, economics, and occasional representatives from industry and labor, have convened, reviewed the problem, and their conclusions concerning the "causes" of crime and recommendations of steps to be taken to "cure" the problem have been widely disseminated and publicized. In general, the outcome of this search has been a reemphasis of the "multidimensional" nature of the subject matter and of the necessity of attacking crime and delinquency on a wide variety of fronts. It is now generally accepted that this country must move more vigorously toward the elimination of those conditions that have been demonstrated to be correlates of crime: unemployment, poverty, the ghetto, ignorance, injustice, and discrimination in its multitudinous forms, to cite only a few items on a seemingly unending list of social, economic, and political ills.

It must be emphasized that the data upon which the conclusion that these conditions are antecedents of crime are based are, by and large,

correlational in nature, and that to infer cause-and-effect relationships
from such associations is to court error. Within this context, Morris and
Hawkins (1970) have presented evidence which indicates that the
amelioration of these conditions may not result in as significant a decrease in the incidence of crime as would be predicted if one were to
deduce cause-and-effect relationships from the available data. In addition, the structuring of investigations into the origins of criminal behavior along lines which, either implicitly or explicitly, predispose us to
search for identifiable sócial, economic, occupational, educational, or
political "causes" of crime is to propagate an untenable myth. As Morris
and Hawkins have so cogently stated,

> criminals and delinquents cannot be distinguished from noncriminals on the
> basis alone of their physical constitution, intelligence, or economic
> background. And although many different factors have been shown to be
> associated to a greater or lesser degree with crime, it has not proved possible
> to organize and integrate them in a causal theory of criminal behavior. This
> point is sometimes concealed by suggesting that the causes of crime are
> multifactorial or multifactorial-dynamic. But no matter what linguistic ar-
> tifices are employed, the truth is there are no more causes of crime than
> there are causes of human behavior. Or, perhaps put more accurately, the
> causes of human behavior are the causes of crime. (P. 47)

It is not necessary, however, to postulate that the inequities which exist
in America are causally related to crime in order to justify an intensified
effort directed toward their elimination. Indeed, the proper basis for the
advocacy of programs designed to remedy the ills of our society should
not be their apparent close association with crime, but rather that it is
unthinkable to maintain conditions that force people to exist in a deplor-
able state when this country has at its disposal resources which, if
mobilized, would enable us to drastically improve the quality of life of a
substantial proportion of our population. It is a "given," therefore, that
the correction of these conditions is a desired end, an end toward which
we must direct all our available resources, an end toward which we must
start moving *now;* and that if the attainment of this end does indeed
result in a reduction in the incidence of crime, so much the better.

Our present concern is with what we must do to correct our criminal
justice system. We need a system that is administered in an expeditious,
impartial, and reasonable manner. But this system must also benefit
those who experience it, in that they leave it better prepared to
adequately function in our society.

A variety of programs and procedural innovations have been proposed to accomplish this. Some experts have stressed the necessity of

redefining the various components of the criminal justice system itself and, within the context of this redefinition, point out that the effectiveness of the police and the efficiency of the courts must be drastically upgraded. Others have recommended the wide-scale implementation of programs designed to provide preventive intervention for those individuals, both juvenile and adult, who appear likely to engage in antisocial behavior. Still others have urged more extensive utilization of pretrial diversionary procedures incorporating the services available from the various community referral agencies. Similarly, it is frequently pointed out that more and more effective use should be made of probation and parole procedures.

Although professional criminologists may not agree about the specific changes that must be made, most do agree that the criminal justice system itself requires thorough examination and overhaul; that the scope of its efforts is to narrow and requires careful expansion; and that the services it provides are, at best, of marginal quality and require redirection and improvement. Moreover, it appears that corrections, long neglected by both the public and the professional community, demands the closest examination; and its policies, procedures, and mission require almost complete revision.

CONFLICTING ROLES OF CORRECTIONS

A major obstacle to examining and improving correctional efforts is the marked lack of agreement within both the criminal justice system itself and the public at large concerning what the roles and objectives of corrections in society are and how they may best be realized. This is not a new phenomenon. Criminologists have long recognized the problem of disagreement and its effect on program planning, funding, and implementation:

> Our modern prison system is proceeding in a rather uncertain course because its administration is necessarily a series of compromises. On the one hand, prisons are expected to punish; on the other they are supposed to reform. They are expected to discipline rigorously at the same time they teach self-reliance. (Federal Bureau of Prisons, 1948, p. 3)

Indeed, little has changed in this repsect in the past quarter of a century as evidenced by John P. Conrad's more recent observation:

> The dilemmas of corrections have never been so apparent. We hear more often than ever before that the correctional mission is to rehabilitate. It is

obvious that we do not succeed to an extent that satisfies either well-wishers or critics. At the same time a succession of seismic disturbances in the institutions which are central to the apparatus painfully demonstrate our difficulties in even controlling those who are to be rehabilitated. The correctional administrator indeed lives in hard times, made harder because of the enormous expectation now directed at him. (Conrad, 1971, p. 67)

For some, prisons exist simply to mete out retribution upon those who have violated the rights of fellow citizens and see the threat of prison as a crime deterrent. Others advocate imprisonment as a means of protecting the members of society from those who would do them harm. Still others look to the period of imprisonment as the last hope society has of rehabilitating convicted offenders so that they may find a satisfying and productive place in the community. These conflicting views will not be resolved easily, for each contains sufficient truth to ensure its continued advocacy and sufficient error to ensure its continued opposition. The threat of imprisonment undoubtedly does deter some from engaging in criminal acts, if only under certain conditions, such as in the presence of a police officer. Confinement does indeed protect society from the offender, if only for the period of confinement. The services provided within correctional institutions most probably do rehabilitate some offenders, if only the smallest of minorities. However, the present crime rate demonstrates that few potential offenders are effectively deterred by the threat of imprisonment. Additionally, confinement permanently protects the public from only the most dangerous, for more than 95% of those who have been imprisoned eventually return to the community. Finally, most would agree that the hope that prisons will rehabilitate a significant portion of those whom they serve is far from being fulfilled. Recidivism figures indicate that between one- and two-thirds of those who have been imprisoned and released will soon be imprisoned again.

It should not be surprising, therefore, that the confusion surrounding the role of corrections in society and the inadequacies of the criminal justice system in general, have prompted a variety of contradictory and often times incompatible recommendations from members of both the professional community and the concerned citizenry. Some urge a greater emphasis upon the apprehension and conviction of the offender (Murphy, 1972); others demand long prison sentences and harsh conditions of imprisonment (Hoover, 1970); and still others argue for more humane treatment of the imprisoned offender (Menninger, 1968) and a greater emphasis upon rehabilitation through psychotherapy, education, and vocational training (Clark, 1970). A small but growing minority have despaired of corrections' potential and now advocate the abolition of all correctional institutions and the release of those who are currently imprisoned (Mitford, 1973). Not even this is a new recommendation: The great penologist, Frank Tannenbaum (1922), wrote:

> We must destroy the prison, root and branch. That will not solve our problem, but it will be a good beginning . . . . let us substitute something. Almost anything will be an improvement. It cannot be worse. It cannot be more brutal and more useless. A farm, a school, a hospital, a factory, a playground—almost anything different will be better. (P. 12)

Correctional agencies appear to have taken Tannenbaum's plea to heart. Indeed, the current scene in corrections can be characterized as a potpourri of novel and commonsensical but, unfortunately, transient and unvalidated efforts in this direction. A sample of programs that are representative of these efforts has been culled from various newspaper and magazine reports and now follows.

In an attempt to normalize the in-prison environment, it appears that several institutions have initiated coeducational programs whereby men and women offenders are allowed to mingle and study together. Sexual intercourse, however, between any couples is forbidden, even if they are married. The sexes are housed in separate facilities and, at the Fort Worth Correctional Institution, the women's dormitory is locked at night. The Massachusettes Correctional Institution at Framingham is closely patterned after the Forth Worth Prison. Both are minimum-security prisons providing programs for education and vocational training. Other programs include work-release and furloughs. Couples, unless already married, cannot take leave at the same time. The prison population is selected. All participants must be within two years of release, not serious escape risks, not considered predatory, and must be willing to accept the restrictions of the coed concept. They must also participate in intensive training and programming.

The only maximum-security prison where the coeducational program has been effected is at Connecticut's Chesire where men and women are separated in cottages, but share facilities for work, school, job training, medical services, and religion. This type of program is expected to raise morale and deportment, decrease homosexual activities, and give prisoners a better chance of successfully rejoining society.

Somewhat related to the coed concept is the conjugal visit program. In the United States, the State Penitentiary at Parchman, Mississippi, pioneered the program of conjugal visits for men several years ago. They are now offering the same privileges to its women prisoners. Participants must use oral contraceptives and other birth control measures.

Officials claim that this program represents an attempt to preserve the marriges of all their inmates.

Several prisons have begun programs that allow children to visit their parents for an entire day in a less restricted setting. New York State penitentiaries have been the leading proponents and initiators of the project. Bedford Hills Correctional Facility for Women held a "Children's Day" carnival-type affair including 60 inmates and 120 children. Touching was actively encouraged and considered an important aspect of the outing since on regular visits mothers and children are allowed only a short embrace. Similarly, Green Haven Correctional Facility, New York's largest maximum-security prison, holds annual father–son picnics, and New York State's Rikers Island Correctional Institution holds Mother's Day activities.

Several special programs have been initiated by the prisons themselves, interested community groups, and by individuals. These projects cover a diverse area of attempts to help the offender realize the good in himself as well as in society as a whole. Most are attempts to restore some of the dignity that persons have lost as a result of incarceration. At Walla Walla Prison in Washington, "The Bridge, Inc." selects skilled craftsmen to repair and manufacture furniture. The furniture is sold to various organizations and individuals. All participating inmates have at least two years remaining in their sentences and three-fourths of the corporation's employees are serving time for crimes of violence. The men travel statewide, escorted by a guard, to buy, sell, and deliver furniture. They earn hourly wages for their work and officials maintain that they also learn social and business skills to compete in the outside world.

Inmates are taught how to train animals in a rehabilitative program called "Animal Psychology" at the maximum-security California Institution for men in Chino, California. Using Skinnerian methods, a myriad of animals are trained—from dogs to sea lions. Officials feel that participants acquire a new attitude and self-image and, at the same time, acquire skills that can put them at the top of their profession when they leave prison.

At Rahway State Prison in New Jersey, a volunteer organization produced a recording made by "The Escorts." The musical group consisted of five vocalists and two instrumentalists serving time in the maximum-security prison for crimes ranging from breaking-and-entering to murder. They formed the musical group and made an album within the prison. Although some of the men are scheduled for parole, they will be allowed to return freely so that the group can stay together. The president of the volunteer organization "Pathroad" says that the musical venture has pointed the way to further projects to make constructive use of prison time.

Work-release programs have been strongly emphasized. They attempt to rehabilitate prison inmates by enabling them to acquire training and experience outside the prison. Most work-release programs require that the prisoner have some marketable skill before being admitted to the program. Paradoxically, this seems to contradict one of the objectives of work-release—to develop marketable skills. Men at minimum-security Fishkill Correctional Prison in New York must be within one year of release, and have a history of good conduct and a marketable skill before being allowed to participate in the program.

Another work-release program is used in the Morris County Jail in New York. They do not make a marketable skill mandatory; thus labor there is generally unskilled or semiskilled. Inmates must pay board, help with their families' support, help with car costs and taxes. The remaining amount is put into a savings account for them after their release.

Similar to the work-release programs are the education-release programs effected in several institutions across the United States. The objectives are the same: The offender is expected to make a better go of it on the outside if he is equipped with social skills, education, and vocational training. Unfortunately, every prisoner is not given an opportunity. The Virginia State Convict Road Camp provides education-release, but most of the participants have already attended some college. Some men may have even been charged with drug offenses at that very college before being sentenced. As a rule, men who are sent to this camp are younger and more intelligent than the average prison population. Other men who are allowed in similar programs elsewhere are selected on a similar basis.

Many persons convicted of crimes are selected to serve some portion, or perhaps the full length, of their sentences in halfway houses. These residences are usually located in the community. Residents most often are required to work or attend school during the day and to report back to the house at night. No sex or drugs are allowed. Group homes operate on the same basis except that there are fewer residents, usually only 10. Differences between programs are more likely to be due to the clientele rather than to its basic objectives which, for the most part, are related to providing the offender with a more normal social environment, thereby avoiding the dehumanizing effects of institutional incarceration. There are numerous examples of this approach to resocialization.

Yoke Crest in Pennsylvania houses 25 male first-offenders who, officials believe, can be rehabilitated by a halfway program. All are in their teens or twenties and are serving time for crimes such as attempted murder or rape. They are either transferred from other prisons or sent to Yoke Crest directly. Reportedly, participants are not "psychotic," but suffering from "lesser personality disorders." The idea of the encounter group is extended there through a constant peer therapy 24 hours per day. The aim is for the men to face up to themselves and to realize that every inmate is concerned about what happens to the other.

Boys 16 and 17 years of age are sent to Highfield in New Jersey by juvenile courts for periods ranging up to six months. The Director attributes the effects of the program to the pressure that the encounter group sessions bring to bear on the boys, and partly on their realization that, if they are caught again, they will be sentenced to serve time in a conventional reform school.

Besides the encounter group there are other techniques that halfway houses use to effect appropriate behaviors. These may include restriction as punishment or, more effectively, restriction in conjunction with peer pressure. When Washington D.C.'s therapeutic community rehabilitation program for young offenders was about to falter because of increased incidents of crime, drugs, and alcohol and curfew violations, drastic disciplinary measures were taken to prevent the program from being discontinued. If a youth had five positive urine tests for narcotics use he was expelled and sent to Lorton Youth Center. At the first evidence of narcotics, weekend passes were withdrawn for the offender as well as for his fellow house residents. After that, punishment consecutively doubled and tripled for each new drug offense. The narcotics use decreased while inflexible rules for other offenses were legislated. If an individual did not confess his actions, the whole community had privileges suspended. By means of peer pressure, offenders admitted guilt and peers handed down punishment by consensus; for example, signs to be worn around necks, and no telephone use or visitors.

Even in those instances whereby new, innovative, and even effective programs of rehabilitation are implemented, public reaction to them is sometimes unfavorable. Americans, to a large extent, seem to be concerned more with removing the offender from society, than with rehabilitation. In an attempt to improve public attitudes toward one group of offenders, Minnesota has initiated a program of restitution. The Restitution Community Correctional Center can handle 25 adult men and women property offenders who volunteer for the program. They reside in a halfway-house setting in the ghetto community where the offenders come from and will return to. Those accepted into the program repay their victims and at the same time they support themselves and their families. They pay room and board at the center. According to the commissioner of corrections, the major goal of the project is to retain offenders within a community setting in order to provide them an opportunity to take the initiative in redressing wrongs done through deviant acts and to improve the nature of community attitudes.

Similar efforts at finding new solutions to offender rehabilitation are illustrated in innovative sentencing by court judges. Such an example is the case of a New York City Queens criminal court judge who feuded with and even threatened the city correctional commissioner with a stay in one of his own jails if he did not accept a prisoner given a special sentence. The offender was ordered to serve 45 weekends in prison for possession of stolen property. The judge passed the unusual sentence because the defendant was attending school and taking part in a methadone maintenance program—neither of which should be interrupted, the judge said. A Florida judge, on the other hand, gave two youths, aged seventeen and nineteen, the option of teaching black prisoners to read and write or of going to jail. The judge reportedly sees illiteracy as one of the major causes of crime.

Programs have also been effected which attempt to improve relations between offenders and those persons who come into closest contact with them such as probation officers, judges, and prison guards. For example, in San Bernardino, California, a new program was begun to bring young offenders and their probation officers into closer personal contact—they go fishing. "New Horizons" has two objectives according to the coordinator: (a) to lower the barriers between youths and probation people, and (b) to introduce youths to a wholesome kind of recreation they can pursue for the rest of their lives. Reportedly, youths who participate still go fishing regularly with former probation officers after their release.

A somewhat more comprehensive program was implemented at the Connecticut Corrections Academy. Persons who will work as guards, probation officers, judges, and others who will be dealing with prisoners or sending people to prison are involved in a new aspect of training. The weekend project creates prison conditions for them and they, as the prisoners, are purposely given rough treatment to hasten the feelings of frustration and alienation.

Perhaps a less dramatic example is the case of a New Jersey judge who created a program to offer people convicted of minor offenses an opportunity to avoid a full sentence or fine by working for civic or municipal projects. He prefers the "work aspect" of his program because he believes in punishment and feels that his program is merited because he expects it to reduce the number of people graduating from misdemeanors to felonies.

The criminal justice system's new emphasis on accountability has revealed that its eclectic and commonsense beliefs concerning offender rehabilitation are of questionable validity and that the unsystematic intervention programs based on those beliefs are of little utility. Although disappointing, it should not be surprising that, when evaluated, institutional and community correctional programs such as those described previously have little, if any, effect upon recidivism (Crowther, 1969; Glaser, 1964; Lerman, 1968). There is nothing inherent in pretrial diversionary procedures, probation, adult basic education, vocational training, graduated release, parole, and so on, that should lead one to expect that they alone will serve to rehabilitate the offender. If they are to contribute to the solution of the problem of crime in America, they can serve best as vehicles for the systematic application of procedures designed specifically to effect change in the behavior of the offender.

TOWARD REHABILITATION OF THE OFFENDER: TWO SYSTEMATIC
APPROACHES

The criminal justice sysem is now in the position that the mental health profession found itself in a half century ago; both professionals and the informed public alike realize the inadequacies of current practices and are actively engaged in a search for more viable alternatives. The criminal justice system can traverse again the arduous and discouraging paths already explored by the mental health professions, or it can profit by the hard-earned experiences of those in the mental health field. By examining the successes and failures of the psychologist and psychiatrist, the criminologist can circumvent the tangle of inadequate approaches to the understanding of human behavior which has characterized mental health's recent history and from which that field is only now beginning to free itself. It is appropriate, then, to conclude this introduction with a brief overview of the objectives and conclusions stemming from evaluative research in mental health and its allied professions.

Evaluative research in the mental health field has sought to compare the effectiveness of treatment procedures deduced from two influential models of human behavior: the "mental illness" model and the behavioral model. Essentially, adherents to the mental illness model interpret deviant behavior as symptomatic of some underlying personality disturbance in much the same manner as aberrant clinical signs, such as irregularities in pulse and temperature, are taken as symptoms of an underlying physical dysfunction. Successful therapy, according to the mental illness model, calls for diagnosis of the exact nature of an underlying disturbance and subsequent prescription of a proven treatment of choice. The primary objective of treatment is the resolution of the postulated psychic disturbance underlying the deviant behavior through catharsis and insight. The belief is that if the primary symptoms were not dealt with, secondary symptoms or "symptom substitution" would emerge from the inside "diseased" state. By eliminating the "cause," it is hypothesized that both symptoms and any symptom substitution will be precluded and a permanent "cure" insured (e.g., Harrison & Carek, 1966, Greenson, 1967).

Adherents to the behavioral model, on the other hand, view deviant behavior as learned. The principles underlying its acquisition and maintenance are viewed as no different from those governing the acquisition and maintenance of any other behavior. Both deviant and nondeviant behavior are conceptualized as "normal," that is, the same basic laws and principles are assumed to underlie all forms of human behavior (Sidman, 1960a). It is the unique experiences of individuals which determine in large measure, differing patterns of behavior. The implied dichotomy in the mental illness model between deviant and nondeviant behavior and, by extension, between those who have and have not been labeled "mentally ill," is therefore denied. Diagnosis in the behavioral model requires precise specification of the presenting behavior and the environmental conditions, both social and nonsocial, which control and maintain it. The objective of treatment is elimination of the presenting behavior as well as to preclude the uncontrolled learning of additional undesired behavior. Replacement of it with adaptive alternatives is achieved through instruction and training in concert with the introduction or rearrangement of appropriate environmental contingencies (e.g., Bandura, 1969; Franks, 1969; Yates, 1970).

Behavior modification, then, is the systematic application of proven principles of conditioning and learning in the remediation of human problems. This, the original and proper definition of behavior modification establishes the boundary conditions of the discipline. It delineates those strategies and techniques that can and those that cannot be legitimately considered within its working domain. A variety of medical techniques, such as psychosurgery, chemotherapy, and electrode implantation, are frequently attributed to the behavior modifier when, in fact, they do not fall within the scope of this discipline. Although these procedures do indeed result in behavior change, they should not be confused with behavior modification procedures for they are not applications of the principles of conditioning and learning. Techniques such as these involve instead physiological alterations which fall within the domain of the medically trained individual. For example, the physician, the surgeon, and the psychiatrist—certainly not the psychologically trained behavior modifier.

The following chapters first compare and contrast the medical and behavioral model in terms of their effectiveness in dealing with both mental health problems in general and offender rehabilitation in particular. Subsequent chapters present in detail the procedures followed and the results obtained from two behaviorally based programs implemented in maximum-security correctional institutions.

Chapters 2 and 3 of this book explore and criticize the theoretical bases and empirical results of major contemporary treatment strategies and programs. While these programs have paved the way for a psychological approach to crime and delinquency, it has proved difficult to extend traditional concepts of the causes and cures of mental illness to the understanding and treatment of delinquents and offenders.

The next chapter describes the behavioral alternative to mental illness formulations. This alternative involves an environmental–behavioral orientation to the understanding and remediation of problems in corrections. Although this approach has only recently been employed in the criminal justice system its initial success justifies a systematic exploration of how it may be employed and what it may accomplish.

Chapters 5 and 6 describe the principles and techniques of behavior modification within the context of offender rehabilitation and procedures that may be employed to evaluate its effectiveness. Chapter 7 explores the ethical considerations involved in any rehabilitation effort and attempts to set forth guidelines for the development of an ethical and humane treatment program. Chapters 8 through 10 describe the basic procedures employed by two separate behaviorally oriented prison programs and how they interfaced with remedial education and vocational training efforts.

Irrespective of theoretical orientation and empirical evaluation, any effort concerned with inmate rehabilitation will be severely limited if it is rejected by the staff or the inmates themselves. Chapter 11 offers a supplementary evaluation of the two programs with emphasis upon the views, attitudes, and individual experiences of inmates participating in the behavior modification programs. The last chapter attempts to put into perspective the array of current correctional programs operating in this country, and suggests how correctional practices might be reorganized and integrated into a unified humane and effective system of offender rehabilitation.

CHAPTER

2

THE MENTAL ILLNESS MODEL
IN PSYCHIATRIC TREATMENT

To date, the mental illness model has been the dominant force in deter-mining the course and direction taken by the helping professions in their attempts to deal with the whole spectrum of human problems. The all-pervasive influence of this model can be appreciated when one examines the arts in general from a psychoanalytic interpretation of Hamlet to an analysis of sexual symbolism of surrealistic paintings.

Indeed, the mental illness model is the warp and woof of each one of us. From birth to dying our deviant behavior and that of those around us is explained and interpreted by us and for us in terms of this model. Because of its influence it is useful to review the major characteristics of this model and attempt to determine whether or not its uncritical accep-tance is warranted.

The mental illness model involves a number of basic postulates con-cerning the origins and treatment of behavior labeled "deviant." First of all, there is an almost universal acceptance of the concept of mental illness. Persons exhibiting a wide variety of behavioral problems—from those labeled criminal or delinquent to those labeled neurotic or psychotic—are considered to be mentally ill. Originally, the various forms of behavior taken as indicators of mental illness were thought to

17

be the effect of a true organic illness or physical defect, much like the relation between general paresis and the syphilitic spirochete. Indeed, the demonstration of this relationship strengthened the belief that it would eventually be possible to discover an organic basis for *all* unusual behavior. More recently, the concept of illness has shifted from that of a diseased brain to that of a diseased mind. This conceptualization of the origins of deviant behavior has also come under attack, and Szasz (1969) has argued that the whole concept of mental illness is more fantasy than fact:

> I submit that mental illness is a myth. Bodies are physical objects; minds, whatever they may be, are not physical objects. Accordingly, mental diseases (such as depression or schizophrenia) cannot exist in the same sense in which bodily diseases (such as broken bones or ulcerated skins) exist (p. 30).

Despite this, and other convincing arguments to the contrary (e.g., Krasner & Ullman, 1965; Stuart, 1970; Szasz, 1961, 1970), the "mental illness" model still maintains that deviant behavior may be viewed as either a product of diseases of the brain (the organic syndromes) or as a product of diseases of the mind (the functional syndromes). The latter is now dressed in the more acceptable and sophisticated garb of the disordered or disorganized personality. That there are indeed physical or organic dysfunctions which underlie some behavioral deviancy cannot be argued; but to use this as a basis for a metaphorical analogy in which all behavioral deviancy is so conceptualized is to commit an epistemological error.

Although most theories of personality have moved from the purely organic position, they continue to assume that a wide range of internal processes are operative, and that in order to understand deviant behavior, it is necessary to understand the underlying disturbance of these processes. According to Bandura (1969):

> In these theories, the conditions supposedly controlling behavior continue to function analogously to toxic substances in producing deviant responses; however, the disturbing agents comprise a host of inimical psychodynamic forces (for example, repressed impulses, energized traits, psychic complexes, latent tendencies, self-dynamisms, and other types of energy systems) somewhat akin to the pernicious spirits of ancient times. Many contemporary theories of psychopathology thus employ a quasi-medical model fashioned from an amalgam of the disease and demonology conceptions which have in common the belief that deviant behavior is a function of inimical inner forces. (P. 2)

The second characteristic of the "mental illness" model involves a heavy emphasis on diagnosis. If it is assumed that behavioral deviance is a sign of an internal problem, it then becomes necessary to specify the nature of the personality disturbance. Various kinds of abnormal behavior are taken as symptoms of specifiable internal problems. Although an attempt to categorize any pattern of behavior as symptomatic of an inferred personality defect is a challenging endeavor which involves a complex set of criteria, it is deemed necessary if the causes of the deviancy are to be understood. Diagnosis is supposedly a tool which is used to "make sense" of the complexities involved in the "mental illness" model of deviant behavior. Ideally, diagnosis serves four functions: (*a*) Diagnosis identifies the etiology of the disorder, the causes or origins of the disease. (*b*) It typically specifies how an individual differs from others also manifesting disease. (*c*) It provides a prognosis of what the course of the illness will be. (*d*) Diagnosis specifies the choice of treatments relative to each disease entity. To the degree that diagnosis fulfills these four functions and, consequently, reduces ambiguity and complexity sufficiently to allow the practitioner to improve the caliber of his work it will have fulfilled its objectives. To the degree that it does not, it undoubtedly does nothing more than instill in the practitioner or decision maker a variety of self-fulfilling prophecies which retard rather than advance the goals of therapy or rehabilitation. As Toch (1970) has so correctly stated:

> Classifying people in life is a grim business which channelizes destinies and determines fate. A man becomes a category, plays an assigned role, and lives up to the implications. Labelled irrational, he acts crazy. Catalogued dangerous, he becomes dangerous, or he stays behind bars. (P. 15)

Rarely is the "textbook example" ever encountered in the field, and rarely is diagnosis in the field as straightforward a matter as it is depicted to be in the classroom. As we shall see, interrater reliability of expert diagnosticians has been found to be far from perfect, particularly as the diagnosis becomes less general (Schmidt & Fonda, 1956; Beck, Ward, Mendelson, Mock, & Erbaush, 1962).

Research conducted to date has failed to support contentions that diagnosis does do more than affix labels to individuals in an unreliable and often potentially deleterious manner. Concerning the etiological function of diagnosis, Kanfer and Saslow (1969), Bandura (1969), and Costello (1970) concur that the differential diagnosis of mental illness in terms of etiological factors is, at present, an impossible task. As far as can now be determined, no aspects of individuals' past histories, be these events occurring in early childhood, "traumatic" experiences, family dynamics, environmental conditions, school situations, differential peer group affixations, or constitutional characteristics have been identified as precursors of assignment to existant diagnostic categories.

The inability of etiological factors to function as predictors of nosological categorization has forced the diagnostician to rely heavily upon the presenting problems of individuals coming before him as the basis of differential diagnosis. Diagnosis is therefore largely based upon reports of the individual and others in terms of subjectively felt and displayed emotions and behaviors, experiences, moods, failures, and interpersonal problems. A further indicator is the performance of these individuals on various diagnostic instruments such as the Minnesota Multiphasic Personality Inventory (MMPI), the Thematic Apperception Test, and the Rorschach.

THE MENTAL ILLNESS MODEL IN PSYCHIATRIC DIAGNOSIS

Reliability

Although only a limited number of studies have been performed which adequately assess the reliability of the preceding form of diagnostic regimen, results indicate that prevalent diagnostic practices are markedly imprecise. An early study by Schmidt and Fonda (1956) compared the degree to which the diagnoses given by psychiatric residents agreed with those by chief psychiatrists of patients entering a state mental hospital over a six-month period. In all, 462 patients were evaluated both by one of three chief psychiatrists and by one of eight psychiatric residents. The degree to which the residents agreed with the chief psychiatrists was relatively high with respect to two major categories of mental illness: There was 92% agreement with respect to those classified as manifesting one of the various forms of psychosis; and 71% agreement with respect to those showing a characterological disorder. However, the agreement between the residents and the chief psychiatrists dropped markedly when the degree to which they agreed with respect to the specific type of illness was examined. Agreement ranged from a high of 80% for the chronic brain syndrome subtype of organic disorder to a low of 6% for the personality trait subtype of characterological disorder. Overall, the residents agreed with the chief psychiatrists only on 55% of their diagnoses. In effect, a resident and a chief psychiatrist were about as unlikely as likely to agree on the specific form of mental illness manifested by an individual whom they both independently examined and diagnosed.

A possible shortcoming of the Schmidt and Fonda (1956) study was the comparison of experienced diagnosticians (the chief psychiatrists) with diagnosticians in training (the psychiatric residents). It is possible that the percent of agreement would have been found to be greater if comparisons had been made between only well-experienced staff members. Sandifer, Pettus, and Quade (1964) present data which bear upon this possibility. The authors attended diagnostic conferences in three mental hospitals in which each patient's work-up (case history, present level of functioning, laboratory tests, psychological tests, etc.) was presented and followed by an interview with the patient. The conferences were attended by 10 experienced psychiatrists, and following the presentation of a case each rendered a judgment concerning the nature of the psychiatric disorder presented by the patient. A total of 91 patients were evaluated in this manner. In 30 instances, nine of ten or ten of ten of the psychiatrists agreed concerning the nature of the illness; in 32 instances between six and eight of the psychiatrists agreed; and in the remaining 29 instances, three to five of the psychiatrists were in agreement. An overall reliability figure of 59% agreement among the various psychiatrists was derived from the preceding data; this figure being almost identical to that arrived at in the Schmidt and Fonda (1956) study. Again, the probability of agreement among diagnosticians concerning the diagnosis of the mental illness of any particular patient was approximately equal to the probability that they would disagree.

Other studies have reported similar results. Both Kreitman (1961) and Zubin (1967) have reviewed the literature pertaining to the reliability of psychiatric diagnosis and conclude the agreement between the independent diagnoses of skilled diagnosticians is typically low. Zubin's (1967) review indicates that concerning the subtypes of functional psychoses agreement may be as low as 26%; for the subtypes of functional neuroses as low as 60%; and for characterological disorders as low as 8%. In addition, multiple diagnoses of the same individuals show little consistency over time (Kaelbling & Volpe, 1963; Zubin, 1967). Finally, comparisons of samples of psychiatric patients drawn from the same populations indicate that the relative incidence of various types of disorders is lacking in consistency; and that this lack of consistency may be attributable to differences in the diagnostic practices or predilection of different psychiatric wards within the same hospitals, or of those of various hospitals within the same community (Zubin, 1967; Pasamanick, Dinitz, & Lefton, 1959; Jenkins, Bemiss, & Lorr, 1953).

Since the "mental illness" model depicts behavioral deviancy to be symptomatic of underlying personality disturbances, it is appropriate to assume that persons assigned to the same diagnostic category should show similar patterns of behavior; and that these patterns of behavior should be different from those manifested by other individuals who have been assigned to alternative categories. This, however, does not appear to be a valid assumption. Ullman and Krasner (1969) have reviewed a number of factor analytic studies (e.g., Wittenborn, Holzberg, & Simon, 1953; Lorr, Klett, & McNair, 1963; Eysenck, 1961a) of the dispersion of specific psychopathological symptoms across various diagnostic categories and have concluded that:

> . . . the behavior of patients given the same diagnostic label is not homogeneous, but rather comprises different subclusters; that some of these behaviors are contradictory with each other so that the presence of one would empirically reduce the probability of the manifestation of the other; and that there is a wide spread of high scores on certain clusters across patients given different diagnostic labels. (P. 227)

Additional studies have produced the same conclusions. The work of both Freudenberg and Robertson (1956) and Zigler and Phillips (1961) supports the contention that assignment to a particular diagnostic category provides little, if any, accurate information concerning the behavior that is manifested by patients. The behavior of individuals assigned to one diagnostic category is frequently as *unlike* the behavior of others assigned to that category as it is *like* that of individuals assigned to alternative diagnostic categories.

Relatively little attention has been directed to the prognostic utility of the diagnostic procedures advocated within the context of the "mental illness" model. Ideally, a system that includes a prognostic component would enable the practitioner to determine who is most likely to recover with mininal or no treatment, those who require only supportive treatment, those who are most likely to profit by intensive treatment, and, pragmatically, those who are least likely to profit from treatment. Based upon decisions derived from proven prognoses, the mental health profession could allocate its resources in the most practical and economic manner. Although these goals are sound, there is little reason to assume that existant diagnostic procedures provide an avenue through which these goals may be realized:

> The prognostic–predictive approach appears to have the most direct applicability. If continued research were to support certain early findings, being able to predict outcome of mental illness from a patient's premorbid social competence score (Zigler and Phillips, 1961), from his score on an ego-strength scale (Barron, 1953), or from many of the other signs and single variables which have been shown to have some predictive powers, it would indeed be comforting. It is unfortunate that these powers are frequently dissipated in cross-validation. (Kanfer & Saslow, 1969, p. 425)

Finally, diagnostic procedures are typically depicted as aiding in the treatment process. Once the personality disorder underlying deviant behavior has been specified, the "mental illness" model ideally prescribes treatments of choice which maximize the probability that correct procedures will be employed to remediate, or cure, that disorder. Again, there is very little evidence to support the contention that this does indeed transpire. Kreitman, Sainsbury, Morrissey, Towers, and Scrivener (1961) have examined the degree to which psychiatrists agree on the treatment of choice for the major diagnostic categories. They reported that there was 77% agreement with respect to prescribed treatment for functional psychoses; 54% agreement for the neuroses, 51% agreement for organic syndromes, and only 33% agreement for the remaining diagnostic categories. In this same vein, Bannister, Salmon, and Leiberman (1964) determined the relationship between diagnostic category and treatment for 1000 psychiatric patients. The patients were classified in three ways: in broad diagnostic categories (e.g., psychotic, neurotic); in more specific subtypes (e.g., schizophrenic, hysteric); and on the basis of the precise nosological system provided by the World Health Organization. Their analysis, based upon the type treatment actually received by patients assigned to the various categories, indicate that it is possible to predict treatment from diagnosis with 18, 33, and 31% accuracy at best for the three categorization procedures. They conclude that:

... the findings are not consistent with the notion that each particular diagnosis leads logically (or habitually) to a particular treatment. It suggests that variables other than diagnosis may be as important as, or more important than, diagnosis in predicting choice of treatment. (P. 731)

Validity

Little has been said in regard to the validity of current diagnostic practices. Whereas reliability deals with the repeatability of assessment (either by the same individual employing different measures of the same phenomenon, or by different individuals employing the same measure of a phenomenon), validity is concerned with the extent to which diagnostic practices determine that which they claim to determine. It is axiomatic that diagnostic practices must be reliable in order for them to be valid: Reliability is a necessary but not sufficient condition for validity (Nunnally, 1967), and in this respect, it is obvious from the previous discussion on the reliability of diagnostic procedures that this requirement has not yet been met. When (or if) this requirement is met, the question of the validity of diagnostic practices will remain.

The necessity of validating psychological variables is a function of the abstractness of these variables. A highly concrete variable, such as the number of fights an individual engages in over time, is adequately specified once the reliability of measurement has been determined. A more abstract variable, or construct, such as the antisocial personality, is not so easily specified. Constructs are things that the diagnostician puts together in his own imagination, not something that exists as an isolated, observable dimension of behavior. They are hypothetical! In essence, three procedures may be employed to assess the validity of constructs that have been conceptualized to explain human behavior.

The first of these is content or "face" validity and involves a judgment as to whether the materials involved in the diagnostic regimen would be logically expected to perform the functions that are claimed of them. This form of validity is most appropriate when attempting to determine proficiency or ability (such as general spelling or mathematical skill), or to assess the effects of some form of training in which a sample of the skills which individuals are thought to have mastered are presented. Performance is then measured in terms of percent correct, speed, and so on. This approach is of little value when attempting to validate diagnostic constructs:

> Most aptitude and personality tests bear less resemblance to the behavior area which they are attempting to measure than do achievement tests . . . under such conditions, content validity is especially likely to degenerate into a substitution of test labels for objectively determined validity. (Anastasi, 1954, p. 123)

The second validation procedure, predictive validity, possesses the objectivity which is lacking in content validity. It involves a determination of the degree to which a *predictor,* in this instance the various diagnostic categories, allows one to predict a past, present, or future state or condition (criterion measure). The term "prediction," therefore, is not limited to the prediction of future events, but refers instead to the identification of a given condition prior to the obtaining of direct knowledge of it. In practice, the predictive validity of diagnostic procedures is concerned with the prediction of outcome of illness for a given diagnostic group. From it should come the prediction of specific characteristics and behavior from the diagnosis and the selection of therapy to maximize positive outcome (Zubin, 1967). The previous discussion of the degree to which current diagnostic practices attain the objectives of diagnosis in general indicates that the various diagnostic categories, when evaluated in terms of these criteria, have not yet been demonstrated to be valid, or useful, entities.

The third form of validation, construct validity, is perhaps most appropriate when viewing the theorizing which has emerged as a function of the "mental illness" model of the causes of human behavior. As has been noted previously, these constructs are invented abstractions based upon theories and inferred from observations of behavior and, as such, are "something more than" behavior itself. It is possible to describe these abstractions in verbal terms, and from these descriptions devise, in a logical manner, operations that may be used to identify and quantify them. So defined, constructs become autonomous entites and, other than the operations that have been developed to identify them, there are no alternative operations that precisely describe or measure them. Without such alternative operations, validation becomes an impossible task. This impossibility is circumvented, in theory, by postulating relationships between the construct in question and other constructs (Ghiselli, 1964). As a result, constructs are generally validated by demonstrating interrelationships with other constructs which, in turn, are validated by demonstrating interrelationships with other constructs (or, perhaps, the construct with which we were initially concerned). This circle is rarely, if ever, broken. Strictly speaking, one can never be sure that a construct has been measured or that a theory has been tested (Nunnally, 1967). Any discipline that relies heavily upon such practices is of questionable value.

The weight of the evidence now available fails to support the contentions of adherents to the "mental illness" model that diagnostic practices are valuable tools which enable them to discharge their responsibilities in a more effective manner. Yet diagnostic practices persist and flourish. Phillips and Draguns (1971) have attempted to explain the endurance and reassertion of the constructs of mental illness in the face of cogent and incisive critiques in terms of the fact that most popular and professional conceptualizations of behavior are couched in the language and constructs of traditional psychopathology. Graziano (1969) offers an alternative and more pessimistic possibility. He claims that:

> . . . the contemporary United States mental health professions have developed viable community-based professional and lay power structures which are composed of mutually benefiting bureaucracies. Scientific and humanitarian ideals are incompatible with and have been supplanted by the professionals' primary loyalty to the political power structure itself. By virtue of their focus on self-preservation, these power structures (a) maintain a dogmatically restrictive view of human behavior and the roles of the professionals within that structure and (b) prevent the development of true innovations. (P. 17)

A third basis for the continued adherence to the "mental illness" model appears to be the role that the concepts and constructs of mental illness plays in our society. The medical diagnosis of mental illness which justifies involuntary civil commitment ranks second only to the criminal justice system as a means by which society deals with individuals manifesting "troublesome" behavior. Historically, this practice is an outgrowth of the attempts of early reformers to insure that individuals showing disturbing (to others) behavior receive humane treatment. This practice is potentially dangerous, for it permits the easy revocation of any individual's civil liberties. It is reported (Wolf, 1971), for example, that the Soviet Union makes extensive use of this procedure to quiet political dissenters. Levinson (1970) has studied the civil commitment process and reports that, in those cases which he reviewed, complete consensus by examining physicians on diagnosis was reached in only one case in five, and that the physicians' examinations resulted in total diagnostic disagreement in almost three cases of ten. The same symptoms were cited as evidence of from 5 to 22 different diseases, with an average of 12.9 different diseases inferred from each symptom. The inclusion of a patient in a particular diagnostic category conveyed only minimal information concerning the symptomotology of the patient, and a particular set of symptoms did not allow a reliable prediction of the diagnostic label which would be attached to the patient. He concludes that involuntary civil commitment is based upon diagnostic assessments and categories which are, at best, unreliable and, at worst, invalid. Consequently, involuntary civil commitment, premised on diagnostic labeling, is without sufficient legal justification, and should be considered a deprivation of liberty without due process of law and in violation of the Fifth and Fourteenth Amendments.

UTILITY OF THE MENTAL ILLNESS MODEL
IN THE TREATMENT OF THE MENTALLY ILL

Theories, be they in the physical sciences or the behavioral sciences, are neither proven nor disproven. Instead, old theories give way to new when the new are demonstrated to be more efficient, effective, or more inclusive than the old. Within this context, the future of any theory of human behavior is determined by how well it, with reference to alternative positions, equips its adherents to deal with the people whom they encounter in the course of their professional lives. Quite often practitioners will justify their adherence to a particular theoretical orientation in terms of the amount of time they have spent perfecting their techniques, the degree to which they feel comfortable and effective using them, as well as the extent to which the orientation emphasizes the value of man.

In the final analysis, the value of a theory is *not* dependent on how much time an individual has devoted to it or how comfortable it makes him feel, or even how effective the practitioner perceives it to be. It is, instead, how effective it is in enabling practitioners to change the behavior of the people with whom they work. This is an empirical question, not a subjective one, and until recently little effort has been expended on the experimental investigation of the effectiveness of the various therapeutic approaches.

The procedures used to evaluate the effectiveness of any psychotherapeutic regimen are no different from those used to evaluate any form of therapeutic intervention. The basic strategy involves a minimum of two groups of subjects; one group, the experimental group, is subjected to the therapeutic procedure while a second group, the control group, receives no such treatment. A third group, the placebo group, should be employed whenever possible. This group is treated in the same manner as the experimental group (the subjects are seen on the same basis as are the experimental subjects, are led to believe that their encounters with the practitioner are therapeutic in nature, and they and their families and friends are informed that it is expected that the "therapeutic" procedures will be successful, etc.), but no therapy is actually administered. This third group controls for the possibility that change may occur as a function of the role expectations which are embedded in the therapeutic process rather than as a function of therapy *per se* (Ullman & Krasner, 1969), or as a function of changes in others with respect to the subjects.

Individuals who would be considered for treatment should be assigned to the comparison groups in a random manner or, if certain variables (such as age, sex, race, socioeconomic background) are known to influence outcomes, matched in such a manner to insure that the comparison groups are comparable along these dimensions. Quite often moral or ethical questions are raised concerning practices that involve deliberately withholding treatment from individuals who are in need of such treatment, and deliberately developing in others the expectation that they will be benefited when in fact they are receiving no therapy. Implicit (or explicit) in these objections is the assumption that the therapeutic procedure is in fact therapeutic; that it is something more than a mere placebo effect; and that it is certainly more effective than no intervention at all. These, of course, are the questions that must be answered rather than accepted as "givens." Indeed, the advocacy of untested and unproven therapeutic practices raises even more serious moral and ethical questions than do the procedures that are necessary to evaluate these practices. As is discussed shortly, research suggests that the bulk of what now passes as "therapy" is little or no more effective in remediating human problems than is the mere passage of time.

As in the experimental analysis of any phenomenon, careful attention must be directed to the selection of outcome measures to assess the effect of therapeutic intervention. The preoccupation of adherents to the "mental illness" model with inferred processes as determinants of deviant behavior and their consequent structuring of therapy in terms of these inferred processes, has quite naturally led to the selection of outcome measures that stress changes in internal states. In light of the previous discussion, diagnostic procedures that attempt to specify dimensions of personality lack the reliability, validity, and precision necessary for assessment. Instead, outcome measures must be objective in nature, and must lend themselves to quantification. Rather than evaluating therapy in terms of changes in hostile or aggressive personality traits as determined by personality tests, introspective reports, ratings of others, and so on, a more precise procedure involves the objectification of the inferred traits as behavioral phenomena which are quantifiable in terms of frequency, intensity, duration, rate, and so forth. Valid objectification of hostile or aggressive personality traits would involve the specification of just what is considered to be hostile or aggressive behavior: noncompliance with requests or orders, destruction of physical property, fistfights, and so on, which may then be quantified by counting. Indeed, once the referents of the inferred personality traits are objectified, it becomes clear that such traits are nothing more than fictions which are employed in a circular manner to explain the behavior from which they are inferred (and as such add nothing to our understanding of that behavior).

Assessment must be performed a minimum of five times: prior to the initiation of treatment; midway through the treatment process; upon termination of treatment; midway through a follow-up period; and at the termination of follow-up. The first three measures allow us to track the course of behavior change that occurs under the treatment, placebo, and no treatment procedures; the latter three measures (with the measure taken at the termination of treatment performing a double function) allows for the determination and extrapolation of the long-term effects of intervention. One of three things may occur during both the intervention and follow-up periods: Individuals may improve, remain the same, or deteriorate. Only by comparing the measures that have been collected on individuals in the three groups with which we are concerned is it possible to adequately assess the effects of treatment. Quite often, research is directed toward a comparison of two (or more) treatment procedures, and it is argued that when this is the object of inquiry the placebo and no treatment control groups are unnecessary. Bearing in mind the three possible outcomes of treatment, one realizes that such a research strategy cannot accomplish this end. If the two procedures do not differ in their effectiveness, it is impossible to determine whether the two procedures are equally beneficial, have no effect, or are equally harmful. Stuart (1970) refers to the latter as "iatrogenic illness as a consequence of psychiatric treatment" (pp. 14–15). If one is demonstrated to be superior to a second, is this because the first is indeed beneficial while the second is of no effect; because the first is of no effect while the second is harmful, etc.? Without the appropriate experimental controls, conclusions drawn from such research are, at best, of no value and, at worst, provide justification for the propagation of useless or harmful "therapeutic" practices.

Considering the importance of such research, surprisingly few studies have been completed which meet these minimal requirements. Meehl's (1955) criteria for acceptability were less stringent than those outlined previously in that he required only (a) a no treatment control group, (b) pre- and postintervention evaluation which was either objectively or judgmentally uncontaminated, and (c) some follow-up of both groups. Yet Meehl reviewed over 200 journal articles and a dozen books on psychotherapy. Of these, only one paper approximated these requirements. Relaxing the follow-up requirement, but still insisting upon appropriate controls did not change this figure. Since the collection of Meehl's data, some additional studies have appeared which do meet these criteria. Brill and Beebe (1955) analyzed data collected on servicemen who were either discharged from the army for neurotic disorders or returned to duty as cured. They reported that men who received individual therapy and returned to duty served somewhat longer, on the average, than men who received routine hospital care, or men who received essentially no psychiatric treatment. However, men who received only rest and sedation also served longer than the latter two groups. In fact, the rest and sedation group served even longer than did the individual therapy group. An examination of men who were discharged for psychiatric reasons revealed that their adjustment in civilian life was independent of the type of treatment they had received while in the service, the judged severity of their illness, and their military experience in general. The overall tendency of the sample was in the direction of improvement.

A second study (Barron & Leary, 1955) compared the pre- and post-therapy MMPI profiles of 85 patients receiving group therapy, 42 patients receiving individual therapy, and 23 individuals who were rejected for therapy because of staff and facility limitations. (They were, however, tested at intervals approximating those of the treated groups.) The three groups were comparable in terms of initial diagnosis, prognosis, severity of condition, age, sex, and education. All groups showed improvement when their initial test profiles were compared to their second profiles, and none of the differences among the three groups on the psychiatric scales approached significance. The authors concluded that the changes in the two treatment and one no-treatment groups tended to be in the same direction, and of the same magnitude. Eysenck (1966), criticizing this study, concluded that "in so far as we can regard the MMPI as a reasonable measure of psychiatric status this study would appear to indicate a complete failure of psychotherapy to produce any effects whatever" (p. 17).

A further study conducted by Walker and Kelley (1960) compared 44 male schizophrenic patients who received short-term psychotherapy to a no-treatment control group of 38 similar patients. When assessed in terms of symptom improvement, general ward behavior, the percentage of each group discharged from the hospital and general adjustment 90 days following release from the hospital, no differences were found between the two groups. Only one difference was found between the two groups: A greater percentage of the patients receiving no treatment were released from the hospital within six months of admission than of those who did receive psychotherapy.

A detailed review of the success rates of therapy conducted within the framework of the "mental illness" model has been conducted by Eysenck (1952, 1966). Eysenck's (1966) criteria of success was each author's report of the percent of patients who showed improvement, much improvement, or were cured. When taken at face value, the success rates appear highly encouraging. An examination of 18 reports of psychotherapy with children (which involved a total of 3399 cases) yielded a mean success rate of 67% with a range of 41 to 77%. The most traditional, psychoanalytically oriented therapy, which was excluded from the preceding figures, fared somewhat more poorly. The five reports of psychoanalytic therapy which Eysenck reviewed (which involved a total of 760 cases) produced an overall success rate of 44%, with a range of 39 to 67%. It is tempting to conclude from these data that psychotherapy results in general improvement or in complete cure in approximately two-thirds of all cases, and that psychoanalysis is slightly less successful, producing improvement or cure in approximately one-half of all cases. Such a conclusion would be unwarranted, however, for the studies from which the preceding figures were derived did not employ the requisite control procedures which would allow an adequate assessment of the effects of therapy.

In an attempt to overcome this deficiency, Eysenck also searched the literature in an attempt to arrive at some valid estimate of the rates of spontaneous remission (recovery without treatment) from mental illness. An analysis of data drawn from a variety of sources (e.g., a comparison of the prevalence of psychoneuroses with the incidences of new cases; the percentage of patients discharged without appreciable treatment from state mental hospitals; claims filed against insurance companies) showed remarkable consistency: ". . . about two-thirds of severe neurotics show recovery or considerable improvement, without benefit of systematic psychotherapy, after a lapse of two years from the time that their disorder is notified, or they are hospitalized" (1966, p. 29). A comparison of this figure with that derived above for a similar population which did receive psychotherapy, led Eysenck to an unavoidable conclusion:

> . . . the therapeutic effects of psychotherapy are small or non-existent, and do not in any demonstrable way add to the non-specific effects of routine medical treatment, or to such events as occur in the patient's everyday experiences. (1966, p. 40)

Eysenck's conclusions have not stood unchallenged. The most objective critique of Eysenck's work and the most comprehensive updating of research pertaining to the evaluation of therapeutic outcomes are provided by Bergin (1971). He first noted the problems inherent in any attempt to compare the effects of a variety of studies that claim to assess therapeutic outcomes. These include: (a) a lack of precisely comparable cases across studies; (b) the lack of equivalent criteria of outcomes; (c) large variations in the type of therapy practiced; (d) equally large variations in the quality of therapy practiced; (e) differences in the duration of therapy; (f) large variations in the follow-up (when present at all); (g) variations in the nature of onset and in the duration of the disturbance; and when comparable cases and outcome estimates are employed; (h) impreciseness in the definitions of the disorders; and (i) equal imprecision in the definitions of the criteria for improvement, the latter two rendering the reliability of the data questionable. In light of these difficulties, any reviewer must recast the data presented in the various studies into one system that does allow comparison. As Bergin has noted, the individual reviewer then ". . . usually winds up with three *different* views of the same case material (the original author's, Eysenck's, and one's own), a fact which unfortunately reduces the objectivity and credibility of the information being summarized" (p. 220). Of course, the system employed strongly determines the conclusions drawn.

Bearing this in mind, Bergin has developed his own system for analysis and criteria of success. These are, in general, somewhat more liberal than those employed by Eysenck, but when one considers the multitudinous views of the nature and objectives of the therapeutic process, they are most probably the most thoughtfully developed of those (including Eysenck's) advocated. Be that as it may, reviews of evaluative research are still dependent for the most part on each author's criteria for success, and include such questionable measures as changes in MMPI profiles, self-concept measures, self-administered checklists, self-ratings, therapist ratings, psychiatric diagnoses. The lack of adequate reliability, the problems involved in validation, and the susceptibility of these procedures to unintentional bias, raise the question of the utility of the basic data upon which the overall conclusions are based. Despite this, and on the basis of his criteria of success, Bergin feels justified in concluding that:

> It now seems apparent that psychotherapy, as practiced over the past 40 years, has had an average effect that is modestly positive. It is clear, however, that the averaged group data on which this conclusion is based obscure the existence of a multiplicity of processes occurring in therapy, some of which are known to be either unproductive or actually harmful. (P. 263)

In summary, the traditional mental health approach, and the approach of those in related fields who would employ the "mental illness" model in the remediation of the particular problems with which they are faced, depicts deviant behavior as caused by processes analogous to those that have been demonstrated to underly organic or physical illness. Within this context the behavior in which an individual engages is viewed as symptomatic of some underlying psychic imbalance (often referred to in general terms as a disturbed or disorganized personality), and the emphasis of therapy is upon the identification and treatment of that disturbance. Only by so doing is it possible to effect a permanent cure.

Embedded in this approach to deviancy are a multitude of abstract concepts and constructs such as unconscious dynamics, repression, complexes, transference relationships, insight, and defense interpretation. Because these appear reasonable and are integrated into formalized and internally consistent theories, they have assumed an aura of face validity. In addition, through their constant and unquestioned repetition and elaboration they have now attained "truth" status. When examined objectively, however, it becomes apparent that the theories that have been deduced from the "mental illness" model are constructed in such a manner as to render them all but impervious to validation or invalidation. In addition, the diagnostic practices that stem from these theories have been demonstrated to be so unreliable as to render them useless in any practical sense. Indeed, it has been suggested that the utilization of these practices to justify commitment is unconstitutional. Finally, an examination of therapy conducted within the framework of the "mental illness" model reveals that such therapy has not been demonstrated to be markedly more effective than the mere passage of time and/or everyday life experiences. It appears, therefore, that there is little empirical basis for the continued and unquestioned advocacy of this model of the causes of human behavior as a medium through which it will be possible to effectively deal with either the problems of particular individuals, identifiable groups of individuals, or of society itself.

CHAPTER

$$\boxed{3}$$

THE MENTAL ILLNESS MODEL IN OFFENDER REHABILITATION

An examination of current trends in correctional research reveals that those concerned with the treatment of the offender have, in general, adopted the mental illness model as their own. The rationale for this is captured by Warren (1971) in her discussion of the necessity of applying diagnostic procedures to the offender population:

> One of the few facts agreed upon in the field of corrections is that offenders are not all alike. That is, they differ from each other not only in the form of their offense, but also in the reasons for and the meaning of their crime. Some individuals violate the law because the peer group, upon which they depend for approval, is of a deviant subculture. Other individuals break the law because of insufficient socialization, which leaves them at the mercy of all but the most protected environments. Still others delinquently act out internal conflicts, identity struggles, or family crises. This list is, of course, illustrative, not exhaustive. (P. 239)

It might be noted that such a list is not only not exhaustive, but is potentially without end. The use of such inferred intrapsychic characteristics as "inadequate superego" (Argyle, 1961), "overinhibited"(Jenkins & Hewitt, 1944), "neurotic; anxious" (Jesness, 1969), "aggressive; psychopathic" (McCord, McCord, & Zola, 1957), "neurotic; disturbed" (Quay, 1964), "psychopath" (Reckless, 1961), "weak ego control" (Reiss, 1952), "situational emotional reaction" (Warren, 1971) and, most recently, "criminal personality" (Yochelson & Samenow, 1976) is the hallmark of the diagnostic procedures that are now being advocated as tools for the efficient management and effective treatment of the offender.

The applicability of the mental illness model to all or part of the offender population, as well as the concepts and constructs developed within that model, must be evaluated on the same basis as their counterparts in the mental health movement: Are the diagnostic procedures reliable; are the constructs involved valid; and is treatment conducted within this framework effective? To date, only the most rudimentary attempts have been made to determine the reliability of diagnostic procedures as applied to corrections, and these have dealt not with the reliability of diagnosis *per se*, but rather with the reliability of specific diagnostic instruments such as the Jesness Behavioral Checklists (Jesness, 1969), the tri-level assessment instruments developed by Quay (Quay & Parsons, undated), and the Interpersonal Maturity Level (I-level) regimen developed by Warren and her associates (Warren, 1969).

It appears that the instruments developed by Jesness and by Quay have been refined to such a degree that the various forms of test reliability (split-half, part–whole, internal consistency, linear components, etc.) are of an acceptable level. The present authors have not, however, been able to uncover any systematic evaluation of the reliability of Warren's I-level classification regimen which has been adopted by the California Youth Authority and is, consequently, the most widely utilized of all correctional classification schemata. Commenting on this, Palmer (1970) notes:

CTP (California's Community Treatment Project) has never undertaken an independent study of sub-study of I-level reliability as such . . . . Studies of reliability have not received higher priority at CTP for a number of reasons. First would be certain later mentioned tactical/strategic factors. For example, the entire Phase 1 intake, diagnostic and staffing procedure has been designed primarily to meet certain joint research-and-operations objectives which had little to do with questions of reliability as such. Instead, they centered around the accurate and rapid processing of individual subjects. The resulting procedure did not allow for an adequate and consistent use of 'blind' or other essentially independent cross-rater techniques. (P. 18)

It is disquieting to know that CTP found it expedient to employ the I-level classification schema for the rapid processing of individual subjects during Phase 1 of their operation. The lack of any systematic attempt before or during this phase to investigate the accuracy with which individual subjects are processed is, at best, unfortunate, for without such an investigation, CTP failed to take even the most rudimentary step in determining the utility of their classificatory system with respect to their charges (above and beyond the immediate needs of the Youth Authority). Phase 1 (preceding) refers to the period between 1961 and 1965. The priorities of subsequent phases of CTP have not appeared to have changed appreciably, and only passing reference has been made to informal or anecdotal reliability estimates scattered throughout the many in-house publications and research reports generated by CTP. It is indeed unfortunate that the Youth Authority has not encouraged its staff to organize their findings and submit them to professional journals so that their work would be readily available to the correctional community.

If it is decided that assessment instruments have the potential of advancing the classification process, ascertaining the reliability of measurement of these instruments is only the first step in determining the reliability and, eventually, the validity of the whole classification system. The reliability of measurement of the MMPI, probably the most widely utilized and most extensively researched of all psychodiagnostic instruments, is comparable or superior to that of the observer-administered and self-administered Behavior Checklists which comprise Jesness classification process, and to that of the Personal Opinion Study, Behavior Problem Checklist, and Behavior Checklist for the Analysis of Life History scales which comprise Quay's tri-level classification schema. However, it became apparent that decisions based solely upon the MMPI were not adequate for classification purposes, and it is now considered as only a part of a broader diagnostic regimen. As has been indicated previously, the psychodiagnostic process, despite the availability of reliable assessment instruments, is markedly imprecise. The instruments that have been developed to aid in the correctional classification process have not yet been fully validated. Therefore, it is not unreasonable to assume that they, too, will come to be employed within the context of a broader diagnostic process which, in turn, must be subjected to close scrutiny in order to determine its reliability, validity, and utility.

THE RELIABILITY AND VALIDITY OF
DIFFERENTIAL DIAGNOSIS IN CORRECTIONS

The general objective of classification is to distinguish one form of "pathology" from another, and then to "prescribe" treatment of choice for each form of pathology. As was discussed previously, the most common form of validity is one that involves a determination of the degree to which differential classification and treatment increases the probability that intervention will be successful. It is ironic that there appears to be an inverse relationship in corrections between the effort that has been expended to produce reliable classification methods and the effort that has been expended to validate diagnostic categories. Both Jesness and Quay have developed reliable instruments, but little attempt has been made to validate them; and while no systematic effort has been made to determine the reliability of Warren's diagnostic procedures, there has been an attempt to validate the I-level classification system (to be discussed in a later section).

Jesness' Behavioral Checklists

The Jesness assessment system is based upon two 80-item behavior checklists: one completed by a rater after he has had an opportunity to observe the target individual in a variety of settings; the second a self-rating scale which the individual fills out himself. The checklists measure 14 bipolar factors (unobstrusiveness vs. obstrusiveness; friendliness vs. hostility; responsibility vs. irresponsibility; considerateness vs. inconsiderateness; independence vs. dependence; rapport vs. alienation; enthusiasm vs. depression; sociability vs. poor peer relations; conformity vs. nonconformity; calmness vs. anxiousness; effective communication vs. inarticulation; insight vs. unawareness and indecisiveness; social control vs. attention seeking; and anger control vs. hypersensitivity) which were derived primarily from several factor and cluster analytic studies (Jesness, 1969, 1970). Although there has been no formal attempt to construct diagnostic categories based upon these 14 factors, such categories could presumably be developed by the sorting and matching of profiles in a manner analogous to that which has been employed with the MMPI.

Jesness has employed his behavioral checklist in the comparison of the differential effectiveness of two approaches to the institutional treatment of juvenile offenders. His project involved the O.H. Close School for Boys and the Karl Holton School for Boys, both California Youth Authority institutions located in Stockton, California. Treatment at O.H. Close stresses transactional analysis (TA), a psychodynamically oriented strategy; while treatment at Karl Holton involves an application of the principles of behavior modification, primarily through the medium of the token economy. The objectives of the program are twofold: The study, which has not at the time of this writing been completed, is expected to provide data regarding (*a*) the feasibility of applying these two contrasting approaches to the treatment of the entire population of wards in large institutions, and (*b*) the relative effectiveness of the two treatment strategies in changing the behavior of different types of juvenile offenders as identified via the Jesness classification regimen.

There were minor differences between the two groups on the pretest scores of the 14 traits. These differences may be attributable to chance factors since youths were assigned to the two schools in a random fashion and because data from other sources showed no differences between the two groups. Analysis of covariance (to control for these differences) of posttest scores revealed that both groups showed significant changes in the favorable direction on six traits. When the results of the observer-administered and self-administered posttest behavior checklists were compared an interesting finding emerged: The observer-administered checklists, although showing the preceding reported improvement for both groups, did not reveal any differences between the two groups in the amount of change which occurred. The self-administered checklists, which also showed the aforementioned change for both groups, indicated that the O.H. Close youth changed more than did the Karl Holton youths. The disparity between the results of the observer and self-administered checklists is not explained. It is tempting to focus upon the results of the self-administered checklist and claim that TA is the more effective treatment procedure. An alternative interpretation would focus upon the comparison of the observer- and self-administered checklists and posit that the TA youths have "lost touch with reality."

Although a formal 12-month follow-up of youths released from the two schools is planned, information currently available covers success on parole for only three- and six-month intervals. The data indicates that parolees from O.H. Close and from Karl Holton are doing equally well, with an overall recidivism rate slightly below that which is to be expected for California Youth Authority parolees of their age group.

Quay's Tri-level Classification Schema

The Quay diagnostic procedure is based upon four dimensions of personality (inadequate–immature, neurotic–conflicted, unsocialized–aggressive or psychopathic, and socialized or subcultural delinquent) which are deduced from a composite analysis of three assessment instruments: a checklist of behavior problems which is executed by an observer who rates the individual as he interacts with others; a true–false self-report questionnaire which is completed by the individual himself; and a checklist for the analysis of the individual's life history as revealed by available records of his past behavior. An individual is placed in one of four diagnostic categories based on his most elevated personality dimension score (Quay & Parson, undated). Although these four groupings are termed "behavioral categories," they parallel the four dimensions of personality upon which they are based and go beyond the behavioral data from which they are presumably deduced. Behavior Category 1 (BC-1) individuals are depicted as mildly neurotic and egocentric, BC-2 individuals are characterized as anxious and withdrawn, etc. (Federal Bureau of Prisons, 1970), and as such retain the markedly "psychiatric" flavor of current correctional diagnostic procedures.

Quay's approach to the classification of the juvenile offender has been adopted as the basis for treatment at the Robert F. Kennedy Youth Center in Morgantown, West Virginia. Work conducted there has led to the development of an additional diagnostic category which is a subcategory of two of the original four (inadequate–immature/BC-1 and socialized or subcultural delinquent/BC-4). Differential treatment is prescribed for the resultant five diagnostic groupings. Youths assigned to each of the categories live together in homogeneous groups, attend school together, work together, and engage in leisure-time activities together. Little contact is allowed with others of differing diagnoses. Specific objectives are prescribed for each group (e.g., the program for inadequate–immature/BC-1 youths stresses basic social skills, "growing-up," problem solving, and so on; the program for neurotic–conflicted/BC-2 youths aims at the reduction or resolution of internal conflicts and the reduction of fear of their own needs and impulses, etc.), and an attempt is made to match the characteristics and strengths of the treatment personnel to the characteristics and needs of the offenders in the various diagnostic categories (Federal Bureau of Prisons, 1970).

As was indicated previously, the reliability of the Quay assessment instruments appears adequate. At the Kennedy Youth Center these are a major part of the diagnostic regimen, but it appears that additional considerations such as additional assessment instruments and in-depth interviews also weigh heavily in the classification process. The reliability of the diagnostic process has not yet been examined. In addition, decisions concerning the treatment of offenders are based upon what is essentially an unvalidated diagnostic schema, and the decisions themselves are more "common sense" than they are tested and proven. The Kennedy Youth Center staff is obviously aware of these limitations, and provisions have been made for the long-term follow-up of releasees. Such follow-up will provide initial assessment of the validity of the diagnostic process and the utility of the treatment model. The results of the follow-up study are not yet available.

The I-Level Classification System

The Interpersonal Maturity Level Classification System (also referred to as integration level or "I-level" classification) employed by the California Youth Authority's Community Treatment Project (CTP) is based upon a general theory of personality development which distinguishes seven successive levels of interpersonal maturity (Sullivan, Grant, & Grant, 1957). Approximately 99% of CTP's delinquent adolescents have been found to fall within the second or "lower," third or "middle," and fourth or "higher" levels of integration or maturity (Palmer, 1971). Each maturity level has a number of subtypes (the subtypes of Maturity Level Two (I_2) are Asocial, Aggressive (Aa) and Asocial, Passive (Ap); of I_3, Immature Conformist (Cfm), Cultural Conformist (Cfc), and Manipulator (Mp); of I_4, Neurotic, Acting Out (Na), Neurotic, Anxious (Nx), Situational–Emotional Reaction (Se), and Cultural Identifier (Ci)) yielding a total of nine diagnostic categories, with a tenth (I U) reserved for unclassified cases. Classification is based upon detailed interviews, psychometric data, and case history information aimed at determining the level of perceptual differentiation or degree of complexity which characterizes the way in which an individual views himself and others, and the way in which the individual responds to his perceptions of the world (Warren, 1967; Palmer, 1971). As has been discussed previously, the reliability with which individuals may be diagnosed with respect to these various inferred personality dimensions has not yet been systematically investigated.

THE UTILITY OF DIFFERENTIAL DIAGNOSIS IN CORRECTIONS

Warren (1971) presents a well-reasoned argument for the utility of differential diagnosis and treatment. She contends that there is, perhaps, an interaction between diagnosis and treatment variables in which the same form of treatment might be beneficial to members of one diagnostic grouping, neutral with respect to a second, and actually detrimental to a third. Conversely, a second form of treatment might have an opposite effect. If this were indeed the case, by grouping all individuals without regard to their diagnoses or treatments the possibility of identifying the beneficial and detrimental effects of specific forms of treatment upon particular diagnostic groupings would be lost. In addition, these two effects would tend to cancel each other, and lead to a conclusion that treatment *per se* has no effect.

Warren (1971) posits that such a phenomenon may underly the apparent ineffectiveness of existent treatment programs in both mental health settings in general and in correctional settings in particular. She cites two studies in support of this position. In one (Adams, 1961), delinquent youths were classified as either amenable or nonamenable for treatment on the basis of pooled clinical judgments. Treatment-amenable youths were characterized as bright, verbal, and anxious, as showing evidence of awareness of problems, insight, desire to change, and as accepting of treatment. The amenable and nonamenable youths were then randomly assigned to treatment and control status.

Those earmarked for treatment were referred to an experimental Pilot Intensive Counseling unit (PICO I) while those designated as control subjects were routinely processed by the California Youth Authority. Youths in the treatment conditions received traditional individual and group therapy administered twice weekly by correctional caseworkers with advanced course work in either clinical psychology or psychiatric social work. Both treatment and control subjects were followed for 36 months following their release. The treated amenables showed a significantly lower reinstitutionalization rate than did the treated nonamenables which, in turn, did not differ from the reinstitutionalization rates of either nontreated amenables and nonamenables. The implication of these findings is that one form of treatment (in this case traditional insight therapy) will be effective with certain types of offenders but not with others, and that differential diagnosis allows the identification of such individuals and the deployment of available resources in the most efficient manner.

The second study cited by Warren in support of the utility of differential diagnosis and treatment is the Camp Elliott study by Grant and Grant (1959). It is also viewed as providing validating information for the I-level classification schema. Military offenders at Camp Elliott were classified in terms of their interpersonal maturity level and assigned to differing types of treatment teams. Treatment was deemed successful if a man was returned to active duty. In her summary Warren (1971) concluded:

The most important finding from this study was that the interaction between the maturity level of the subjects and the supervisory characteristics significantly affected later success rate of subjects. Not only were the treatment methods of some internally-oriented supervisory teams effective in increasing the success rates of the high maturity offenders, but also, the treatment methods were markedly detrimental to the success rates of low maturity offenders. Furthermore, the externally-oriented supervisory team had the reverse effect on high and low maturity subjects. (P. 245)

It appears, then, that one form of treatment benefits one type of subject and is detrimental to a second, while a second type of treatment is detrimental to the first type and is beneficial to the second. These conclusions do not appear to be warranted from the data which is presented in the referenced study. Grant and Grant do analyze their data in terms of the type of supervision individuals received (these are termed "predicted best supervision," "predicted next best supervision," "predicted worst supervision," and "companies with changing supervision" (p. ‑133). However, neither Grant and Grant nor Warren discuss how the quality of supervision was determined, and the terms "internally-oriented supervisory team" and "externally-oriented supervisory team" do not appear in the original study.

An examination of the data presented by Grant and Grant indicates that there is indeed an interaction betwen type of supervisory team and diagnosed maturity level. This interaction is due to the differential effect of treatment upon low-maturity offenders: A significantly *lower* proportion of low-maturity offenders receiving better treatment are returned to active duty than those receiving poorer treatment. When high-maturity offenders are examined, the type of treatment that is provided appears to make little difference, with approximately the same proportions of these individuals returning to active duty under all types of supervision. In addition, there appears to be no difference between the success rates of low-maturity offenders receiving no treatment and the success rates of both treated and nontreated high-maturity offenders. Finally, no evidence can be found to support Warren's contention that internally and externally oriented treatment have opposite effects upon high- and low-maturity offenders.

The results of the Grant and Grant study leads to a provocative conclusion: Since the major demonstrable effect of differential classification and treatment is a regressive one in the case of the low-maturity offenders provided the better treatment, would it not be preferable to omit classification and provide all with poor treatment? By so doing the probability of successful intervention would appear to be maximized.

Taken together, these two studies suggest there is an interaction between diagnosis and treatment. Adams' (1961) research indicates that a particular form of treatment might benefit one discernable group while leaving another unaffected. It is interesting that the success rate of even the group with the poorest postrelease performance is remarkably high, for at the end of the 36-month follow-up, only 15% had been reinstitutionalized. This suggests that his sample consisted of exceptional youths (which Adams denies in his characterization of the sample as representative of the highest age groups in the custody of the California Youth Authority), or that factors other than those that are accounted for by institutionalization, diagnosis, and treatment are operative. In contrast to the work of Adams, the research of Grant and Grant (1959) indicates that a particular form of treatment (vaguely defined) might be detrimental to one discernible group while leaving a second unaffected. It is risky, however, to view military corrections, with its peculiar characteristics, demands and expectancies, as an analog of civilian corrections. In addition, Grant and Grant's criterion for success (the return of the military offender to active duty) is questionable. It is not unlike considering all inmates paroled from civilian institutions "successes," and all those who are rejected for parole as "failures," for subjective biases and idiosyncratic requirements which shade the decision process are undoubtedly operating in both settings. A more appropriate criteria would, of course, be the successful adjustment of the offender upon his return to duty and/or to civilian life. Any firm decision concerning the role of differential diagnosis and treatment derived solely from these two studies would be, at best, of questionable validity and generalizability. The lack of any adequate data base upon which such decisions may be based highlights the void that separates theory and practice in modern corrections. Until a firm commitment is made to experimental correctional research this void will remain unbridged, and corrections will retain its position as the most primitive of the "helping disciplines."

The data derived from Phase 1 of California's Community Treatment Project (Warren, 1967a, b) is commonly taken as an experimental validation of the I-level diagnosis and treatment system. In Phase 1, first-time commitments to the California Youth Authority were designated as either eligible or ineligible for the projects; the eligibles were then randomly assigned to either the Community Treatment (Experimental) Project or to the regular Youth Authority (Control) Program. Approximately 73% of the juvenile males and 90% of the juvenile females having first-time commitments have been found eligible for CTP; those deemed ineligible are typically seriously assaultive cases and cases to which there is considerable community objection.

Following diagnosis, CTP youths were provided differential treatment. Each CTP case worker (Community Agent) was "matched" on the basis of his personality characteristics to one or two delinquent subtypes and carried a caseload of 12 youths. The prescription for I$_2$ youths typically involved placement in a "supportive environment" (usually foster homes) in an attempt to meet some of their unmet dependency needs while helping them to learn to perceive more accurately and respond more appropriately to the demands of society and its institutions. The treatment program for I_3 youths involved an adult who expressed concern for the youth by controlling his behavior. Group treatment was also employed, thereby taking advantage of the youth's dependence upon peers to control behavior, change attitudes, and increase social perceptiveness. Treatment for I_4 youths was aimed at the reduction of internal conflicts and an increased insight into personal and family dynamics which are taken as an important part of their acting-out behavior (Warren, 1970).

The comparison of the effectiveness of the Experimental and Control programs was based primarily upon failure rates on parole. The failure rate, which included all revocations of parole, recommitments from the courts, and unfavorable discharges, for Control youths was 52% after 15 months' exposure time and 61% after 24 months' exposure time. The failure rate for the Experimental youths was 28% after 15 months and 38% after 24 months. Of the nine diagnostic sybtypes, four show a failure rate difference favoring the Experimental program, one favoring the Control program, with no difference between the two for the remaining four types. Hypotheses concerning the reasons underlying the apparent differential effectiveness of institutional and community treatment of the juvenile offender have been constructed within the framework of the assumptions underlying the I-level classification system (Warren, 1967a, b).

In summary, CTP stressed three aspects of correctional practice: differential diagnosis and treatment; treatment within the community; and an exceedingly low staff-to-client ratio. It has been successful in its mission, for CTP youths showed a significantly lower rate of parole revocation than did their institutionalized controls. It is difficult to interpret these findings, however, for Warren (1970) comments:

> Experimental cases were rarely revoked for minor offenses, while Control cases were fairly often revoked for such offenses as placement failure, poor home or school adjustment, truancy or runaway. Even when a more serious offense is involved, Experimental Agents more often requested the youth's restoral to parole if some growth has been shown. (Pp. 676–677)

Do these differences account for a significant portion of CTP's apparent success rate? Not surprisingly, Warren thinks not: "While these differences in restoration practice may account for some revocation-rate differences, it is unlikely that it explains away all Experimental–Control failure rate differences" (P. 677). This conclusion may well be unwarranted.

A second problem in interpretation is involved in the comparison of community and institutional placement *per se*: If, as Meninger (1968) and Clark (1970), among others, have claimed, correctional facilities have regressive effects upon their charges, community placement may preclude this possibility and result in higher success rates. Warren does not address herself to this question, but Palmer (1971) does:

> . . . the community-located (Experimental) program is found to perform better with reference to 24 month follow-up than what may be termed the community-located (Control) program (traditional parole, with prior in-stitutionalization omitted or greatly reduced). At the same time, the direct parole/early release group of (Controls) perform slightly but not significantly worse on parole follow-up than (Controls) who have experienced the regular (institutional) program. (P. 90)

It appears, then, that CTP is more effective than either "typical" community treatment and institutionalization, with no great difference in success, as measured by parole revocation, between the latter two forms of treatment.

A third problem in interpretation revolves around an inability to determine the effectiveness of differential diagnosis and treatment beyond that which should be expected as a result of reduced case loads and the expectation that case workers provide "treatment" rather than more traditional "supervision." Warren (1970) argues that differential diagnosis and treatment accounts for a major share of CTP's success, for:

> Probation and parole departments everywhere use some or all of the (CTP) treatment methods. Some experiments have even used highly intensive, low case load programs without improved success rates. Because intensive treatment by competent personnel does not, of itself, guarantee results that differ from those of routine, nonintensive programs, it was assumed that the Project must include something more than skilled workers, small case loads, and even good intentions. (P. 673)

This "something more" is, of course, I-level classification and treatment.

It is indeed correct that a variety of intensive community intervention programs (to be reviewed in following sections) have proven ineffective. In some instances the lack of well-structured and directed treatment programs may have accomplished nothing more than increasing the efficiency with which violations were detected. In the bulk of such intervention programs, however, intensive treatment is synonomous with wide-scale deployment of the mental illness model in the form of differential diagnosis and the subsequent individual and group counseling and psychotherapy which they prescribe. While this is also true of CTP,

Palmer (1971) indicates that there have been departures from this model in the form of extensive surveillance, accredited school programs operated by CTP within their community-based treatment centers, small group tutoring, structured recreational and coeducational programs both within the treatment center and in the community, and so on.

California's Community Treatment Project appears to have implemented, on a wide scale, techniques that others have only advocated or employed on a limited scale. Namely, the treatment strategies employed by CTP have moved beyond traditional therapy conducted within the confines of the case worker's office and now are incorporated procedures which deal with the youthful offender in his "natural environment." In so doing, they have not only moved away from the mental illness model and toward the behavioral model of deviancy and intervention, they have also called into question the validity of the I-level classification system which depicts the causes of problematic behavior as lying within the individual. In addition, the degree to which specific intervention strategies have been keyed to the behavioral problems of individual offenders may account, in large part, for the success of CTP. Conversely, the utility of differential diagnosis and treatment procedures which prescribe general procedures for groups of individuals has been decreased.

Although there has been, in corrections, a long history of advocacy of the value of differential diagnosis and treatment in the mode of the mental illness model, little evidence can be found in support of this position: The reliability of the various diagnostic procedures has not yet been established; the validity of the various nosological categories has not yet been determined; the utility of this particular form of diagnosis and treatment has not yet been demonstrated; and the effectiveness of the treatments of choice has not yet been proven. It must be concluded that the applicability of the mental illness model of diagnosis and treatment to the practical problems faced by corrections has not yet been demonstrated.

THE MENTAL ILLNESS MODEL
IN THE TREATMENT OF THE OFFENDER

As was indicated previously, a number of studies have sought to determine the effectiveness of intervention strategies derived from the mental illness model upon youthful and adult offenders. Among the most rigorously designed, carefully executed and thoroughly evaluated of these is the Cambridge–Sommerville Youth Study (Teuber & Powers, 1953a, b). Subjects in this study consisted of 650 male youths who had been identified as delinquency-prone by welfare workers. The boys were divided into matched pairs on the basis of such variables as age, IQ, ethnicity, socio-economic background, and delinquency ratings. The toss of a coin decided which youth in each matched pair would be assigned to the group to receive treatment, and which would be assigned to a no-treatment control group. Treatment, which lasted between two and eight years in individual cases, consisted of either traditional psychoanalytic therapy or Rogerian client-centered therapy. Follow-up was carried on for five years following the end of the treatment period.

Ratings performed by the counselors indicated that about two-thirds of the youths had been substantially benefited by treatment, and that half of these had derived outstanding benefit from the program. These impressions were supported by the self-ratings of the youths, of whom 65% indicated that the program had aided them, kept them out of trouble, and so on. Unfortunately, the follow-up data failed to confirm the subjective reports of the therapists and their clients. McCord and McCord (1959) report that of 253 matched pairs traced into adulthood, 107 of the treatment youths were convicted of a total of 315 crimes, while 95 of the control youths were convicted of 344 crimes. Neither of these differences was found to be statistically significant. Powers and Witmer (1951) suggested that the treatment youths would evidence better adjustment as they matured. This does not appear to be the case, for a slightly, but not significantly, higher percentage of treatment youths had criminal records in each of three categories: those convicted only as juveniles; those convicted only as adults; and those convicted as both juveniles and as adults. Neither the length of treatment (more than six years in some instances), the number of therapists who worked with a youth, nor the frequency with which youths met with their therapists had any influence upon the patterns of delinquent and criminal behavior which emerged.

Commenting upon the results of this study, Teuber and Powers (1953) state:

> Such an outcome of the delinquency prevention program of the Study appears to be not only negative, but paradoxical. Instead of confirming the expectation that the treatment group would be less delinquent than the matched control group, there is a slight difference in favor of the control group . . . . Unless further developments change the picture . . . the direct comparison between T[reatment] and C[ontrol] groups fail to show that the major hypothesis can be sustained; treatment did not . . . reduce the incidence of adjudged delinquency in the treatment group. (P. 145)

McCord and McCord (1959) add: ". . . using the standard of 'official' criminal behavior, we must conclude that the Cambridge–Sommerville Youth Study was largely a failure. Some individuals undoubtedly (it is assumed) benefited from the program; but the group, as a whole, did not" (P. 96).

It is interesting to note that when the therapists were informed of the results of the study and provided the opportunity to comment upon the outcome, individuals of both therapeutic persuasions responded in a similar fashion:

> . . . those who were analytically trained and oriented asserted that the results would have been positive, had analytic principles been applied by all staff members, consistently, throughout the course of the treatment period. Conversely, those counselors, who were followers of Carl Rogers' non-directive approach averred that a systematic use of non-directive methods would have produced more definite success. (Teuber & Powers, 1953, P. 146)

Be this the case or not, the burden of proof lies with those who claim either specific or general effects of any form of treatment. Although the Cambridge–Sommerville Youth Study was a failure in that it did not demonstrate such effects, it was an unqualified success in that it emphasized the necessity of subjecting criminology's many myths and shibboleths to experimental validation. Studies that do not lend themselves to such analyses must be either reformulated so that they may be properly investigated or discounted as being of no value. To do otherwise is to continue to talk science and practice philosophy.

Admittedly, the mental illness model has influenced the training of psychiatrists and psychologists and defined their approach to the offender. What is more, the mental illness model lies behind the treatment practiced by social workers and the parole strategies implemented by probation and parole officers. Lemert (1971) has traced the evolution of the philosophical biases of social work from its early beginnings as a reformation-oriented endeavor to its current status as a discipline involved primarily with the delivery of supportive services and traditional therapy:

> Early-day social work was moralistic and reform oriented. It uncritically identified itself with middle class values and sought to induce conformity among clients who deviated from moral and legal standards of the community. The use of authority was not uncommon. As social work became more "scientific" or professional it sought to become amoral rather than moral. Work with the individual, particularly at the level of his feelings and attitudes, became the focus of social work techniques. Under the influence of psychiatric theories, social work in large part absorbed and adhered to this belief that deviant behavior is symptomatic and that its task is dynamic therapy, i.e., to get at the deep rooted, "real" problems of the clients. From

this point of view, overt deviance was relatively unimportant and, therefore, might have to be ignored in order to achieve some kind of individual growth or self growth. Social workers took the position like that of the psychiatrist, that it was not their job to enforce the law or even report law violations of their clients. To do so ran a serious risk of destroying the delicately cultivated rapport between them and their clients. (P. 49)

Although the role of the social worker in our society has now become institutionalized, and large staffs (and increasing sums of money) are devoted to this approach to the betterment of the human condition, little attempt has been made to determine the effect of what social workers do upon their clientele. When this has been done the results are far from encouraging. Meyer, Borgatta, and Jones (1970) investigated the outcome of social casework and group counseling services with girls who had been identified as potential problems and as a consequence were enrolled in a special vocational high school. Experimental and control girls were selected at random from those enrolled at the school, and the experimental girls were provided intensive casework and counseling by professional social workers in consultation with psychiatric and group therapy consultants. The control girls did not receive any special treatment. The program was operative for four years and its effects were assessed in terms of a number of different variables. There was no difference in the percentage of girls who were suspended or discharged from school. There was no reduction in "undesirable" associations. There was no difference between the attendance records of the experimental and control girls. The authors conclude that:

The personality tests, questionnaire responses, and sociometric data have failed to detect substantial differences between experimental and control cases. We must conclude that, with respect to all measures which we have used to examine the effects of the treatment program, only a minimal effect can be found. (Pp. 615–616)

A similar lack of effect was found in the midcity delinquency control project (Miller, 1970), a 4-year project with the objective of reducing the amount of illegal activity engaged in by adolescent residents of a lower-class district of Boston. A number of treatment techniques were employed. Psychiatrically-oriented social casework (under the supervision of psychodynamically trained psychiatrists) was provided families with histories of repeated and long-term utilization of public welfare services. The detached worker approach (Crawford, Malamud, & Dumpson, 1970) was employed in working with area gangs. An effort was made to develop and strengthen local citizens' groups and encourage them to take direct action in regard to local problems, including delinquency. Finally, an attempt was made to secure cooperation between the professional agencies of the community that were in any way involved with adolescents (settlement houses, churches, schools, psychiatric and medical clinics, police, courts, and probation departments, corrections and parole departments, etc.). A control group was constructed by identifying youths who had no contact with the project and matching them on the basis of age, race, ethnic status, social status, and gang membership in the same area of the city to youths who did receive services. The results of the comparison of the treated and control groups is provided by the author:

> It is now possible to provide a definite answer to the principal evaluative question—"Was there a significant measurable inhibition of law-violating or morally-disapproved behavior as a consequence of Project efforts?" The answer, with little necessary qualification, is "No." All major measures of violative behavior—disapproved actions, illegal actions, during-contact court appearances, before-during-after appearances, and Project-Control group appearances—provide consistent support for a finding of negligible impact. (P. 652)

Finally, most "enlightened" probation and parole strategies, at both the juvenile and adult levels, are modeled after the psychiatric casework approach to intervention and treatment. The justification for this approach has a long history, and the words spoken in its behalf a half century ago are indistinguishable from those spoken today:

> . . . the place of the medical expert in dealing with juvenile delinquency in the courts has been assured. Mental and physical defectiveness, next to defective environment and training, is probably the greatest cause of delinquency. Though recent studies have demonstrated that only a small proportion of children coming before the juvenile courts are feeble-minded, a much larger proportion are physically or mentally diseased or psychopathic, and all have tendencies and conditions which the expert psychiatrist and psychologist only can fully appreciate. The probation officer in his work of social investigating and treatment ought if possible to have had psychiatric training or at least a knowledge of the principles of this new science. (Chute, 1923, P. 225)

It is now an accepted or, perhaps, preferred practice to select probation and parole officers from those who have received undergraduate and advanced training in the social sciences; training which, by and large, continues to lay heavy emphasis upon the mental illness model as a medium through which the deviant individual may be understood as well as treated. As a consequence, these individuals bring with them, and perpetuate among themselves, this traditional conceptualization of the causes of criminal and delinquent behavior and how it must be dealt with as they work with their charges and interact with their professional peers. Adherence to this model is virtually unquestioned, and those who do question its validity or utility are, at best, tolerated or, at worst, viewed as poorly trained, stupid, or incompetent and dealt with accordingly. The mental illness model continues as the dominant force in contemporary probation and parole work, despite evidence from other areas of therapeutic endeavor (and for which the model appears more appropriate) that indicates that it is of doubtful value.

In summary, a number of treatment programs conceived within the framework of the mental illness model, involving a variety of psychiatrically trained professionals and directed toward the prevention or remediation of delinquent behavior have been reviewed. A large number of treatment programs have not been included in this review because they did not adhere to minimally acceptable principles of experimental design and, consequently, do not permit an assessment of their effectiveness or utility. The emphasis upon delinquency-oriented programs has not been by choice, but reflects instead general research and intervention priorities. The inescapable conclusion that must be drawn from this evaluative research is that intervention strategies deduced from the mental illness model of human behavior have had little, if any, success in dealing with criminal and delinquent behavior. Evaluative research in both the fields of mental health and in corrections leads to the same conclusion, namely, that the validity of the mental illness model and the utility of intervention strategies derived from that model have not yet been demonstrated.

Shah (1971), in explaining his general disaffection with and abandonment of the traditional psychotherapeutic approach to the offender population, cites its unsuitability, ineffectiveness, and inefficiency. He contends that the abject failure of the traditional approach may be attributable to the differences between offenders and others commonly depicted as aided by the psychotherapeutic process. The clients of most therapists enter therapy voluntarily with the goal of remediating troublesome behavior or feelings. Offenders, however, do not feel troubled and do not seek to change their patterns of behavior. They are, in short, not motivated to change. In addition, the requirements for successful therapy (the patient should talk freely, seek to understand the underlying causes of his problems, and not be resistive to therapy or act out, etc.) are reflective of a middle class value system and not, by and large, appropriate for, nor to be expected of, the vast majority of those adjudicated criminal or delinquent by our courts.

An alternative explanation, and one not offered by Shah, is that the failure of the traditional psychotherapeutic approach is not restricted to "special" populations such as the offender, but is, as has been discussed previously, a general phenomenon. The accountability built into the criminal justice system perhaps makes the failure of therapy more obvious to workers in the correctional field than it is to those working under the more vaguely defined criteria (if any) employed to determine "success" in the mental health fields. In addition, the distinctions made by Shah between good and poor risks for therapy may reflect more upon the liklihood that an individual will improve with or without therapy rather than the amenability of an individual to therapy. Viewed in this manner, it would be expected that comparisons of the success of therapy with offenders to that of other groups would indicate that therapy is less successful with the offender, when, in fact, the nonoffender population is simply more likely to show improvement over time, as a function of daily life experiences, than are the offenders.

Although one would hope that those charged with the responsibility of formulating crime and delinquency control programs would profit from these studies, this does not appear to be the case. As Burns and Stern (1967) have noted:

> There are few things sadder than producing a sound evaluation study over all obstacles and then watching its conclusions ignored. Evaluators often assume that "the facts will speak for themselves," but the history of evaluation in delinquency prevention—as in most other fields—shows that things seldom work so rationally. Decisions about the future of programs are affected by organizational self-protection, ideological fashion, practitioner defensiveness, and a host of other factors unrelated to program outcomes. Yet, if evaluation is to be worth its salt, it must get a hearing from the information it has produced. (Pp. 406–407)

Not only must evaluative research get a hearing, but its message must be acted upon. If effective intervention programs are to be developed, professionals in every field must overcome their theoretical/philosophical biases and in a truly pragmatic sense design and evaluate programs on the basis of a proven potential or ability to meet specifiable objectives. The failure of evaluative research to document the utility of the mental illness model in mental health has moved workers in that field to search for alternative approaches. The results of the evaluative research reviewed in this chapter should encourage professionals in corrections to do the same.

The preceding critique of the value of the medical model in the diagnosis and treatment of individuals, be they termed mentally ill, emotionally disturbed, delinquent, criminal, or whatever, should not be viewed as an indictment of either the motives of counselors and therapists or their clinical observations concerning the many differences among the clients with whom they work. These professionals are certainly committed to providing their clients the highest quality service possible. Moreover, they are correct in their observation that each client requires an individualized program tailored to the client's unique characteristics. What is being questioned is whether this individualized program should be based upon inferred attributes of the client's "personality." The evidence that is currently available indicates that those who have attempted to do so have met with little success. The following chapters describe an alternative approach to the development of individualized programs based upon the unique characteristics of clients. In doing so, however, we will not reexamine the personalities of our clients but we will instead look elsewhere for these distinguishing attributes.

CHAPTER

$$\boxed{4}$$

THE BEHAVIORAL MODEL: AN ALTERNATIVE APPROACH TO PSYCHIATRIC TREATMENT AND OFFENDER REHABILITATION

Tharp and Wetzel (1969) have observed that:

> The winds of discontent are gusting over the lands of helping professions. Psychology, social work, corrections, psychiatry, education, rehabilitation nursing; hospitals, clinics, schools, prisons, psychotherapists, pastoral counselors, teachers, probation officers; criticism, self-examination, and the hard facts of research evidence bring to each of these the courage to change and the anxiety of ambiguity. The dogmas of the last century's orthodox psychology do not stand before the challenge of this century's human condition. . . . Certainly among us there is much self-satisfaction and reluctance to disturb the comforts of routine and old habits. But beyond that, the thrust towards excellence and the dedicated desire to extend help is discernable—

to authentically extend the helping enterprise in ways that are more effective for a much broader portion of the spectrum of human misery. (P. 1)

No evidence exists to support the contention that the mental illness model of human behavior has produced a technology of behavior change applicable to the problems facing the practitioner in either mental health in general or in corrections in particular (Eysenck, 1952, 1966; Rachman, 1971). It is now apparent that those in the helping professions must search for and perfect alternative conceptualizations of the causes of human behavior if they are to effectively serve those who come under their care, as well as society itself.

The behavioral model (Ullman & Krasner, 1969) has the potential of succeeding where the mental illness model has failed. This potential is clearly outlined by Brown (1971) following his review of the effectiveness of the behavioral model in dealing with a variety of psychological problems in all areas of mental health. He concludes that the behavioral model, when contrasted to the mental illness model, appears to offer:

1. Greater *effectiveness* as a treatment method; i.e., at least for some emotionally disturbed behaviors the results are often clearly superior.

2. Greater *efficiency* as a treatment method, i.e., in general, it takes less time and fewer sessions to bring about desired changes in the patient's life adjustment.

3. Greater *specificity* in establishing goals and outcome of therapy; i.e., the specific end result of therapy is specified at the beginning of therapeutic work.

4. Greater *applicability* to a wider segment of the population; i.e., it covers a broad spectrum of maladaptive behaviors rather than, for example, being limited more or less to upper class neurotic patients with above average intelligence, etc.

5. Greater *utilization* as a treatment method by various groups; i.e., the [behavioral model] can be used not only by the practitioners of the basic mental health disciplines themselves but by public health and other nurses, case workers, counselors, adjunctive therapists, teachers, etc., and even by parents. (P. 32)

Just what, then, is the behavioral model in both theory and application? Reynolds (1968) provides an excellent description of the basic orientation of operant conditioning, the laboratory science upon which behavior modification, the applied science of human behavior, is based. He responds to the question: What is operant conditioning?

Operant conditioning is concerned with the relationship between the behavior of organisms and their environment. Research in operant conditioning gathers knowledge about behavior from the experimental study of the effects on behavior of systematic changes in the surrounding environment. Operant conditioning attempts to understand behavior by gaining knowledge of the factors that modify behavior. As an objective science, it is restricted to the study of the factors that can be observed, measured, and reported. The science of operant conditioning has accumulated an enormous body of knowledge and has taken great strides toward a complete answer to the question: What makes organisms behave as they do? (Pp. 1–2)

The behavioral model holds to these same fundamental precepts. As such, it represents a veritable revolution in the manner in which human behavior is examined, understood, and dealt with. Unlike the mental illness model, it is the result of a rapprochement between psychology as a basic and as an applied science. This therapeutic orientation retains the rigorous scientific approach to its subject matter—the analysis and remediation of complex human problems—and employs and validates, in practice, the basic principles and laws of behavior identified in the experimental laboratory.

Within the context of the mental illness model, persons manifesting deviant behavior are depicted as mentally ill and, as such, qualitatively different from those not manifesting such behavior. This approach leads the traditional practitioner to focus his attention upon the individual or, more specifically, upon inferred internal processes that are thought to underlie his manifest deviancy. In contrast to this orientation, the behavioral model postulates that the differences between persons labeled deviant and nondeviant lie not within the individual, but are a function of the interrelationship between the behavior of the individual and his environment (broadly defined). Furthermore, this model posits that these differences are quantitative rather than qualitative in nature. That is, persons are brought to the attention of the various social agencies not because their behavior *per se* is markedly different from that engaged in by other members of society, but because they engage in that behavior to a noticeably greater or lesser degree than does a majority of the population, or because the behavior is considered an inappropriate response to existant times, places, or social contexts. For example, little attention is paid to the youth who occasionally "skips school." It is the youth who engages in this behavior at a high frequency who earns the attention of the juvenile court and the title "truant." In a similar manner, the behavior of a soldier in the heat of battle and the looter in the midst of a riot, although similar in many ways, is reacted to in a considerably different fashion by society.

With the artificial distinction between sick and healthy individuals rejected, both deviant and nondeviant behavior is conceptualized as "normal"; that is, the same basic laws and principles underlie all forms of human behavior. It is the unique and idiosyncratic experiences of individuals which determine, in large measure, their mode of behaving. More specifically, by conceptualizing deviant or antisocial behavior as behavior that is acquired, maintained, and modifiable in accord with the same principles by which other behaviors are learned, it is possible to marshal these principles in order to weaken or eliminate undesirable activities while at the same time providing for, strengthening, and maintaining constructive, nondeviant behaviors in their place.

If, as in the case of the mental illness model, disapproved behavior is considered symptomatic of some underlying disorganization of personality, intervention is logically directed toward the remediation of that disorganization. Diagnosis within this framework is an attempt to identify the specific nature of the inferred disturbance so that appropriate treatment strategies may be determined and implemented. As has been discussed previously, the utility of this approach, in terms of its reliability, validity, and effectiveness, has been examined in both mental health in general and in correctional contexts in particular, and has been found lacking in both areas. The behavioral model offers an alternative conceptualization of the causes of human behavior, one which stresses the nature of the interrelationship between behavior and environment. This model is offered as a more effective vehicle for the understanding, prediction, control, and modification or change of human behavior than has heretofore been available to those charged with the difficult task of solving the problems facing Americans in the homes, schools, ghettoes, and factories of this land.

A major emphasis of the behavioral model is upon overt, measurable behavior as a primary datum or subject matter. Indeed, this aspect of the model is commonly taken as its sole defining characteristic. This is unfortunate for at least two reasons. First, the subject matter of the behavioral model encompasses considerably more than *just* the behavior of individuals. Also of concern are the affective components of behavior (Wolpe, 1976). Secondly, the term "behavior" has gained such popularity among nonbehaviorists in both professional and lay circles that its original and appropriate meaning has all but been lost. Schaefer and Martin (1969) have commented upon this strange phenomenon:

> The word "behavior" has become such common coin that like all common coin it is shiny but faceless. Over the last forty-years its use has increased twenty-fold in the titles of scientific articles alone, but the number of behavioral scientists has not. And all that is called behavior today is not necessarily behavior in the sense in which a behavioral scientist uses the word. (P. 3)

The term "behavior" refers to that which is publicly observable, either directly or with the aid of special instrumentation that allows measurement of physiological processes such as heart rate and blood pressure. Used as such it allows procedures that have been validated in one setting to be applied in a second. Research that attempts to deal with unobservables is not only logically impossible (Ramp and Hopkins, 1971), but tends to employ vaguely defined criteria and procedures that lessen the chances for replication.

The major objective of the behaviorist has been the specification of the manner in which environmental phenomena influence or control behavior. Closely related to this approach has been a general reluctance to turn to inferred but unobservable "inner" agents or processes to explain phenomena that may be most parsimoniously understood in terms of identifiable relationships between behavior and its antecedents or consequences. The acquisition and maintenance of behavior may be viewed as a natural outcome of two distinct arrangements of environmental events. In one, respondent conditioning, behavior is elicited by its antecedants; in the other, operant conditioning, behavior is maintained by its consequences.

Respondents are relatively fixed responses to specific stimuli, such as orienting in the direction of a sudden, loud noise, tearing in response to an irritant in the eye, and salivating when food is placed in the mouth. These relationships between this class of stimuli and responses is not dependent upon physical maturation. Pavlov is generally credited with the first systematic investigation of the manner in which reflexlike behavior may be acquired. In the respondent conditioning paradigm (also termed classical conditioning, Pavlovian conditioning, and Type-S conditioning) a relatively neutral stimulus (i.e., one that does not elicit the to-be-conditioned response) comes to elicit a response similar to an unconditioned response through its repeated pairing with the unconditioned stimulus which regularly does elicit that response. The previously neutral stimulus is termed the conditioned stimulus while the response it now elicits is termed the conditioned response. Although it is sometimes implied that the respondent conditioning paradigm results in "new" reflexes, this does not appear to be the case and, indeed, this was not the contention of Pavlov. Conditioned responses do not follow the same laws as do unconditioned responses, indicating that they are distinctly different phenomena. In addition, close examination of the conditioned response reveals that it is seldom, if ever, identical to the unconditioned response despite their unusual similarity.

The importance of respondent conditioning is its postulated close relationship with the emotions, for it is generally accepted that this paradigm underlies the acquisition of most emotional behavior. It has been observed that environmental conditions or objects (including people) regularly associated with pleasant or unpleasant events appear to generate corresponding emotional characteristics to the degree, at least, that these characteristics may be inferred on the basis of verbal reports and overt behavior. Fear and aggression are viewed as the product of unconditioned aversive stimulus and the conditioned stimulus which precedes it. The tender emotions, such as affection and kindness, have not been as closely examined as have the more violent emotions. When viewed from this perspective they would be postulated to be elicited by unconditioned appetitive stimuli and the conditioned stimuli that regularly precede them.

Although it is most common to view emotions as a product of the respondent conditioning, it is equally possible that emotional behavior may be a function of its consequences. That is, emotional behavior may be operants that are maintained by their effects on the environment. Within this context, the aggressive behavior of a particular individual would be explained in terms of what function that behavior has served for the individual in the past. In like manner, the consequences of affection would be viewed as determining the degree to which an individual exhibits affection. A past history of positive consequences for displaying affection would explain the behavior rather than the conclusion that the individual has a "loving personality."

The term "operant" refers to specifiable classes of responses, or acts, which operate upon the environment to produce certain consequences for the operator. The consequences of operants, in turn, affect the probability that classes of operants will be repeated in the future.

Functional definitions of operants group a variety of morphologically different behaviors together into a class. This given class will have a common effect upon the environment. For example, threatening, hitting, kicking, and so on, are commonly grouped together as a single behavior class ("antisocial" behavior) without regard to their effect upon the environment. However, these activities can have a variety of different effects—forced compliance of another, escape from the persecution of another, approval of the peer group, attention *per se,* and so on. By examining the behavior and its effect, we avoid the error of labeling and treating the same behavior in different individuals (or within the same individual at different times) as the same when, in fact, it is functionally different (i.e., results in differing consequences for different individuals or for the same individual at different times).

When first encountered, the principles that make up this discipline often appear either misleading or seductively simple. Some first find it difficult to appreciate the manner in which the principles may be employed to explain the broad expanse of complex behavior in which man engages. Others feel that they have a firm grasp of the principles and hurry to apply them. It verges upon the impossible to detail in a limited amount of space just how psychologists can and do employ these principles to both understand and change a wide range of human behavior. It is possible, however, to urge those who are so impressed to study the field in more depth. Similarly, it is not possible to communicate to the enthusiast that the ability to successfully employ these principles requires an understanding and appreciation of a host of subtleties only hinted at in brief introductions to the discipline. Contrary to what is becoming a more and more common belief, Michael and Meyerson (1962) have warned:

> A behavioral approach to human control does not consist of a bag of tricks to be applied mechanically for the purpose of coercing unwilling people. It is part of a highly technical system, based on laboratory investigations of the phenomena of conditioning, for describing behavior and specifying the conditions under which it is acquired, maintained, and eliminated. (P. 382)

The application of "behavior modification" by those who view the technology as nothing more than a "bag of tricks" and/or by those who have not had extensive training and supervision is undoubtedly more harmful than beneficial for both the individuals subjected to "treatment" and for the behavioral approach itself.

A basic proposition of the psychological model is that the therapists, by nature of the position and role they have assumed, must also assume responsibility for conducting treatment and its eventual success (or failure). It is their role to identify critical initial behaviors, select realistic and appropriate terminal behaviors, devise and implement intervention strategies, insure that their prescriptions are fulfilled, ascertain their effectiveness, and institute changes if it is determined that their original formulations are lacking. All too frequently change agents seek to abrogate this responsibility by maintaining that they can work effectively with only those individuals who "are ready for help," or "want to help themselves." The "facilitative" role of the change agent is a central characteristic of most psychotherapeutic systems, and is captured in Ford and Urban's (1963) description of what Carl Rogers considers to be an "effective therapist":

> An effective therapist does not manipulate events to produce specific changes in the patient's behavior. He does not change the patient, the patient changes himself. At the most, the therapist creates a set of conditions under which it becomes possible for the patient to overcome faulty learnings and acquire new ones. The learning that occurs in therapy is self-discovery. (P. 400)

Indeed, it is frequently argued that for the change agent to attempt to do otherwise is unethical and/or immoral.

That the change agent does indeed do otherwise has been suggested by Truax (1966). He obtained audiotape recordings of Rogers' therapeutic sessions with a long-term patient and analyzed and categorized the patient's verbal productions on the basis of their content. Nine categories were identified. He then analyzed Rogers' responses to these verbal productions. This analysis revealed that Rogers responded differentially following verbal productions classed in five of the nine categories, providing responses that communicated understanding, warmth, and affirmation to "healthy" statements while withholding this tacit approval if the productions were "unhealthy." In addition, it was discovered that the statements that earned approval (the "healthy" statements) increased in frequency, while the statements that were ignored (the "unhealthy" statements) decreased in frequency. Whaley and Malott (1971), in their review of this study, concluded:

> The patient is reinforced for saying the right things. He receives reinforcement as long as he stays "on the right track," but not when he makes statements which are confused, self-depreciating, pessimistic, or generally unhealthy. As therapy continues, the patient's healthy verbal behavior begins to generalize to areas outside the session. He is more optimistic, relaxed, and clearer than before. Friends and acquaintances see this change and respond to it favorably, thus reinforcing his new personality. Soon it can be maintained by persons other than the therapist, and therapy may be terminated. (P. 71)

It appears, then, that this form of analysis reveals that even the most nondirective of the non–directive therapists exerts considerable, albeit "unintentional," control over the behavior of his clients. Therapists, in general, must, therefore, come to grips with this possibility and its consequent responsibilities despite any ethical, moral, or systemic predispositions to the contrary. More important, however, are the implications of these findings for the training of new therapists. If the behavior of successful therapists may be understood as a process involving the careful application of the principles of operant conditioning, it logically follows that the most effective manner in which to teach individuals to become effective therapists is to instruct them in these basic principles and their application to human problems. Until this is done, the preparation of most therapists will continue to consist of instruction in vague generalities deduced from untested theories followed by on-the-job practice during which the contingencies operative in the therapeutic session sometimes produce (and often times fail to produce) effective change agents. This is painfully evident in a description of psychotherapy cited in Raimy (1950): "Psychotherapy is an undefined technique applied to unspecified problems with unpredictable outcome. For this technique we recommend rigorous training" (P. 93).

THE UTILITY OF THE BEHAVIORAL MODEL
IN THE AREA OF MENTAL HEALTH

The treatment of institutionalized schizophrenic patients presents a major challenge to the mental health professions. While the introduction of phenothiazines and the development of community treatment centers has contributed to a decline in the number of hospitalized mental patients, it appears that this is not as hopeful as it first appeared. There are apparently two psychiatric populations. One population responds well and turns over fairly rapidly. Another population, however, does not move in and out of the hospital rapidly, and becomes the source of chronic patients.

The first group of short-term patients accounts for most of the reduction in institutional population size. Unfortunately, this subgroup consists of only about one-third of the total population. The second and chronic subgroup is much larger. This group has a very low probability of discharge, and when these patients are released they are usually readmitted in a matter of months (Fairweather, Sanders, Maynard, & Cressler, 1969).

The first attempt to investigate the behavior of chronic, institutionalized psychiatric patients, using the methods of operant psychology, was that of Lindsley and Skinner (1954). Since this initial investigation, an operant approach to the treatment of the hard-core institutionalized mental patient has evolved. This approach has developed, essentially, into two treatment strategies: (a) ward-wide group treatment programs; and (b) individual treatment programs. The following is a brief discussion of the outcomes of these two strategies beginning with the group programs. A description of the specific procedures employed in these group programs is provided within the context of the token economy in a subsequent chapter.

GROUP PROCEDURES

Ayllon and Haughton (1962) and Ayllon and Azrin (1965) were among the first to apply group contingencies to hospitalized schizophrenic patients. Ayllon and Azrin (1965) developed the token economy to bring the behavior of chronic psychiatric patients under the control of ward contingencies.

Briefly, a token economy is a structured motivational environment based upon positive reinforcement in which individuals "earn" tokens by engaging in specified activities and then exchange the tokens for the opportunity to partake of privileges available in the treatment milieu. Their behavioral program was effective in increasing performance of assignments, maintaining job performance, and increasing self-care behavior. These results were found for 58 of a total of 65 patients.

Steffy, Hart, Draw, Torney, and Marlett (1969) set up a behavioral program to improve eating and self-care behaviors and to reduce disruptive behaviors in a group of psychiatric patients with a mean term of hospitalization of 20 years. At the end of one year of treatment, 16 of the 36 patients were placed in community boarding homes. After two years only four of the patients had been returned to the hospital. Similarly, Lloyd and Abel (1970) developed a behavioral program that emphasized personal care, work, and social interaction. At the end of the study, 21 months after it began, 13 of 52 patients had been discharged and 9 had been moved to wards for less severe patients.

Another study dealing with chronic psychiatric patients was one reported by McReynolds and Coleman (1972). The clients in this program were "back ward" patients with a mean hospitalization time of 13 years. A behavioral program was implemented to foster a variety of behaviors including eating, grooming, dressing, and recreational activities. Significant gains were reported for most of the target behaviors. After one year of treatment, 12 of the 48 clients had off-ward jobs, 11 were in occupational therapy, 13 were on open wards, 5 had made home visits, and 9 had been placed in the community.

McReynolds and Coleman also investigated the difference in attitudes toward and perception of patients between the staff on the behavioral ward and other wards. The staff on the behavioral ward had more positive attitudes toward the patients and perceived the patients as having greater potential for positive treatment outcome, as being more normal, and as more likely to receive discharge. These effects were attributed to the program's focus on positive observable behaviors. The program also gave staff members a sense of being involved in a productive treatment.

The behavioral approach has been demonstrated to be effective with a wide variety of behaviors in chronic institutionalized patients. Among the behaviors affected by this treatment procedure have been personal care, work behavior, social behavior, recreation, apathy, and aggression. In addition, behavioral programs appear to positively affect discharge rates, recidivism, and staff attitudes. The question which next arises is: How does the behavioral approach compare with other treatments?

A common problem in chronic psychiatric patients is apathy. Schaefer and Martin (1966) compared a behavioral program to a routine psychiatric treatment and their effects upon apathetic behaviors. Apathy was construed as a very limited behavioral repertoire relative to environmental stimuli. The target behaviors were hygiene, work performance, and social interaction. Significant results were obtained only for the behavioral treatment group. Further, the recidivism rate for patients in this group was cut in half. A similar study that also demonstrated the effectiveness of a behavioral program for apathy was that of Atthowe and Krasner (1968).

A comparison study which used patients on other wards for a contrast group, thereby reducing the problem of keeping treatments separate, reported significant results in favor of the token economy (Gripp & Magaro, 1971). The other treatment, however, was not specified. The measurement procedure was indirect, and the treatment staff was selected on the basis of their willingness to try new techniques and their optimism toward patients.

Birky, Chambliss, and Wasden (1971) compared a behavioral program with a traditional psychiatric program. Traditional treatment was chemotherapy, weekly groups, and individual therapy in some cases. The behavioral program focused on self-care, work, and living skills. The results revealed that the behavioral program was more effective than the psychiatric program in discharging long-term patients.

Finally, Maley, Feldman, and Ruskin (1973), conducted a study in which subjects were randomly assigned to behavioral treatment and control groups (which consisted of) whatever routine treatment was available on the control subjects' wards. The assessment was by means of ratings and revealed superiority of the behavioral program in terms of "normal" behavioral parameters. In conclusion, then, the comparison studies reviewed have generally favored the behavioral approach.

INDIVIDUALIZED PROCEDURES

Studies employing behavioral procedures with groups have constituted a great deal of the behavioral research with schizophrenics. Another major focus has been research on specific psychotic disorders using individualized procedures.

The first study along these lines was by Ayllon and Michael (1959). They trained psychiatric nurses to modify certain problem behaviors of chronic schizophrenics. The behavioral procedures of extinction, reinforcement of incompatible behavior, escape and avoidance conditioning, and stimulus satiation were used to modify specific behaviors. Each undesirable target behavior was reduced following the application of behavioral techniques. Since 1959 behavioral techniques have been successfully applied to a variety of psychotic disorders.

Verbal Behavior

Verbal behavior has been studied by several researchers. Isaacs, Thomas, and Goldiamond (1960) successfully reinstated speech in two psychotics, who had been mute for extended periods of time. This study strongly suggests abnormal behavior can be decreased by the selective increase of normal behavior. Other studies have also demonstrated reinstatement of verbal behavior (Baker, 1971; Sherman, 1965).

Social Skills Training

Some current researchers are concerned with the development of social skills in schizophrenics. This work is related to Zigler's findings on posthospital adjustment (Zigler & Phillips, 1961; Levine & Zigler, 1973). Specifically, the better a person's social skills and adjustment prior to the onset of hospitalization, the better his/her posthospital adjustment will be.

Social skills have been behaviorally defined as "the complex ability to maximize the rate of positive reinforcement and minimize the strength of punishment from others" (Libet & Lewinsohn, 1973, p. 311). Skill training emphasizes the positive, educational benefits of therapy. Skill training usually employs one or all of the following behavioral strategies: instructions, feedback, modeling, behavior rehearsal, social reinforcement, and homework assignments.

A few researchers have been concerned with assertiveness skill training with schizophrenic patients (Hersen, Eisler, Miller, Johnson, & Pinkston, 1973; Eisler, Hersen, & Miller, 1973). Wisler et al. (1973) compared the effectiveness of behavioral treatment and two control procedures. The behavioral group was significantly improved, relative to the other two groups, on five of eight components of assertion. Hersen et al. (1973) followed the same design as Eisler et al. and replicated their findings.

An elegant, well-controlled study by Goldsmith and McFall (1975) compared interpersonal skill training, a pseudo therapy control group, and an assessment-only control group on the development of social skills, with psychiatric in-patients. The skill training was found to lead to greater pre–post differences than the other two conditions. In addition, greater generalization was observed with the skill training group.

These studies are illustrative of the training of schizophrenics in socially important behaviors. Instead of training the patients simply to conform to hospital conduct standards, they are trained in behaviors that are extremely important for posthospital adjustment.

Self-Control

Newly developed techniques of self-control are being applied to schizophrenic patients. Behavioral self-control is a means for training individuals to exert more control of the contingencies controlling their behavior (Thoresen & Mahoney, 1974). Epstein and Hersen (1974) were able to get a reduction in cigarette smoking, lip biting, and finger picking by teaching a patient how to self-monitor and contingently self-reinforce. Hallucinations have been reduced by self-monitoring (Rutner & Bugle, 1969).

Meichenbaum and Cameron (1973) were able to improve the performance of schizophrenic patients on several sensorimotor tasks by self-instructional procedure, relative to attention-practice and no-treatment control groups. Patients in a second study were compared to a yoked practice control group. Self-instructional patients showed significantly more improvement than the controls on measures of abstract thinking and percentage of "sick talk" (i.e., bizarre, incoherent, or irrelevant responses in an interview).

In conclusion, group and individualized behavioral procedures offer considerable hope for helping schizophrenic patients overcome some of their debilitating problems. The behavioral approaches appear to be more effective than other approaches or no treatment (Gripp & Magaro, 1971; Eisler et al., 1973; Meichenbaum & Cameron, 1973). Social skill and self-instructional training procedures are being used as techniques for modifying extremely complex maladaptive behaviors.

THE BEHAVIORAL MODEL IN THE TREATMENT OF THE OFFENDER

Although the effectiveness of applied behavior analysis procedures has been amply demonstrated in a variety of mental health, health-related, and educational settings (*Journal of Applied Behavior Analysis,* 1968 to present), only recently has there emerged the beginnings of a concerted effort to determine how they may be best applied to the problems facing workers in the areas of crime and delinquency. The "street corner research" or "subject–experimenter psychotherapy" of Slack and his associates (Slack, 1960; Schwitzgebel, 1964; Schwitzgebel & Kolb, 1964) is among the earliest examples of this movement. Their work in metropolitan Boston illustrated how the principles of applied behavior analysis can be employed in the community to encourage "unreachable" delinquents to participate in traditional forms of counseling and psychotherapy, acquire the skills necessary to secure and hold employment, and seek out and establish new friendships with nondelinquent peers.

Juvenile Offenders

Cohen, Filipczak, and Bis (1967) examined the feasibility of employing behavior modification procedures in the form of a token economy (Ayllon & Azrin, 1965) as the basis for a rehabilitative regimen for delinquent juveniles incarcerated at the National Training School for Boys, Washington, D.C. Cohen et al. (1967) were concerned primarily with developing and maintaining educational (study and learning) behavior and, within this context, noted that their population did not have the acquisitional and attitudinal patterns (study habits, the honoring of commitments, etc.) that are necessary for learning in the classroom. Through the use of the token economy it was possible to overcome these deficiencies and the students, typically classified as "unmotivated" in other educational settings, averaged a 2.7 year grade gain as measured by the Scholastic Achievement Test over the course of the six-month project.

Based upon the success of this program, which was operative only during "normal" school hours, the scope of the program expanded to 24 hours per day, seven days per week (Cohen & Filipczak, 1971; Cohen, Filipiczak, & Bis, 1967). Architectural and behavioral modifications and procedures were introduced in a four-story structure of the National Training School to fulfill the students' requirements of rest, nourishment, hygiene, and recreation. A complete educational program was also developed, and these activities, as well as family visits and furloughs, were integrated into a system designed to maintain educational behavior patterned after the model developed during the initial study. The program was voluntary and individualized in that students were not required to participate in any of the activities offered by the program, nor to engage in any of the routine housekeeping chores involved in the maintenance of the training facility. However, such activities did earn tokens—the structure upon which the program operated. The major way in which tokens were earned was by participating in the education program. Here, programmed instructional material was used extensively, and a criterion of 90% accuracy in the material was required before the students could take an exam covering that material and subsequently earn tokens. Students who wished to supplement their income could work part-time in the kitchen and dining room, and perform routine janitorial, maintenance, and clerical work. Finally, the correctional officers assigned to the program could award tokens as bonuses for exemplary social behavior. Backup reinforcers (those privileges and commodities for which the tokens were exchanged) included, among other things, soft drinks, milk, and potato chips, purchased from the store; entrance and time in a lounge or library; smoke breaks; rental of private room; rental of books and magazines; the purchase of private tutoring; and the purchase of furloughs.

The results of employing such a technology in this setting were highly encouraging. For every 150 hours of schoolroom instruction students gained, on the average, between 2 and 4 months' grade level increase (approximately three times the standard expectancy for general public school children). Nineteen students involved in the entire year-long program showed a mean IQ gain of 16.2 points as measured by the Revised Beta. The authors, in commenting on some of the nontangible results of the behavior modification approach as compared to the common mode of institutional control, note that in their program the individual made his own decision. They note that it is critical that the delinquent boy learn to make these decisions because, in our society, he has to accept the consequences of his decisions. Programs that do not give him that opportunity, or which do not provide a structure in which consequences regularly follow behavior, fail to prepare him to cope in the "real" world. It is through a system in which an individual makes decisions and experiences success and failure that the youth can begin to evaluate his own performance, begin to take responsibility for his own behavior, and prepare himself for a world that is not under constant parental, penal, or political monitoring. An evaluation of the program revealed that academic skills and IQs increased, as measured by standardized tests, and positive attitudinal changes were observed in the youths as well. Moreover, the program appeared to have a positive effect upon the youths' adjustments following their release from the school even in the absence of a transitional program. The youths stayed out of trouble and out of institutions for longer periods of time than the national average.

However, the eventual level of recidivism was the same as that of comparable releases (Filipczak & Cohen, 1972).

The behavior modification approach has also been employed with considerable success at Achievement Place, a residential, community-based home-style living center for predelinquent boys (Phillips, 1968; Bailey, Wolf, & Phillips, 1970; Phillips, Phillips, Fixsen & Wolf, 1971). Achievement Place, in cooperation with the Juvenile Court, the County Department of Social Welfare, school officials, and teaching-parents, is developing a model program designed to improve the academic, social, and self-care behaviors of youths who are (or are about to be) suspended from school, who are in trouble in the community, or who are thought to be "uncontrollable by their parents." As has so often been noted, each youth's problem exists in his community, and the treatment procedures, if they are to be successful, must focus on his behavior where it is problematic: in his school, in his home, and in his peer group. The goal of Achievement Place is to help the boy become a secure, well-adjusted, and useful citizen, and to achieve this goal the program is designed to modify undesirable and antisocial behavior while developing new and appropriate behavior patterns. To accomplish this, Achievement Place adopted the token economy as the most efficient medium of treatment.

The token economy allows the youths to earn tokens for appropriate behavior and to lose tokens for inappropriate behavior. In addition, the token system provides the boy immediate and concrete feedback when he first enters the program. As the boy's skills and self-control develop, he may earn his way out of the highly structured token system. As this system is gradually withdrawn, it is replaced by more natural (teacher–parent, peer, and academic) feedback conditions. If a youth's behavior indicates that he needs more experience with the structure of the token system he can lose his new status and return to the token system. Once he has demonstrated his ability to exercise self-control, to take responsibility for his own behavior, and to work productively in the home and school, he is ready to be returned to his own home or to a foster family. To maintain the gains which have been made at Achievement Place, each family receives training in behavioral management techniques. The boy's progress with his family is closely monitored for several months following his release, and he may be returned to Achievement Place if it is deemed beneficial.

The Achievement Place program examines important areas of social concern including verbal interaction in the form of aggressive statements, poor grammar, and articulation errors. It also encourages the development of appropriate study skills including completion of homework as well as academic performance in school. Good work habits such as following rules, punctuality, and tidiness are also fostered through this program. Finally, prosocial behaviors including self-control and social responsibility are instilled.

In the first project, the frequency of aggressive statements and poor grammar were decreased through the token economy, and tidiness, punctuality, and the amount of homework completed were increased. The program was continued and resulted in repeated demonstrations of the effectiveness of the token procedure including improvements in awareness of current events and promptness at evening meals (Phillips et al., 1971). Scheduling effects were examined by delivering points contingent upon room-cleaning behaviors and gradually decreasing the number of days when the reinforcement was delivered. The behavior increased and remained at a relatively high rate for over six months even when points were delivered on only 8% of the days. Money saving was increased but was not maintained when points were not delivered for deposits.

Within the same setting, small groups of adolescents participated in a number of projects using peers. One such study involved the modification of articulation errors of two boys by their peers (Bailey, Timbers, Phillips, & Wolf, 1971). Error words involving particular consonants and consonant combinations were treated by peer modeling and approval, contingent points and feedback by groups and individual students who were, in turn, given points for training. Generalization to other, non-trained, words occurred and the results were replicated.

Since previous work has shown the significance of peer influence for delinquents, a series of studies at Achievement Place was conducted utilizing peer control for prosocial behaviors. The first study examined the reliability of self-reports and peer reports of room-cleaning behavior (Fixsen, Phillips, & Wolf, 1973). Although reliable reporting in both cases was improved by training on behavioral definitions and points contingent for agreement with a second peer observer, neither kind of report produced a systematic effect on the target behavior.

The democratic decision-making process in a small group of students was also studied and the variables affecting participation were investigated. In the Achievement Place, semi-self-government system, youths established many of their own rules of behavior, they monitored their peers' behavior to detect violations of their rules and they conducted "trials" to establish the guilt or innocence of rule violators and to determine the consequences for the violation. Results indicate that more boys participated in the discussion of consequences for a rule violation when they had complete responsibility for setting them during the trial rather than having the teaching parents do it for them. However, more trials were called when the teaching parents were responsible for calling trials on rule violations reported by the peers than when the boys were responsible for calling trials. Contingent points for calling trials resulted in increased frequency but for more trivial rule violations.

Another series of studies was conducted to compare several arrangements for assigning routine tasks and for providing token consequences for task performance. Effectiveness in completing the tasks and task preferences were evaluated (Phillips, Phillips, Wolf, & Fixsen, 1973). Results of the analysis indicated that the system most preferred and most effective included a peer manager who was democratically selected and who had the authority to award and take away points for his peers' performances.

Home-style treatment facilities are not an uncommon phenomenon–how does this one differ from the vast majority of others operative in this country? At Achievement Place the emphasis is upon behavior, and upon a technology that enables the practitioner to change behavior. Both desirable and undesirable behavior is specified and its frequency of occurrence is determined. Individual and group treatment procedures are implemented; and these procedures focus upon the relationship between the behavior in question and their consequences. The identification of these behaviors and monitoring of performance allows constant assessment of the effects of treatment and provides the basis for the determination of their success and/or failure. By so doing, it is possible to develop alternative programs when the one in effect is found lacking, and to progress to the next stage of treatment when initial objectives are met. Finally, the extrinsic reinforcers provided by the token economy are gradually faded out, and new behaviors, now occurring at a relatively high frequency, come to be maintained by their natural consequences— those that the individual will encounter in the "real" world.

The training of individuals in the natural environment (real or foster parents) in behavior modification techniques and the appropriate use of social and other reinforcers, maximizes the probability that the behaviors will indeed be maintained once the youth leaves the treatment facility. The success of this approach, as reported by the authors, is highly encouraging. Once the boys enter the Achievement Place program, there are virtually no unpleasant contacts with the law. The schools report that they are "new boys." They take pride in their achievements and enjoy their new-found responsibilities. The success of the boys has been great enough to lead the authors to believe they are on the right track in their efforts to develop a rehabilitation program for disadvantaged youths who are high risks for a future of antisocial behavior (Phillips, Phillips, Fixsen & Wolf, 1973).

Many of the procedures and results obtained from the projects at Achievement Place have been replicated. For example, Liberman, Ferris, Salgado, and Salgado (1975) used token reinforcement to modify savings, conversational interruptions, and table setting in a similar treatment setting. Response-cost procedures decreased the frequency of conversation interruptions and token rewards improved table setting. However, savings were not increased even with large rewards. Similarly, Boren and Colman (1970) effectively modified a number of behaviors within a psychiatric ward for delinquent soldiers, while Cohen, Keyworth, Klanert, and Brown (1974) demonstrated that academic performance of delinquent adolescents living at home could be improved by programmed instruction and token reinforcement procedures.

A variation of the Achievement Place model in a correctional institution, as reported by Karacki and Levinson (1970), included the token system with a number of additional factors. First, bonus points were awarded for particularly noteworthy and socially valuable behaviors in the cottage, school, and work detail. This contingency was added in order to shape these behaviors using immediate reinforcement. Secondly, the maximum number of points earned depended on "class level." Promotions were determined by weekly staff ratings. Thirdly, there were involuntary charges in the form of mandatory savings accounts with the amount of each deduction dependent upon the class status of the youth. For example, mandatory savings were deducted from trainees' accounts at a rate of 40%, apprentices' at 20%, and honor students' savings were completely voluntary. There were also differences in room rental fees since the accommodations of the rooms varied. Highest-level students were also allowed to wear street clothing daily whereas others had to rent the street clothing, and then only for weekends and special occasions.

A number of token programs have been effected with prisoners and probationers with modifications of the usual point contingencies to allow either accumulation of points toward parole consideration, reductions in probation time, as well as for access to regular backup reinforcers. For example, Sloane and Ralph (1973) implemented a token system whereby points could be earned for immediate backup reinforcers. However, in order to be recommended for parole, youths had to earn a predetermined number of "social points." Furthermore, as a punitive measure, the amount of social points necessary was increased by some percentage, contingent on inappropriate behaviors, rather than taking the social points away.

A similar program was implemented, with extensions, in a school for delinquents by Jesness and DeRisi (1973). In this project, three general categories of behavior were reinforced: (*a*) convenience behaviors (those that help to run a "smooth" institution), (*b*) academic behaviors, and (*c*) "critical behavior deficiencies" (CBDs) which were behaviors assumed to be the most likely to increase the probability of the subject's failing or succeeding on parole. All behaviors earned "Karl Holton dollars" which were exchangeable for backup reinforcers. The CBDs earned behavior change units (BCUs). The number of BCUs necessary for parole varied for the individual and the price was set for the youth upon entry into the program.

In summary, the token economy has been of demonstrated effectiveness in increasing a wide variety of desirable targets including both academic and social behavior. Other procedures can be used concurrently to decrease inappropriate behaviors. Furthermore, the procedures have produced positive behavior changes in institutions, residential treatment centers, and psychiatric wards. In addition, group contingencies and consequences and peer management have been shown to be useful.

The use of behavior modification techniques with offenders has not been restricted to institutions, nor centered primarily in residential treatment facilities. Tharp and Wetzel (1969), Thorne, Tharp, and Wetzel (1967) have developed and proven a model which allows treatment to be carried out in the individual's natural environment—in the community, the home, the school, and so on, in which the deviant behavior in its most extreme form occurs. The foundation of their treatment procedures lies in the realization that there are not enough trained and competent professionals available to carry the burden of this form of treatment.

To overcome this deficiency they relied on trained subprofessionals to supervise the behavior modification strategies implemented in this program. Commenting on the selection requirement, the authors state:

> Selected specifically for their lack of previous training in any of the helping professions, their requisite characteristics included only intelligence, energy, flexibility, and qualities of personal attractiveness. The (supervisors) have included sociology majors, an ex-football player, an ex-stevedore and carpenter, a returned Peace Corps volunteer, a housewife, a cocktail waitress, and the like. (Tharp & Wetzel, 1969, P. 62)

As a consequence, these individuals came into the project with little if any personal bias concerning the "treatment of choice" for the problems with which they were to deal. Training for the tasks they were to assume consisted of an intensive three-week course in the principles of behavior modification and their utilization in the applied setting followed by equally intense on-the-job training.

All treatment procedures were within the "triadic model" consisting of the supervisor, various mediators, and the client. The supervisor component of the treatment triad has been discussed previously. It should be pointed out, however, that the supervisor was not completely autonomous with respect to the treatment procedures constructed for the varying problem behaviors dealt with. In addition to the three-week course and on-the-job training these individuals received during the beginning of the project, the supervisors met with the professional staff on a regular basis to discuss strategies, explore new approaches, and review data pertaining to the course of treatment.

The clients were 77 youths who were referred to the treatment program. Of these, approximately one-third (or 26) had police records of one sort or another. These records ranged from one to 13 offenses, consisting of virtually everything from minor curfew violations to armed assault.

The mediators consisted of "significant others" in the lives of the target individuals: parents, teachers, neighbors, social workers, and so on. They were identified on the basis of two criteria: (a) The mediator had to possess incentives of high value for the client; and (b) the mediator had to be able to dispense those incentives on the basis of an established agreement. All other information was considered irrelevant to the designation of a mediator according to Tharp and Wetzel (1969). In the traditional psychotherapeutic approach the target individual is depicted as the client, and the therapist works directly with him in an attempt to modify his behavior. In this program the client of the treatment program was the mediator. By working with and through the mediator the staff worked most effectively with the problems experienced by the youths.

The value of any particular intervention strategy can only be assessed in terms of the degree to which its stated objectives are realized. For the 26 youths who had police records, the effect of intervention was a decrease in the number of police contacts. In actual fact, only 5 of the 26 youths committed any offenses during the six months following intervention; of these, 3 youths were subsequently committed to an institution.

Although it is not possible to draw any firm conclusions concerning the long-range effects of the treatment program, the immediate effect of the intervention strategies, as indicated by the six-month follow-up, was to reduce the number of youths who were committing offenses by 81%, and the number of offenses committed by 68%. It is also impossible to determine what would have transpired if no intervention strategies had been instituted. It does appear, however, that these procedures, for a majority of such youths, have the potential of breaking the chain of activities which eventually lead to incarceration in a juvenile correctional facility and then, all too often, to a life of adult crime.

Adult Offenders

In corrections, the juvenile offender has been the focus of most behavior modification programs, while the adult offender has been virtually ignored (a state that undoubtedly reflects the felt priorities of our country in general). The adult offenders are, more often than not, the products of juvenile justice system. They are, in short, its failures. They typify a cross-section of the disadvantages of our land: poor, disproportionately black, undereducated, underskilled and, in too many cases, without real hope. To return these individuals to society with these same disadvantages plus the added stigma of imprisonment is to sentence them to the revolving door of the criminal justice system. To be sure, not all those who are imprisoned return but, as is so often noted, this may be more in spite of the prison experience than as a function of it.

Recently, a beginning has been made in the utilization of the principles and technology of applied behavior analysis with adult offenders in institutional settings. The Walter Reed ward for delinquent soldiers was established at Walter Reed Army Hospital, Washington, D.C., to treat male soldiers who had been diagnosed as having "characterological" behavior disorders (Boren & Colman, 1970; Colman & Boren, 1969). The treatment program was based on the assumption that these men had failed in the military and, previously, in civilian life because of deficiencies in their behavioral repertoire. The program's objective was to teach the soldiers the education and recreation skills, personal habit patterns, such as planning and performing consistently, and interpersonal skills that would make their presence and performance important to other members of their military unit.

In follow-up, the performance of 46 men released from the Walter Reed project was compared to that of 48 comparable soldiers who received either routine disciplinary action or general psychiatric treatment. Of the soldiers in the Walter Reed group, 7 had completed their tour and 25 were functioning in a unit (69.5% success), while 14 had either been administratively discharged from duty, were AWOL, or were in a stockade (30.5% failure). Results from the comparison group showed that only one had completed his tour, 12 remained on active duty (28.3% success), while 33 were administratively discharged or in a stockade (71.7% failure) (Colman & Baker, 1969).

The early work of the Experimental Manpower Laboratory for Corrections (EMLC), operated by the Rehabilitation Research Foundation and located at Draper Correctional Center in Elmore, Alabama, concentrated upon the development and implementation of efficient and effective methods of encouraging adult offenders to excel in remedial academic instruction and vocational skill training (Clements & McKee, 1968). Contingency management procedures were developed that generated increases in both the quantity and quality of academic work performed in the classroom. Overall progress in the program was substantial: Offenders enrolled in the projects averaged gains of 1.4 grades per 208 hours of programmed instruction. High school equivalencies were earned by 95% of those who qualified for and took the General Educational Diploma test (G.E.D.), and nine former students entered college after leaving prison (McKee & Clements, 1971).

Studies such as these are only the beginning of a behavioral analysis of the problems confronting the criminal justice system. The scope of the problems to which this approach has been applied is fairly circumscribed, and the evaluative research that has been conducted, although promising, is certainly not conclusive. The work that has been done suggests, however, that this approach has the potential of being as productive when applied to the criminal justice system as it has been in the mental health and educational professions. It is particularly unfortunate, therefore, that the Task Force on Corrections of the National Advisory Commission on Criminal Justice Standards and Goals (1973) suggests otherwise:

> Most techniques of behavior modification have been generated either in the mental hospital or for educational use. Although their application to the correctional situation is not necessarily inappropriate, sufficient attention has not been given to the nature, scheduling, and limits of the reinforcement repertory available in the correctional apparatus. Thus the use of tokens for behavior reinforcement in a reformatory may not be a suitable application of an approach that works in mental hospitals, where the problems of manipulation for secondary gains are not so prominent. (P. 516)

The preceding conclusions are most encouraging because they reflect a refreshing skepticism regarding the adoption of new therapeutic and rehabilitation procedures in corrections. In view of the very limited success of the variety of therapeutic approaches reviewed previously, this skepticism appears not only justified but long overdue. If this skepticism reflects a trend in decision making in the correctional "apparatus," it implies that in the future new or innovative approaches will have to empirically demonstrate their potential before their claims are acknowledged and their programs funded. Moreover, it may herald closer scrutiny of existing programs and administrative policies with an eye toward replacing the ineffective and regressive ones with those holding more promise. Before we turn to recent evidence on the suitability and effectiveness of the behavioral model in prison institutions, it would be appropriate to examine in detail its methodology, principles, and techniques.

CHAPTER

$$\boxed{5}$$

PRINCIPLES AND TECHNIQUES OF BEHAVIOR MODIFICATION

Behavior modification is commonly defined as the application of learning and conditioning principles and techniques to the understanding and remediation of human problems. This approach has documented its contribution to a better understanding of a wide range of problems such as the analysis and treatment of the psychotic and neurotic, the mentally retarded and learning disabled, the delinquent and criminal, and of normal individuals experiencing stress in work, marriage, and social relationships.

Only the principles and techniques of behavior modification most relevant to the correctional field will be reviewed. These represent only a small sample of the large and growing body of principles and techniques within the area of behavior modification (for a more extensive treatment of this area, see Craighead, Kazdin, & Mahoney, 1976; Rimm & Master, 1974; Kazdin, 1975).

The most straightforward way of presenting the basic principles of behavior involves a distinction between procedures that may be employed to *increase* the probability of behavior and those employed to *decrease* the probability of behavior.

Procedures that *increase* behavior would be most welcome where the objective of a correctional program is to motivate the individual to actively participate in his own rehabilitation. Similarly, procedures that *decrease* behavior would be particularly useful where the objective of the correctional program is to eliminate the bad habits and poor attitudes of the offender's old criminal ways.

The major technique for increasing behavior is that of reinforcement. According to this technique, individuals will be *more* likely to engage in certain conduct, activity, or behavior if such conduct results in the *presentation* or continuance of a pleasant or *desired* condition, outcome, or payoff. If the conduct or activity results in the *termination* or avoidance of an *undesirable* event or condition, this conduct will also increase.

To decrease behavior, techniques are used that inhibit behavior in a number of ways. According to these techniques, individuals will be less likely to engage in certain behavior or activity if such conduct results in the *presentation* or continuance of an *unpleasant* or undesirable state of affairs. Similarly, if the behavior or activity results in the *termination* or postponement of a *pleasant* condition or event, this conduct will also decrease.

To summarize, behavior may be increased or decreased in accord with the following four tactics. Each tactic is based upon the contingency which specifies that if the behavior occurs a particular consequence will follow.

Consequences that increase behavior: (*a*) Present something desirable; (*b*) end something *un*desirable.

Consequences that decrease behavior: (*a*) Present something *un*desirable; (*b*) end something desirable.

Discussions of several studies that illustrate these procedures, as well as their effectiveness in correctional settings, follow.

REINFORCEMENT THROUGH RESPONSE-CONTINGENT PRESENTATION

Thorne, Tharp, and Wetzel (1967) discuss the case of Claire, a bright, attractive 16-year-old girl who was experiencing difficulties because of truancy, poor grades, and incorrigibility. When seen, Claire had been staying away from school and had threatened to run away. Truancy appeared to be the most serious problem since the school officials were on the verge of expelling her. Consequently, the objective for the treatment was to reinstate the child into school. The mother in her attempts to control the child's truancy had withdrawn all money, use of the telephone, and dating privileges. Although these were potentially powerful reinforcers, the mother's unsystematic use of them did not result in an improvement in Claire's school attendance.

The behavioral program designed by Thorne et al. involved providing Claire with explicit ways through which she could earn privileges back. The plan had the approval of Claire and her mother. Briefly, each day that Claire attended school, she was allowed telephone privileges that evening. In addition if she attended school for four out of five school days, she was allowed one weekend date. If she attended school every day, she was allowed two weekend dates.

The results of this systematic program were impressive. During the 46 school days before this program began, Claire had missed 30 days. Her school attendance was only about 35%. During the three months of behavioral program, she attended approximately 95% of the time and missed only two class days. Moreover, even after the plan was discontinued, Claire's perfect school attendance continued on throughout the semester of the school year. This case illustrates how a response-contingent presentation of reinforcement can be used to increase behavior, that is, when privileges (reinforcers) are made contingent upon a school attendance (response), the school attendance will increase.

Both the mother and the behavioral program had used privileges. Only in the program did they succeed. What accounts for the different results? The major reasons lie in:

1. Specifying for the child exactly what the mother expected of her, e.g., the time of arrival at school.
2. Specifying for the mother exactly what the child could expect from her in return for improved behavior, e.g., daily telephone privileges.
3. Offering additional reinforcement for outstanding performance, e.g., two weekend dates for five days of school attendance.

Another example of reinforcement through response-contingent presentation is provided by Clements and McKee (1968) who were working with adult male felons in a maximum-security prison. The objective of this study was to increase the academic performance in a remedial education program. They specified for each inmate the academic requirements necessary for reinforcement and upon mutual agreement, completion of each segment of work resulted in access to a special recreational area. There, inmates could relax, have free coffee, cigarettes, shoot pool, listen to the radio, chat with their friends, and so on. Units of academic work were small enough for each inmate to succeed and thereby gain access to the recreational area several times a day. This program also offered additional reinforcement for outstanding academic performance: When an inmate completed an entire day's assignment, he was given the remainder of the day off.

The results of this study showed that the average number of frames of programmed instructional material completed increased from 61 to 134 per hour. In addition, the average test score covering the material studied increased from 71 to 90%, from failing to passing. This illustration of awarding privileges contingent upon the desired behavior parallels the previous example, but it also extends the suitability of the technique to correctional settings.

REINFORCEMENT THROUGH RESPONSE-CONTINGENT TERMINATION

While formal documentation of the effectiveness of this procedure is lacking in the criminal and juvenile justice system literature, it is a procedure commonly employed to motivate inmates. The following example culled from the authors' observations illustrates this technique.

Inmates working on a prison farm were harvesting the cotton crop. Inmate workers checked out in the morning, worked throughout the day, and returned to the institution in the early evening. The farm supervisor was dissatisfied with the speed with which the cotton was being brought in and, therefore, devised the following procedure to correct the situation. He specified exactly how many bags of cotton he expected each inmate to pick each day and told them that when they picked that number they were finished for the day. The farm's supervisor's anecdotal impression indicated the procedure was effective as each worker, generally, picked more cotton in shorter amounts of time. This illustrates how the opportunity to terminate an undesirable activity (the hard work in the hot sun) increased the desired behavior (the number of bags of cotton filled).

BEHAVIORAL INHIBITION THROUGH RESPONSE-CONTINGENT PRESENTATION

An example of the inhibition of behavior by means of response-contingent presentation or continuance of an undesirable state of affairs is provided by Levinson, Ingram, and Azcarate (1968). The study took place at the Federal Bureau of Prisons, National Training School, Washington, D.C., and focused upon the entrenched antisocial leaders of the inmate population who had an established history of continuous rule violation. The standard practice employed to deal with these serious violations consisted of placing the individuals in segregation units for varying periods of time. The lack of effectiveness of this procedure led to the psychologist's exploring a unique modification of an accepted treatment. One of the ways in which penal institutions attempt to rehabilitate the inmates is through enrollment in group therapy programs, the major rationale being that the opportunity to talk through their adjustment problem and gain insight into the psychological dynamics underlying their conduct will contribute to their rehabilitation. Unfortunately, many inmates are not interested in joining such groups and view them as a waste of time. Levinson et al. (1968), aware of the inmate's feelings regarding group therapy, designed a procedure that capitalized upon these feelings. Their procedure consisted of assigning youths who violated rules to group therapy sessions for fixed periods of time and then increasing the time requirement whenever an additional infraction occurred. The result of this procedure showed approximately a 50% reduction in the incidence of rule infractions.

This case illustrates how inhibition of behavior may be accomplished through response-contingent presentation and continuance of an undesired event; that is, when enrollment and extension of group therapy (the undesired event) was made contingent upon rule infractions (the response), rule infractions decreased (or were inhibited). Why did this procedure work with such antisocial leaders when segregation, which is a drastic procedure, had not succeeded? There are three possible and interrelated factors that may account for these results. First, being assigned to an ostensibly benevolent therapeutic program did not signify defiant confrontation between the inmate and the institution. Placement in segregation typically does. Second, participation in group therapy ordinarily does not commend the admiration of adherents to the inmate counterculture. Serving a period in segregation does. Finally, the group therapy was experienced by the inmates as distasteful and a waste of time. As the authors note, inmates typically commented that group therapy had not done anything for them. When inmates were asked why their behavior had improved, they pointed out the undesirable aspects of continuance in group therapy.

BEHAVIORAL INHIBITION THROUGH RESPONSE-CONTINGENT TERMINATION

Tyler and Brown (1968) conducted a study in a school for delinquent boys (age 13 to 15) committed by the courts because of auto theft, assault, sex offenses, and incorrigibility. In the context of a rehabilitation program, they noted that one specific source of conflict that often resulted in physical attack was provocation among the boys.

Interestingly enough, the occasion for such conflict was provided by the game room where the boys played pool. Among the behaviors noted were throwing or hitting with the pool cue, scuffling around the table, "bothering" other players, touching moving balls, bouncing balls onto the floor, and excessive arguing. The staff typically dealt with such conduct by banning the offending youth from the pool table for an hour or so. Those boys who repeatedly got into trouble were not allowed to play for a day or so. Despite these efforts, the staff found that the boys continued misbehaving.

In a new procedure, Tyler and Brown took care to specify to the delinquent youths the behavior and consequences attached to them. In addition, one of the major features of the new procedure was the substitution of a businesslike manner of reacting to the youth's offenses instead of the typical scolding, reasoning, or giving reminders of appropriate conduct, and so on. The staff simply stated to the offending youth that he had broken the rules of the cottage and proceeded to take him to a separate area where he was removed from social contact for 15 minutes. At the end of that time he was allowed to return to the game area.

The results of this procedure were most gratifying to the staff. The youths' offenses averaged 10 per week under the old procedure and about one per week under the new behavioral program. This case illustrates how inhibition through response-contingent termination of a desirable event can decrease behavior.

The youths' offenses (response) were inhibited when they resulted in his removal from the pool room (termination of reinforcement). Moreover, the procedure also insured that he would not go from one enjoyable activity (the pool room) to another and that he would not receive immediate attention from his peers for his expulsion.

CHANGING EXISTING CONDITIONS

To this point, the emphasis of the discussion has been on designing and instating *new* outcomes to reinforce desirable behaviors and to inhibit undesirable behaviors. An alternative, and often complementary, strategy to change behavior consists of identifying and discontinuing the *existing* outcomes that reinforce undesirable behaviors and those that inhibit desirable ones.

Identifying and Discontinuing Existing Outcomes That Reinforce Undesirable Behavior

If a behavior has been occurring because it results in a pleasant state of affairs or outcome, the behavior will decrease in frequency when that outcome or support ceases to follow the behavior.

One of the most powerful influences upon the behavior of inmates within the institution is the approval of the peer group. The adherents of the inmate counterculture who are most resistant to the rehabilitative efforts of the institution are held in the highest esteem and receive the most reinforcement or group support.

For example, Buehler, Patterson, and Furniss (1966), documented the pervasive influence of the peer group on attitudes held by girls residing in a detention home. Behavioral observations were made of a sample of six girls between 4 and 9 p.m., five days per week. The observer focused on the interpersonal transaction of the six girls with each other and with the staff members. The results show that the peer group tended to socially reward delinquent behavior and attitudes with attention or approval. One girl who showed coercive behavior toward her peers was rewarded by them in this manner two-thirds of the time. Surprisingly, she was also rewarded in the same manner by the staff approximately 50% of the time.

A strategy that would attempt to reduce inappropriate behavior would ideally include discontinuing the reinforcement that supports such behavior. In the preceding study, it would be appropriate to train the staff to minimize the attention and reinforcement they provide for delinquent behavior. Moreover, additional procedures would be required to reduce or eliminate the reinforcement provided by peers for undesirable behavior such as that used by Tyler and Brown (1968). It will be recalled that to assure discontinuing social reinforcement provided by the peer group, the rule violator was separated from his peers for a brief period of time following expulsion from the pool room.

A second example of an outcome that reinforces undesirable behavior involves the protection from the administration's disciplinary actions afforded by adherence to the inmates' counterculture. The inmates' counterculture exists because it allows or helps inmates to escape or avoid institutional sanctions.

One way to discontinue the basis for the inmates' counterculture is to design the institution and its administration so perfectly that it becomes impossible to escape or avoid administrative punishment. Indeed, this is the course of action typically followed in correctional institutions, and is illustrated by the proliferation of television surveillance systems and the like. Unfortunately, the inmates' ingenuity quickly overcomes these technical innovations and often results in a strengthening of the inmates' counterculture.

Technically, another way of weakening behavior maintained by escape or avoidance is by drastically reducing the severity of what is being escaped or avoided. As an institution shifts its emphasis from control through punitive sanctions for undesirable behavior to positive consequences for desirable behavior, adherence to the inmates' counterculture would be expected to weaken. While we are a long way from testing this hypothesis the two projects to be described in subsequent chapters represent serious attempts in this direction.

Identifying and Discontinuing Existing Outcomes That Inhibit Desirable Behavior

If a behavior is inhibited because it results in an unpleasant state of affairs or outcome, the behavior will increase in frequency when that outcome ceases to follow the behavior.

One of the most inhibiting influences upon the behavior of inmates is the disapproval of the peer group. The study by Buehler, Patterson, and Furniss (1966) also provides an example of how disapproval is used to discourage desirable (prosocial) behavior. It was noticed that the more domineering and coercive girls tended to disapprove and discourage those girls who attempted to show some socially conforming attitudes, expectations, and behaviors. Behavioral data indicate that the peer group chided one girl 75% of the time for identifying with social norms, while the staff interactions reinforced her 90% of the time. However, the frequency of disapproval by the peers greatly outnumbered the reinforcers dispensed by the staff. This difference in frequency is related to the greater amount of time the individual girl spent with her peers thereby allowing more opportunities for the peers to react to her behavior.

A strategy that would attempt to increase desirable behavior would include discontinuing the consequences that inhibit it. In the preceding study, the staff does not appear to be contributing to the inhibition of desirable behavior but rather appears to be reinforcing it. Although no staff training appears to be called for here, it would be appropriate to encourage the staff to spend more time with the girl thereby increasing the probability of reinforcement.

A treatment program aimed at this problem should focus on the peer group in an attempt to reduce their efforts to inhibit prosocial behavior. This might be accomplished by reinforcing the peer group for prosocial behavior displayed by its members thereby making prosocial behavior significant and something to be encouraged rather than discouraged.

Another method of inhibiting behavior in virtually all social groups involves ostracism wherein an individual is no longer acknowledged. Numerous examples exist. Cadets who violate the honor code of our military academies are excluded from social intercourse with their peers. Similarly, prison inmates who violate the norms of the counterculture are quite often excluded from the group and viewed as pariahs.

The major way of reducing ostracism has been discussed previously in the context of reducing adherence to the inmate counterculture. As the counterculture becomes less important (e.g., to escape or avoid aversive consequences provided by the institution) the use of ostracism would become less common.

MODELING AND SHAPING

From the preceding discussion, one might conclude that behavioral techniques may be used only to increase or decrease *already existing* behaviors. Admittedly, while these techniques are of practical value, their applicability is severely limited to situations in which the behavior already exists in the persons' repertoire of skills. Fortunately, additional behavioral techniques are available that allow the practitioner to develop completely new behaviors. Two general techniques may be employed to achieve this objective: modeling and shaping.

In the context of correctional applications, modeling is the most useful technique. Modeling consists of communicating to the individual the specific behaviors that he is expected to perform. This information may be conveyed in any one or a combination of three methods. (*a*) The instructor, or model, may *demonstrate* for the individual the actual behavior that he is expected to imitate. (*b*) The instructor may *verbally describe* the behavior. (*c*) The instructor may provide the individual a detailed set of *written instructions* detailing the behaviors he is to engage in.

The preceding imitation methods are probably the most commonly used teaching techniques used anywhere—including the prison. When they are used effectively, they produce rapid results with little effort for the model and the imitator. Unfortunately, this technique does not always work. The question then becomes, how to render it effective. From our previous discussion, one way of maximizing the effectiveness of the modeling technique is by reinforcing each imitative response on the part of the learner. Although modeling provides the individual with skills that are required for the behavior to be performed, reinforcement is still required to insure that the behavior will be performed. A second way of maximizing the effectiveness of the modeling technique is by *combining* it with the shaping technique.

The shaping technique involves identification of the individual's initial level of performance upon which we may build new behaviors in a gradual and overlapping progression until the desired behavior has been achieved. For example, an inmate who is always late for his vocational training class could be shaped into coming on time by first identifying the pattern of his tardiness. It might be found that some-times he is only 40 minutes late while at other times he is 90 minutes late. To gradually instill promptness, arrangements could be made to initially reinforce him whenever he was late by less than 60 minutes. The effect of this procedure would be to change the pattern of his tardiness so that arrivals at greater than 60 minutes would decrease and arrivals at less than 40 minutes would begin to occur. Proceeding in this manner, the criteria for reinforcement would gradually move in the direction of prompt arrival until that objective had been met. Although the modeling and the shaping techniques may be used independently, their general effectiveness is maximized if used in combination as is often the case in applied settings. The guidelines for their effective use are:

1. The skill or activity must be broken into small steps which begin with a component-activity which the individual is easily able to perform.
2. The description of what is expected at each step must be detailed and explicit, and care must be taken to insure that the individual is aware of the requirements.
3. The successful completion of performance at each step must be reinforced.
4. Unsatisfactory progress after following these guidelines should lead to a reevaluation of the treatment procedure. The procedural dif-ficulties might include: (a) The steps to master may be too large, or ill described. If this is the case, the steps should be made smaller or the description of what is expected should be made more explicit or precise. (b) Insufficient practice may prevent complete mastery thereby requir-ing additional opportunities for extended practice. (c) The programmed consequences of the behavior may be insufficient to maintain progress. If so, it is necessary to either increase the magnitude of the reinforcer, decrease the requirement for reinforcement, or explore new conse-quences in hopes of finding an effective reinforcer.

THE TOKEN ECONOMY

One of the defining characteristics of the behavioral approach is its emphasis upon intensive study of the individual. It is not surprising, therefore, that the bulk of the early research in applied behavior analysis consisted of one or more treatment personnel working with a single individual. More recently, however, the desirability of employing be-havioral techniques with groups of individuals has been recognized, and increasing effort is being expended in this direction. Research with institutionalized psychiatric patients has led to a technological advancement, formalized by Ayllon and Azrin (1968) and generally referred to by its key concept, the *token economy*. The token economy retains the principles of applied behavior analysis and permits their systematic application in a wide variety of group settings. Indeed, as has been discussed previously, much of the work in applied behavior analysis carried out in the juvenile and adult justice systems has employed the token economy.

The token economy has three defining characteristics: (*a*) a number of objectively defined goals or target behaviors, (*b*) the token itself, and (*c*) a variety of backup reinforcers (Krasner, 1968). The target behaviors are the potential activities or accomplishments of program participants that the staff consider important for treatment or rehabilitation and that they wish to encourage via the token economy. Once defined, these activities are those that will earn tokens when the token economy is operative.

The tokens are the medium of exchange in a token economy. They are earned by performing the target behaviors and expended to obtain the backup reinforcers. The tokens themselves may be tangible or intangible and take many forms: poker chips, green stamps, credits in a credit card system, and points in a checkbook banking system. The token, then, may be any object or stimulus that can (*a*) be easily presented following the occurrence of a target behavior, (*b*) mediate the time between the target behavior and the availability of a backup reinforcer, and (*c*) be exchanged for the backup reinforcer once it becomes available. Like money, tokens are of value because their possession allows individuals within the token system to engage in desired activities or to obtain valued commodities or privileges.

The backup reinforcers are the things of value to the program participants. They can include, among a number of other things, the opportunity to watch a favored television program, special foods, and extra visiting or pass privileges. As has been indicated, the value or *conditioned reinforcing properties* of tokens are determined by the value or reinforcing properties of the backup reinforcers. The number and variety of backup reinforcers must be as large as possible to (*a*) maximize the probability that the reinforcing event menu includes activities and commodities reinforcing to all participants and (*b*) minimize the likelihood that satiation will reduce the token's conditioned reinforcing properties. Indeed, the term *generalized conditioned reinforcer* is appropriately applied to the token, for the token signifies that it may be exchanged for a host of conditioned and unconditioned reinforcers in much the same manner that money is exchanged. Care must be exercised to insure that the tokens and backup reinforcers are obtainable solely through participation in the token economy, for a token or potential backup reinforcer that may be freely obtained by circumventing the contingency management system will render the token economy ineffective.

To be maximally effective, the token economy must be designed and operated upon the realization that the reciprocity inherent in all human relationships (Azrin, Naster, & Jones, 1973; Stuart, 1971) also exists in the relationship between institution staff and program participants, whether the institution is a school, community mental health center, mental hospital, or correctional facility. Virtually all healthy human relationships involve some sort of equitable give-and-take exchange. Each participant both expects something of and provides something for the other. Indeed, those interpersonal relationships that are either themselves pathological or that breed pathology appear to be those in which this reciprocity is either distorted or completely lacking (Patterson & Reed, 1970; Patterson, Cobb, & Ray, 1973).

Two requirements of the token economy foster and protect reciprocity between institution staff and program participants. First, the token economy requires an explicit statement of what each party, staff and participant, expects of the other and what, in return, each is expected to provide for the other. Second, the token economy also requires an accountability system, wherein the degree to which expectations are fulfilled and obligations are honored, is monitored and may be held up to public scrutiny. In meeting these two requirements, the token economy guards against the shortcomings of contemporary institution management and therapeutic endeavors. The clarification of expectancies fosters negotiations between both parties and helps insure that the resultant exchange system is balanced (i.e., fair to both parties). On-line accountability, long neglected by both the health-related and criminal justice professions, allows the continuous monitoring of a program's effectiveness while at the same time protecting each from either actual or false claims of capriciousness, inconsistency, or malevolence on the part of the other (Ayllon & Roberts, 1972).

There are, of course, many differences between the program staff and program participants, in terms of both the decision-making power each wields and the potential backup reinforcers each possesses. The staff decision-making power is, in most settings, absolute. The staff of a residential institution leaves at the end of the workday to return to the "real world." The program participants merely observe the change of shifts as the program in their world continues. All too often the staff views the program from its perspective alone and, in so doing, locks the program participants into a pathology-ridden system. Indeed, recent studies have indicatd that mental hospitals contribute to the ills of many of their patients and correctional institutions increase the likelihood that many of their charges will again engage in criminal activities once they have been released. In a properly designed token economy, systematic safeguards are incorporated, in part, as a result of the attention paid to the reciprocity of human relationships. Such safeguards, as discussed in Chapter 7, provide not only a more effective behavior management system but also optimal protection of the inmate from programmatic arbitrariness and from potentially harmful institutionalized treatment regimens.

In addition to the ethical guidelines to be observed in connection with the safeguarding of inmate welfare, a set of technical guidelines must also be observed to insure optimal effectiveness of the token economy as a tool for fostering inmate rehabilitation. These guidelines follow:

MAJOR REQUIREMENTS OF A TOKEN ECONOMY IN A PRISON SETTING

1. *The tokens must be counterfeit-proof.* This requirement is common to all token economy systems but it is particularly important when the population is predisposed to finding a variety of ways to "beat the system." This requirement may be met in a number of ways, all of which minimize the likelihood of cheating. One way is to use a modified banking system where the tokens exist only as points that are added or subtracted from a checking account balance by a staff member. A second method is to use a credit card system analogous to that used by department stores or gasoline stations. Both earnings and expenditures are processed through the system and monitored by a staff member. Other specific procedures have consisted of using foreign coins or punches of counterfeit-proof symbols and the like.

2. *Tokens must be nontransferable* to avoid stealing from one another as well as possible extortion. This may be accomplished by checking account and credit card systems. Both involve a coding system that enable the staff to identify by name the individual inmate, the amount of points earned each day, how they were earned, the number of points spent, and how they were spent each day. Both systems insure that only the individual involved will receive credit for meeting specified behavioral objectives and that inmates will be able to spend only those points they have credited to their accounts.

3. *The backup reinforcers must include a large variety of special activities and commodities.* By so doing, the chances of offering meaningful incentives to every inmate are maximized. Further, this procedure minimizes loss of interest with subsequent reduction in the desirable performances. In effect, the possibility of satiation (the loss of reinforcer effectiveness

due to its frequent use or presentation) is minimized because the individual has a chance to choose from a variety of reinforcers rather than being limited to one or two.

4. *Balance of point earnings and expenditures must be kept up to date.* One of the advantages of this procedure is that it keeps the inmate informed on where he stands vis-à-vis the availability of backup reinforcers and whether or not he needs to consider additional efforts to secure them. This requirement also prevents inmates from exploiting the token system by spending unearned points.

5. *Loans must not be granted* since the token economy system depends for its optimal effectiveness on high level of motivation. Individuals will be more motivated when their performance leads directly to the backup reinforcers they desire than when their performance accomplishes nothing more than repaying for back-up reinforcers they already have enjoyed. The preceding requirement insures fair treatment vis-à-vis the earning of points and the availability of backup reinforcers thereby preventing the emergence of friction among inmates and between inmates and staff which could occur if the token system is misused or abused.

The five requirements discussed represent a synthesis of findings on the application of behavioral principles in general and token reinforcement in particular. They also represent the experience and observations derived from the projects that are reported in detail in the following chapters. Although observance of these guidelines will not guarantee success in establishing a token economy, their disregard will virtually guarantee failure.

While the guidelines and specific features defining a token economy might suggest a structured and static system, it is in fact a flexible and dynamic one. Indeed, the token economy must be periodically reevaluated in terms of the backup reinforcers as well as in terms of the price structure itself. Specifically, backup reinforcers should be changed, modified, dropped, expanded, and so on, to maximize their attractiveness and general function as incentives. Similarly, to insure that individuals make contact with new incentives, the token economy should provide limited opportunities for freely sampling these new incentives. This procedure, called *priming/sampling,* will enable individuals to expand the scope of their interests and incentives (Ayllon & Azrin, 1968a, b).

MAINTENANCE OF BEHAVIOR CHANGE

From the preceding discussion, one would be led to believe that once a behavior has been developed, its occurrence will require continuous reinforcement or alternatively, that the behavior will continue indefinitely. Neither appears to be the case. Continuous reinforcement is not necessary for behavior to be maintained. If a behavior occasionally results in the same reinforcer as was the case in training, it will be maintained. If a behavior, from time to time, results in some naturally occurring reinforcer, it too will be maintained. However, if the behavior does not result, at least occasionally, in the same or some naturally occurring reinforcer, it will decrease.

In practice, as well as in theory, one major strategy to eliminate individuals' constant dependency on reinforcement is to "wean" them only after they have achieved satisfactory levels of performance. This "weaning" procedure involves gradually reducing the amount and regularity of reinforcement until either a satisfactorily low level of reinforcement has been achieved or until the "natural" reinforcers come to maintain the behavior and programmed reinforcement can be terminated. The latter outcome is, of course, the more desirable of the two.

What is legitimately expected from any rehabilitative effort is that the new skills, attitudes, and so on, that are instilled in the training center be carried over and displayed after training is completed. Such will be the case only if the behavior selected for training is meaningful to individuals once they leave the institution; that is, it earns them reinforcement in the community. Admission to a training program, a well-paying job, development of important social relationships are some of the avenues to reinforcement in the "natural community."

However, no matter how well mastered a skill or behavior is in a familiar setting, an individual will experience difficulty when required to perform it in unfamiliar settings. To minimize this decrement in performance, it is important that transitional programs be established that gradually reintegrate the individual into the new settings in which the established behaviors are to be performed.

What is being suggested here goes beyond the services provided currently in halfway houses that have been established to meet this need. Specifically, in addition to providing shelter, food and opportunities for discussion with a counselor, the halfway house must structure its programs to maximize its involvement through direct supervision. To assist and insure that the individual functions adequately in the community, supervision should be maximal at the start of the reintegration program, should initially involve direct contact and instruction in the actual job and/or social settings of concern, and should be withdrawn in a gradual fashion as competence is demonstrated in these settings.

The specific characteristics of each rehabilitation program would involve the application of concepts and techniques as discussed previously.

Following this behavioral orientation then, the functions of the halfway house should include in addition to their current services, the development of systematic outreach programs that support and maintain skills acquired in the institution and build upon them to teach and instill additional skills that by their very nature cannot be effectively taught in the institution.

For example, skills involving acceptable heterosexual encounters may be simulated and appropriate behavior taught through modeling in the institution, although it is clear that this type of training is severely limited in sexually segregated facilities. Contrast that to training the same skills in the context of nonartificial gatherings outside the institution, For example, demeanor and relevant social behavior in a cocktail lounge, and the preferred mode of instruction is obvious.

Again, the strategy of training would include shaping and modeling suitable social behaviors, prompting their execution, reinforcing successful completion of each component and, finally, gradually withdrawing the artificial support provided so that natural consequences come to support the new social skills. Admittedly, this general strategy would require considerable ingenuity and effort on the part of the rehabilitation team. However, the outcome of this approach would more than compensate for the additional effort required. Moreover, experience with current rehabilitation efforts indicates that they produce little more than marginal result.

CHAPTER

6

EVALUATION IN
BEHAVIORAL PROGRAMS

The basic assumption underlying the practice of behavior modification is that each of the full range of psychological problems that individuals experience may be translated or redefined in behavioral terms. Once this translation has been accomplished the problem behavior or behaviors may be explained in terms of the interrelationships between the to-be-explained behavior and the environmental events that precede and follow it. One major endeavor of the behavior modifier is to advance our knowledge of the ways in which environmental factors influence behavior by discovering and elaborating the general laws and principles that describe the nature of this interrelationship (*Journal of the Experimental Analysis of Behavior,* 1958 to present). A second major endeavor involves the utilization of this knowledge of the ways in which environmental happenings shape and maintain behavior in efforts to remediate human problems. In the latter endeavor, the behavior modifier employs knowledge of the general laws and principles of behavior to understand the unique problems each client experiences and presents. These same laws and principles of behavior are then utilized to formulate an intervention program aimed at the remediation of the problem (*Journal of Applied Behavior Analysis,* 1968 to present).

CHARACTERISTICS OF A BEHAVIORAL APPROACH TO EVALUATION

1. Diagnostic labeling is avoided and psychological difficulties are specified in behavioral terms. Although it is common practice to classify individuals experiencing psychological problems in terms of general nosological categories, such as psychotic depressive reaction, anxiety neurosis, antisocial personality, such labels provide little, if any information concerning the precise nature of the problems experienced by the individuals to whom the labels have been applied. Is the individual who has been labeled as antisocial, aggressive? If yes, is the aggression directed towards others or towards inanimate objects? Is the aggression physical or verbal? Does it involve attacks upon peers or authority figures? Do these attacks occur once an hour, once a day, once a week? Do the episodes of aggression last for a matter of seconds, for minutes, until they are interrupted by another individual? Is the damage that is inflicted minimal, moderate, or maximal? Is the damage inflicted by physical blows or by the use of objects? Kanfer and Saslow (1969) have addressed themselves to the ambiguity implicit in current psychiatric diagnostic practices and concluded that the:

> . . . important fault (of psychiatric classifications) lies in our lack of sufficient knowledge to categorize behavior along those *pertinent dimensions* which permit prediction of responses to social expectations, social stresses, life crises, or psychiatric treatment. This limitation obviates anything but a crude and tentative approximation to a taxonomy of effective and ineffective behavior. (P. 419)

As an alternative to the traditional system of psychiatric classification, these authors have suggested a "behavioral diagnosis" schema which classifies behaviors in terms of (*a*) *behavioral excesses* (what does the individual do too much of with too much intensity, for too long a duration or under conditions which society disallows?); (*b*) *behavior deficits* (what does the individual do too little of or not at all, or without sufficient intensity, duration or form under socially expected conditions?) and (*c*) *behavioral assets*, which are nonproblematic behaviors that the individual does well. Analysis of problems like that of Kanfer and Saslow (1969) address themselves to the "who, where, when, and how much" aspects of behavior. This precise specification of the problem in terms of observable referents allows all, including the individual who is said to be experiencing the problem, to agree on its existence and upon specific instances of its occurrence. Similarly, the quantification of the observable referents of the problem in terms of frequency, duration, intensity, and so on allows all, including the individual experiencing the problem, to agree upon its severity.

2.   As mentioned previously, human problems are seen as developing when particular behaviors occur too frequently, too infrequently, or are situation inappropriate. If the problem involves a behavioral deficit wherein the individual does not engage in important activities or show critical skills, the objective of an intervention program would be to encourage the performance of those activities or to teach the lacking skills. Second, if the problem is seen as involving a behavioral excess wherein the individual shows either an inappropriate behavior or an excessive amount of what might be a generally acceptable form of behavior, the objective becomes one of either eliminating the undesirable behavior or bringing the aberrant rate, duration, or intensity of the acceptable behavior to within normal limits. Third, if the problem involves the inappropriateness of the setting or circumstances in which the behavior occurs, the task becomes one of reducing the occurrence of the behavior in the appropriate settings while maintaining or fostering its occurrence under appropriate conditions.

In most instances it is found that intervention programs incorporate two or all three of these tactics. A program designed to deal with an individual's aggressive behavior, for example, would probably include a component to directly reduce the overall frequency of aggression, but would also involve a second component which taught new skills to be used when confronted with the situations that previously initiated aggressive acts. A third component aimed at fostering the individual's ability to distinguish between those situations in which the old aggressive behavior is and is not called for would also be indicated.

3.   Once the problem has been stated behaviorally, it is explained in terms of the observable antecedents and consequences of its behavioral referent rather than as a manifestation of inferred intrapsychic forces or processes. Explanations that stress such concepts as fixation, overcompensation, or unconscious conflict do not specify the observable referents from which the labels are deduced. These explanations provide little assistance in the development of intervention procedures save the prescription that therapy should be continued until the fixation is identified and resolved, the overcompensation worked through and resolved, and the unconscious conflict made conscious and resolved. In contrast to these explanations, one that takes note of the fact that problem behaviors routinely follow a refused request, a slight from a peer, or a period of inattention from an authority figure provides important information concerning what circumstances may "trigger off" the problem behaviors that the individual shows. Similarly, knowledge that aggression regularly results in capitulation on the part of an authority figure, attention and approval from peers, or the breaking of a period of boredom contains important clues concerning what consequences or rewards might be maintaining the behavior. Based on information such as this, some intervention procedures would focus upon the conditions that precede the problem behavior and would emphasize the teaching of new ways of coping with those situations. Others would focus upon the consequences or rewards that accrue to the individual following the occurrence of the problem behavior and would stress the teaching of new, more appropriate, ways of securing those rewards.

4. Intervention plans are individualized and explicitly stated. The specification of the problem in behavioral terms and the analysis of the environmental events that regularly precede and follow it fosters the development of specific programs for its remediation. Traditional approaches to the solution of human problems typically place individuals in broad diagnostic categories and then prescribe general treatments of choice for all individuals falling within each category. In contrast, the behavioral approach identifies for each individual the unique situational factors that contribute to or underlie the problem behavior and then develops specific programs based upon this information for the remediation of the problem. The rehabilitative program designed for an individual who shows aggressive behavior when thwarted by an authority figure will not be the same as that for an individual who aggresses when ridiculed by peers. Similarly, individuals who steal to assure a top position in the peer group, to support a drug habit, or to support themselves after having lost their jobs obviously require different programs.

5. The approach is self-corrective. After the problem has been stated and analyzed in behavior terms, goals agreed upon and established with the client, and an intervention plan implemented, the client's performance is monitored on a day-by-day basis. The frequency of occurrence of the problem behavior is recorded daily, as is the progress of the individual towards goals established for the component programs (social skills training, basic education, contingency contracting, etc.) of the general treatment plan. The continuous recording quickly reveals whether the client's behavior is improving, remaining unchanged, or deteriorating. Obviously, if components of the intervention plan appear either ineffectual or harmful, a reanalysis of the problem and/or a reformulation of the intervention is called for. Even if the intervention procedures appear beneficial, recording of progress might reveal that change is not occurring at the rate that was anticipated, indicating that additional procedures are called for to accelerate movement.

The approach is also self-corrective in another sense. Not only does the emphasis on the constant evaluation of progress enable practitioners to assess the appropriateness of the procedures that they have developed, but also insures that the field in general will quickly separate newly developed effective procedures from ineffective ones. In addition, it specifies what conditions and with what problems those newly developed procedures are of general use. The careful replication of new procedures across a variety of problems insures against the premature and careless extension of new procedures to areas for which they are unsuited.

EVALUATION PROCEDURES

As the preceding discussion has indicated, a major feature of the behavioral approach is the evaluation of the effects of intervention procedures. The objective of intervention is behavior change. Only by monitoring behavior can we tell if desired improvements occur, if goals are being attained, if the client is ready to move on to a more advanced stage of treatment or to terminate treatment altogether. Some would argue that whether the improvements seen in the client's behavior are a result of the specific treatment procedures utilized or are a result of other, more or less nonspecific changes occurring outside of treatment is of little concern because the major objective, an improvement in behavior, has been achieved.

This is an unfortunately short-sighted view of the rehabilitation process. As important as the improvement of the client is, the growth of each therapist and the progress of the profession in general are equally important, and this is best accomplished by the practitioners themselves. Once a practitioner has proven to his satisfaction that the procedures that he has employed with one client account for the changes in that client's behavior, their utilization with other clients with similar problems becomes sound therapeutic practice. Without such proof, this extension rests only on the therapist's intuitive judgment concerning the effectiveness of the procedures. The possibility then exists that ineffective or harmful procedures that appeared successful only because they were associated with serendipitous improvements in one client's behavior might be erroneously employed with a number of subsequent clients.

Similarly, it is each therapist's professional responsibility to share with others newly developed procedures and new applications of already established methods. This can only be done when the effectiveness of these innovations has been strenuously proven. This characteristic is a hallmark of behavior modification, and probably accounts most for its rapid and continuing growth. The documentation and sharing of new applications provides all practitioners with the skills, encouragement, and direction that contribute greatly to the vigor and enthusiasm of the approach.

Individuals come to the attention of others because of the intrusive nature of their behavior, and this intrusiveness usually stems from an excessive amount of some undesirable behavior rather than an insufficient amount of some desired behavior. The individual who interacts with others constantly and in a physically aggressive manner is more likely to be earmarked as in need of assistance than is the individual who does so infrequently. While an excessive amount of undesirable behavior *implies* an insufficient amount of some alternative desirable behavior, this is often overlooked because of the intrusive and dramatic nature of the presenting problem. As is discussed in detail later, programs that construct and encourage desirable behavior are preferable to those which merely seek to discourage undesirable behavior. For this reason, rather than focusing solely on the undesirable behavior, it is equally important to focus on desired alternatives for the purposes of recording and evaluation. Even in those occasional instances in which such a formulation is not feasible, the intervention procedures that are employed should emphasize the acquisition of new adaptive skills and alternative behaviors rather than just the inhibition of the undesired behavior.

Defining Problem Behaviors

The first step in the evaluation of behavior modification procedures is the translation of the problem that an individual experiences into its observable behavior referents. Two general types of translations and redefinitions are possible. If the occurrence of the target behavior results in some observable and relatively long-enduring effect, such as a completed work assignment, an answered examination, a damaged piece of equipment, or physical injury in the form of broken bones, bloody noses, and so on, it is possible to define the occurrence of the target behavior by specifying and monitoring such effects or outcomes. If, on the other hand, the occurrence of the target behavior does *not* result in any enduring environmental changes, as when an inmate student distracts his classmates, when a worker is insubordinate to his supervisor, when an instruction is not followed, when two inmates argue, and so on, it is necessary to define the specific target behavior in objective and unambiguous terms. This second method of stating problems in behavior terms focuses directly on the behavioral events themselves. For both *event* and *outcome* definitions, the objective is to develop a written description of the target behavior itself or its aftereffects that is sufficiently precise that two individuals, upon reading the description, will agree on each occurrence of the described behaviors.

Obviously, the statement of the problem in global psychological terms, such as aggression, does not facilitate agreement on the part of two independent observers. Although both might agree that a fight in the form of an exchange of physical blows is an incident of aggression, one might exclude verbal threats and the second not, while the second might exclude shoving and the first not. In the case of such global definitions, more precise specification is called for.

A refined definition of aggression, and one that lends itself more to precise measurement and on-line recording, would be one that enumerated the specific actions that were to be considered instances of aggression. Verbal threats, shoving, and exchanges of physical blows might or might not be included in that enumeration, but the enumeration would serve as the working definition of what constitutes aggressive acts. Clearly, the credibility of such a working definition depends upon the particular behaviors that are included and excluded, and is achieved by matching the behaviors actually exhibited by the individual with generally accepted exemplars of the more global psychological problem that is being defined. It is quite possible that during this process it is discovered that the problem is something other than that which it was originally thought to be. Indeed, it is unimportant at this step in the definition of problem behaviors just what label the psychological problem carries; what is important are the particular classes of problem behaviors the individual manifests.

However, an enumeration of these classes is still not a sufficiently precise definition of the actual problem behaviors to insure agreement among observers on their occurrence. There may or may not be agreement upon what constitutes a verbal threat, shoving, or even a fight. What is still required is a precise description of the defining characteristics of the general classes of behavior in which the individual engages that are the referents of the global psychological problem. This is accomplished only when a definition has been constructed that allows an individual unfamiliar with the client and the difficulties that are being experienced to employ that definition to record the occurrence of the problem behaviors and while doing so be in near-perfect agreement with another recorder.

Recording the Problem Behavior

After the problem has been stated in behavioral terms that allow agreement between two independent observers on its occurrence, a recording procedure must be selected. A determination of *when, where,* and *how* the behavior is to be recorded is required. In deciding when to record, we must ask whether a particular behavior is regularly displayed at a particular time. For example, an individual may work industriously in the morning but not in the afternoon. By knowing the time of day the problem is most likely to occur, it is possible to make arrangements to conduct observations economically and with the greatest possibility of observing the behavior by recording it *when* it occurs and discontinuing recording at other times. In deciding *where* to record, we must determine whether the problem is restricted to one or more particular places. Again, an individual may be found to be aggressive in the crowded confines of a dormitory, but not elsewhere. By knowing where the problem occurs, and by restricting our recording to those places, time and energy is conserved and accurate records of the occurrence of the behavior are obtained.

The determination of *how* to record the occurrence of the behavior is more involved than determining when and where the recording is to take place. Several alternative recording methods are possible. The one that is selected should depend upon both whether it is a feasible method and whether it produces information that is representative of the true nature of the problem. Quite often this involves a compromise, for a recording procedure that is most convenient may not produce representative data while one that produces the most representative data may be impractical to employ. The representativeness of the data must take precedence, however, for no matter how convenient a recording procedure might be, the data that is recorded is of no value unless it accurately describes the phenomenon that is being studied. (This is analogous to the situation of the drunk who was looking for his lost keys under a lamppost because that was where the light was.)

The first general method of collecting information on the occurrence of behavior is though *frequency counting.* Frequency counts may be based on tallying the behavior as it occurs, if it has been defined as an event, or on counting the discrete product(s) associated with the occurrence of each behavior, if it has been defined as an outcome. The choice of which method to use depends, generally, on whether the occurrence of the behavior leaves some physical product in the environment after its occurrence. The duration of the recording period can either be constant from day to day (e.g., when a remedial education teacher records problems worked at the end of a standard three-hour class period or a supervisor records people leaving their assigned tasks throughout the daily eight-hour work shift), or it can vary (e.g., when a correctional officer records fights during evenings and weekends or a counselor records positive interactions while in a dormitory). If the recording period is always of the same duration, a simple frequency count consisting of the total number of instances of the behavior during the recording period accurately reflects the occurrence of the problem behavior.

In most instances, however, there will be some variation in the duration of the recording period. If this is the case, a frequency count does not accurately reflect the occurrence of behavior, for the number of instances of behavior that are recorded will depend, in large part, upon the length of the recording period. Comparisons between recording periods would be impossible, for there would be no way of telling whether apparent changes in the occurrence of the behavior reflected actual changes, changes in the duration of the recording period, or both. For this reason, when the length of the recording period varies from day to day, the data collected must be converted to a rate measure. To do so, the length of each recording period must be determined. The total number of behaviors observed is then divided by the total amount of time the behavior was recorded (event recording), or could occur (outcome recording), and the data is reported as the number of responses per minute, behaviors per hour, and so on, for each recording period. In so doing, the representativeness of the data is preserved and comparisons between recording periods become possible.

In addition to frequency counting, a second and third method for collecting data are the interval recording and time sample methods. These procedures are closely related. In *interval recording,* the period during which occurrences of the target behavior are to be recorded is divided into successive equal-size intervals of relatively short duration, typically 10 or 20 seconds. Throughout the recording period the observer indicates in each interval whether an instance of the target behavior(s) occurs. The behavior(s) recorded may consist of either a continuation of those from the preceding interval, the initiation and completion of an instance of the behavior(s) within the interval, or the initiation of an instance of the target behavior(s) that continues into the following interval. The frequency of occurrence of the target behavior within each interval is not recorded, and the resulting data indicates that at least one, or a portion of one, instance of the target behavior has occurred in each scored interval.

The resulting data can be reported either simply as the total number of intervals in which the target behavior was observed, or it may be transformed into a percentage by dividing the number of intervals in which the behavior occurred by the number of observation intervals and multiplying the resulting decimal by 100. The decision concerning which of these two ways of presenting the results of the observations rests upon the same considerations as were detailed in the discussion of the frequency count recording procedure. If the length of the recording period is the same from day to day, and if the person whose behavior is being recorded is present throughout each day's recording period, simply reporting the total number of intervals in which the behavior occurred will produce representative data that permits comparisons between recording periods. If the lengths of the recording period vary or the individual whose behavior is being recorded is absent for varying periods of time, the percentage transformation must be performed to preserve the representativeness of the reported data.

In the *time sample* method, observations are performed at predetermined times, perhaps every 30 minutes or at 15 minutes past each hour. Whether or not the target behavior is occurring at the moment of each observation is then recorded. Clearly, the time sample and interval recording procedures differ in two important ways. First, in the time sample procedure, the target behavior must be occurring at the exact moment for which an observation is scheduled for it to be detected, while in the interval recording procedure an observation is conducted over a brief period of time and if an instance of the target behavior occurs during the interval it will be detected. Second, in the time sample method, observations are usually widely spaced, while in interval recording the observations either follow each other in succession or are closely spaced.

The times at which behavior is to be observed in the time sample method may be fixed, as when an observation is performed every 15 minutes (i.e., on the hour, 15 minutes past the hour, at the half-hour, etc.) or they may vary. If, for example, an average of four observations per hour are to be made during the three hours between 9 a.m. and noon, successive five-minute times beginning at 9 a.m. and ending at noon (i.e., 9:00, 9:05, 9:10, 9:15, etc.) might be written on separate pieces of paper and 12 observation times selected at random each day. By varying the observation times from day to day in such a manner the observations becomes unpredictable, thereby precluding the possibility that those who are being observed will detect the temporal patterning of observations that exists when they are performed at fixed times. Obviously, the unpredictable time samples are more likely to reveal the natural occurrence of the target behavior than are the fixed samples, for it prevents those who are being observed from altering their behavior when an observation is imminent.

Whether fixed or varied time examples are employed, the resulting data may be reported as either the total number of samples in which the target behavior was observed or transformed into a percentage by dividing the number of observations in which the behavior was seen by the number of observations performed and multiplying the resulting decimal by 100. As with the preceding recording methods, the manner in which the data will be presented will depend upon the day-to-day representativeness of the data. If the number of observations that are performed varies from day to day, as is typical in most applied settings, the percentage transformation is required.

The fourth data collection procedure involves controlling the opportunities that the individual has to respond. In this procedure, each opportunity for a behavior to occur and whether or not it does occur are recorded. The *controlled presentations method* is most useful when the number of opportunities for the behavior to occur is dependent upon identifiable antecedents. For example, suppose that the problem behavior is the manner in which an individual responds to constructive criticism from a supervisor. Obviously, the number of times such situations arise can be controlled by the supervisor engaging in constructive criticism. When using this method the possibility of a misleading representation of the occurrence of the behavior (particularly when the number of controlled presentations may vary from observation period to observation period), should be eliminated by converting the data to percent of occurence of the behavior. This is computed by dividing the number of recorded occurrences of the behavior by the total number of opportunities in which the behavior could have been exhibited and multiplying by 100. A common example of this method of reporting data is the percent correct grade employed in the prison school classroom, for it is computed by dividing the actual number of correct answers by the total number of opportunities for a correct answer (the number of questions asked) and multiplying by 100.

In addition to a measure of the occurrence of the problem behavior in the four different ways that have just been discussed, two additional means of quantifying behavior are sometimes employed: latency and duration recording. *Latency* refers to the interval of time between when a behavior is to occur and when it actually does occur. Quite often, individuals can and do perform desired behaviors or engage in required activities, but they experience difficulty in doing so when they are expected to. Common examples are the employee who is consistently late, the inmate student who delays beginning assigned work, the youthful probationer who violates curfew by staying out later than allowed. In each case, the objective is to reduce the time interval between when the behavior is to begin and when it actually does. By timing the interval with a stopwatch or clock, the latency of each behavior is determined. As can be seen from the examples cited previously, the number of latency measures that may be recorded during any particular day is determined by the behavior under examination. There may be one opportunity to record the latency of a response (curfew), there may be two opportunities (arriving at work in the morning and after lunch in the afternoon), or a varied number of opportunities (three classroom assignments on one day, five on the next, etc.). If the behavior can occur only once during each recording period, the actual latency of that response is reported. If the behavior may occur two or more times during each recording period, the latency of each response is recorded and the mean latency of all responses occuring during the recording period is determined. This is accomplished by summing all the latency times and dividing the resulting figure by the number of latency times that contributed to that sum.

A *duration* measure specifies how long a behavior is continued once it has been initiated. An individual may be fully capable of performing a particular behavior; however, he does not engage in it for sufficient periods of time. Common examples of this type of problem would be the worker who moves from task to task without staying with any of them for a sufficiently long period of time to be truly of benefit, the inmate trainee who just barely begins to study before taking a break, the counselee who can only listen for a matter of seconds before interrupting with comments. In each instance, the objective is to increase the duration of the behavior of interest. By timing the period during which the behavior is emitted with a stopwatch or clock, the duration of the behavior is determined. The number of duration measures that are possible during any given day may range from zero (if the behavior is not emitted at all) to many (as in the preceding examples).

In those instances in which only one duration measure is possible, the actual duration of that episode of behavior may be reported. If the behavior occurs two or more times during recording periods, the duration of each episode is recorded and the mean duration of all responses occurring during the recording period is computed by summing all duration times and dividing by the number of duration times that were recorded. If this latter method were selected, it would be necessary to report both the mean duration and the number of episodes of the behavior that were represented by that mean value. By so doing, it is possible to determine whether the figure represents a small number of relatively long episodes or a large number of brief instances of the behavior.

There are no hard and fast rules governing the selection of a recording procedure. As has been emphasized previously, which of the six methods described is selected will depend upon which is most feasible and produces data most representative of the actual occurrence of the target behavior. Moreover, when a compromise between these two requirements is necessary, the representativeness of the data must always take precedence over the covenience of the recording procedure. If, for example, one were interested in the performance of a group of workers, one could choose to look at either the proportion of the work day they devoted to their assigned tasks, or at the products of their labor. If the former indicator of work performance were selected, it would be necessary to develop a molecular definition of "work" so that an observer would easily determine whether a worker was actually "working" rather than being "off task." Once a suitable definition has been constructed, an appropriate recording procedure must be settled upon. Of the six possible procedures, three may be eliminated as clearly inappropriate. First, counting the frequency of each episode of "working" would produce misleading data, for the measure fails to take into account the length of each episode of work. The individual with a few long intervals of work might be working more than the individual with a large number of very short intervals of work, while the data generated through frequency recording of the occurrences of episodes of "working" would indicate the opposite. Second, the nature of the behavior that is being recorded is not amenable to a controlled presentations procedure because we are not offering the workers discrete opportunities to work and, therefore, cannot record how many opportunities result in work behavior. Third, the latency measure may also be excluded from consideration. Although at a later time the interval between when work is to begin and when workers actually begin might be of concern, this factor probably has little influence on just how much work is accomplished. Of more concern is how much time is devoted to work throughout the work period.

The remaining three data recording procedures may be ranked according to their relative appropriateness for determining the amount of time workers devote to their assigned tasks during a work period. The duration measure appears the most appropriate, for by starting and stopping a clock when an individual begins and stops working, an observer will produce a record of exactly how much time the worker devoted to assigned tasks. The identification of just when an inmate began and stopped working might, however, prove difficult. The interval-recording procedure would probably produce data that was nearly as representative of the occurrence of the target behavior as would the duration measure. Individuals typically work steadily for a period of time and then take a work break for a period of time. Because of this, the proportion of intervals during which an individual showed work behavior would closely approximate the actual proportion of minutes that were worked throughout the recording period. This could, of course, be verified by comparing the proportion of time on-task as determined through the duration procedure with the proportion of intervals in which the individual showed at least one instance of work behavior as determined by the interval-recording method.

The time sample method would probably not produce data that approximated that derived from the duration measurement procedure as closely as interval recording would but, depending upon the time between observations, would also probably produce an acceptable estimate of the degree to which a worker was on-task. While observing only once an hour would clearly not produce a representative measure of an individual's work behavior, observing on the average once every three of five minutes probably would.

Although an individual who is virtually never observed to be engaged in assigned tasks can in no way be considered a productive worker, the fact that workers might give the appearance of being engaged in productive labors is no guarantee that they are working efficiently. Indeed, and as anyone who has served in the military can attest; "soldiering" (appearing to be busy but instead merely passing time) is a time-honored and skilled activity in and of itself. Being on task, then, is best viewed as a requisite behavior, one which is necessary for productive labor, but is not sufficient to insure that what appears to be labor is actually productive. Definitions of behavior that look solely at behavioral "form" are referred to as topographical definitions. If productive labor is to be guaranteed, what is required in place of a requisite behavior such as being on-task is a more direct measure of the outcome of such behaviors, for example, assignments completed without error in an office, the number of bushels of cucumbers picked on a farm, the percent of problems correctly solved in a remedial education classroom, the numbers of skills acquired in a vocational training shop.

INDIVIDUAL VS. GROUP DATA

An important question to be answered when formulating a recording procedure for a behavior engaged in by a group of individuals is whether it will be sufficient to report the *composite* behavior of the group, or whether the recording procedure should be *individualized*. Returning to the previous examples, it would be generally accepted that a composite measure of the number of skills mastered by all trainees taken together in a vocational training classroom for a particular week would tell the instructor little about the progress of any particular student. Similarly, the average number of problems solved correctly for all students in a remedial education classroom would be of little assistance as the teacher went about the task of educating each student. What the vocational training instructor and the remedial education teacher both require is individualized data on each of their learners' progress so that curriculum adjustments may be made to insure effective instruction for all. Clearly, then, individual data is required in settings such as these to maximize the educational effort. Composite data would be useful, however, in evaluating the effectiveness of each educator, but that is a separate area of concern.

It is less obvious whether composite or individual data would be most useful in dealing with such problems as either increasing productivity on a farm or the number of clerical assignments completed without error in an office. The farm supervisors might argue with conviction that they are concerned with how many cucumbers are being picked, and any effort on their part would be directed at increasing the productivity of all workers. Similarly, the office managers might contend that they are not interested in singling out any particular employee or employees, but that the objective is to increase the proficiency of all. In both examples, however, information concerning the performance of each worker would permit the farm supervisor and the office manager to more easily meet their objectives.

One reason underlying the poor performance of the workers might be that some lack the skills necessary for their tasks. No matter what is done to encourage increased productivity in farm workers or careful completion of assigned tasks in office workers, production will not reach its potential and errors will not be completely eliminated until such skill deficits are remediated. Individual performance records allow supervisors and managers to identify the poorer performers and, if necessary, provide remedial training in the critical skills that are lacking.

A second reason for poor performance might involve lack of motivation. If only group data is available, the only possible motivational procedure is that based on the group's average performance which would affect all workers in the same way, regardless of their individual contributions to that group average. When such procedures are employed all are treated unfairly: The efficient workers will be unnecessarily penalized, for their level of performance will be above that of the group average, while the inefficient workers will receive more than their due for their level of performance will be below the group average. In the prison milieu, not only is such inequitable treatment poor preparation for what the workers will encounter when they leave the institution, but it reinforces inmate's common feelings that they are being dealt with arbitrarily, thereby contributing to the hostilities, jealousies, and resentments they so understandably exhibit. Clearly, individualized motivational procedures based on individual performance records are required.

Reliability of Measurement

After a problem has been defined in behavioral terms and a recording method has been selected, data collection on the occurrence of the target behavior(s) may begin and the reliability of measurement determined. In essence, the reliability of measurement is an estimate of the degree to which two independent observers agree upon the occurrence of a target behavior. As such, it insures that the definition of the target behavior is objective, and that all those involved with the problem and attempts to solve it are in accord as to what the problem is and how and when it manifests itself. Without the objective definition of target behaviors insured by a high reliability of measurement, it is impossible to remedy the lack of consistency in the manner in which both the same and different staff members interact with each inmate from time to time within the same day or from day to day. All too often, what happens (or fails to happen) to an inmate is more a function of how a staff member feels at a particular time than the behavior in which the inmate is engaged or what has been accomplished at the time.

The training and continued practice in objectivity that is an integral part of the effort towards reliability of measurement increases the likelihood that the typical fluctuations between leniency and strictness are overcome, and judgments regarding whether target behaviors meet predetermined criteria of acceptability are consistent from day to day. Even when each staff member is consistent in dealing with inmates, there is no guarantee that there is consistency from staff member to staff member. Such consistency is particularly important in an institutional setting where inmates are under continuous supervision and a number of different staff members are responsible for each inmate during different hours of the day and at different portions of the week. A concern with reliability of measurement insures that all staff members have mastered the definitions of the target behaviors for those for whom they are responsible and that the manner in which judgments are rendered concerning the occurrence or performance of these behaviors is the same from staff member to staff member.

The importance of refining the definitions of the target behaviors and providing the staff with training in observational and recording procedures until all observers show a high degree of agreement cannot be overemphasized, for such agreement serves a number of critical functions both during the course of intervention and for the general advancement of the profession itself. First, and perhaps most importantly, in terms of the practical considerations of the day-to-day provision of services, a reliable definition of the target behavior minimizes conflict between inmate/clients and supervisor/practitioners. When target behaviors are only vaguely defined and there is little specificity on the part of the clients concerning what they have committed themselves to and/or on the part of the practitioner concerning what they expected, the two parties typically spend more time and energy debating whether or not the client has engaged in or shown the behavior than they do working on a solution to the problem. As a consequence, the inmates' feelings that the staff is always on their back, picks on them, and/or is unreasonable and unfair in their dealings with them are enhanced.

Second, reliability of measurement goes a long way toward insuring that correctional plans will be applied in a consistent manner from shift to shift. Although consistency in the manner in which clients are dealt with is generally encouraged in institutional settings, one of the most important requirements of a behavior modification program is that the procedures that have been formally agreed upon and established by the client and staff be followed scrupulously and without fail. If this is not done, the behavior modification effort is almost guaranteed to fail. Indeed, it is probably safe to say that when behavior modification programs do fail, it is most often because inconsistencies in either the recording of the target behaviors or the honoring of prearranged agreements related to the occurrence of those target behaviors is prevalent. High-reliability estimates and the commitment of the staff to the correctional program insures consistency in the scoring and recording of the target behaviors without which the same behavior will, on some days or during some shifts, be accepted, while on other days or during other shifts, be rejected as unsatisfactory. This consistency plus the commitment of the administration are necessary for the impartial and routine honoring of the agreements relating target behaviors and their consequences.

Third, the consistent recording of the target behavior reduces extraneous day-to-day or recording period-to-recording period variability in the data that are being collected and graphed. The elimination of such fluctuations is important because the recording and graphing of data is commonly employed to determine whether the occurrence of the target behavior is related in any systematic manner to environmental events and/or institutional routine. If such is the case, a correctional program that takes these relationships into account will be more efficient, in terms of the time devoted to recording, the individuals who participate in the program itself, and so on, than one that does not. Large fluctuations in the data resulting from the unsystematic and inconsistent recording of the target behavior commonly mask such patterns, thereby preventing the identification of these relationships and depriving the program personnel of important information that allows the construction of more efficient and effective programs and, in many instances, means the difference between success and failure.

The fourth reason that it is important to insist upon the development of a reliable response measure is closely related to the preceding discussion of the manner in which large fluctuations in data that stem from unreliable measures mask important ongoing behavioral patterns. Here, however, the concern is with the manner in which such fluctuations mask the effects of the correctional programs that have been implemented in order to influence the occurrence of the target behavior. As was indicated previously, one of the important aspects of a behavior modification effort is the practitioner's concern with determining whether the correction plan that has been devised is effective. Just as fluctuations resulting from unreliable recording periods can mask existing patterns of behavior, they can also mask the positive effects of correctional programs, particularly when their impact is a gradual one. If this is the case, effective programs may be discarded, potentially successful ones may be prematurely discontinued, and important information concerning effective correctional strategies will be lost to the professional community.

COMPUTING THE RELIABILITY OF MEASUREMENTS

In general, the reliability estimate represents a comparison of two independent observers' simultaneous recording of the same target behavior, defined either as an event or in terms of its outcome, and is computed by dividing their total number of actual agreements upon the occurrence of the response by their total number of possible agreements on the occurrence of the response and multiplying the resulting decimal by 100. The result of this computation is commonly presented as the percentage of agreement between the two observers. Agreements between the two observers upon the nonoccurrence of the target behavior are always excluded from consideration when the total number of actual and possible agreements are determined, for, as will be discussed, their inclusion however, the concern is with the manner in which such fluctuations typically results in a spuriously high percentage of agreement. In addition, the general formula for determining the percentage of agreement is modified to a greater or lesser degree, depending upon the method of data collection that is being used in the project.

In the case of frequency counting of behavior events, wherein discrete events are being counted as they occur, a common method to determine reliability has been to compare the total count obtained by two independent observers. For example, if one officer counted 8 rule infractions and a second counted 10 during the same recording period, it is assumed they agreed on 8 counts they both reported and disagreed on the remaining 2 counts of the second officer. Based on this assumption the formula for obtaining the reliability would be 8 agreements divided by 8 agreements *plus* 2 disagreements or 8 divided by 10, resulting in a reliability estimate of .80 or 80%. The problem arises when we ask if the two observers actually agreed count by count on the 8 counts. As a hypothetical example, one officer may have counted all the rule infractions he observed during the first half of the recording period while the other counted his during the second half. Although they both reported approximately the same total number of infractions, they never once agreed on any single instance of what constituted a rule infraction. Checking instead instance by instance of rule infraction, their true percentage of agreement was zero rather than 80%. The appropriate procedure to follow to overcome this problem involves breaking the recording period down into smaller units of time (e.g., 5-minute units) and having each observer record his observations by time unit. Similarly, if outcomes, rather than events, are being recorded, the physical space within which the outcomes are observed should be broken down into smaller areas (e.g., quadrants, rooms, buildings, etc.) and the observers record their observations by areas.

In the preceding example, if in the first time unit, one officer recorded three instances of rule infractions and the other recorded only one, it would be assumed that for that five-minute period of observation, they agreed on one infraction and disagreed on two. This procedure would be used for each successive unit. At the end of the recording period the number of agreements and the number of disagreements by units would be summed and the resulting totals would be employed to determine the percentage of agreement in the manner described previously (i.e., total number of agreements divided by total number of agreements plus total number of disagreements). Obviously, the accuracy of the reliability estimate increases as the time units become shorter and shorter. Similarly, in the case of outcome recording, the accuracy of reliability estimates increases as the area units become smaller and smaller. Although this procedure does not completely guarantee instance-by-instance comparison it will produce a more accurate reliability estimate than a mere comparison of the total counts.

As will be recalled, interval recording is a data collection method in which a given period of observation is divided into successive and small time units. The observer simply checks each block in which the behavior occurred. For purposes of accurately determining the reliability of such observations, the number of blocks checked by *both* observers is divided by the number of blocks checked by at least one observer (i.e., blocks checked by either or both observers). As noted previously, blocks that neither observer checks are excluded from consideration and do not enter into the computation of the reliability estimate. Observations made on a time sample basis require that the observer look for the behavior at specified times. The reliability estimate of behavior when using this method is obtained by employing the procedure described under interval recording. That is, the number of time samples at which both observers saw the behavior is divided by the number of samples at which only one observer saw the behavior.

A similar procedure for estimating the reliability of observations is used with the controlled presentations method. In this method, the observer records the number of opportunities that prompt the occurrence of the behavior and whether the behavior occurs at those times. The reliability estimate of observations is computed by dividing the number of opportunities at which both observers indicated the behavior occurred by the number of opportunities at which only one observer indicated it occurred.

When latency data is being collected, instructions provided either by the observer or signalled by a mechanical device (e.g., a clock) inform the inmate that he is to begin a specific performance. The observer then records the time elapsing between the instructions and the start of the designated behavior. To obtain the reliability estimate of *each* latency measure, the latencies recorded by two observers are compared and the smaller is divided by the larger. If more than one latency is recorded per session, the average reliability estimate for all latencies is reported.

Duration data is collected when the object of interest is not how often an individual engages in a given activity but rather how much time is devoted to that activity. In duration recording, the reliability estimate is based on each observer's recording of the real time when the behavior began and when it ended. The reliability itself is obtained by dividing the real time common to both observers by the real time of at least one observer. For example, if one observer recorded the behavior as beginning at 9:05 a.m. ending at 9:20 a.m. while a second observer recorded the behavior as beginning at 9:10 a.m. and ending at 9:25 a.m., they would agree on the occurrence of the behavior for the 10 munutes of real time they have in common (i.e., from 9:10 a.m. to 9:20 a.m.). The amount of real time during which at least one observer recorded the behavior was 20 minutes (from 9:05 a.m. to 9:25 a.m.). The reliability estimate for the above duration measure would be 10 divided by 20 or .50. If more than one duration measure is involved, the average reliability estimate for all measures may be reported.

PROGRAM EVALUATION

Once a measurement procedure has been selected and has been shown to yield reliable data, it is possible to assess the effectiveness of an intervention effort. In order to demonstrate that a particular program or set of procedures is effective, two questions must be answered: (1) Does an anticipated change in behavior actually occur? and (2) Is that change in behavior a product of the program that is being evaluated? The first of these two questions is answered by measuring the behavior of each individual program participant across several days of sessions *before* the program is begun and comparing these "baseline" levels of performance to the performance of these same individuals across several days or sessions *after* the program has been instituted. Typically, measurement is begun sometime before the beginning of the program and is continued on a day-by-day or session-by-session basis during the program until the level of performance has stabilized at its new level. A comparison of each individual's baseline performance with the new stabilized level reveals the degree to which behavior has changed in each individual and in the group as a whole.

The second question, which asks if the change observed may be attributed to the program that is being evaluated, is more difficult to answer. If there is a change in behavior following the introduction of the program, it cannot be concluded with certainty that the change is a result of the program. This is because individuals in general, and those who would become involved in planned rehabilitation programs in particular, are subject to a variety of pressures and changes in their lives. Some of these changes, such as a death in the immediate family, reaching the 40th birthday, or the denial of probation, only influence particular individuals, whereas others, such as a supreme court decision, a change in the weather, or the promulgation of new guidelines governing parole decisions, affect all in the group. It is always possible that changes occurring during a program are a product of these chance happenings rather than of the program itself. If this possibility is not ruled out, it is conceivable that ineffective or regressive procedures will be mistakenly thought effective and advocated as such by those who have developed and implemented them. The result could be the wide-spread use of ineffective procedures that only appear effective because of their accidental association with changes in behavior that would be in reality a reaction to unnoticed or disregarded changes in living conditions or administrative policies.

Although it is a common practice to evaluate programs by comparing the performance of a "treatment" group to that of no-treatment "control" group, such an effort is not only costly, but it typically deprives the control group of a possibly beneficial program, an issue of increasing concern as we consider the legal, ethical, and moral implications of such evaluation procedures. The other possibility, that of assuming that a program is effective and implementing it without also undertaking the difficult task of program evaluation, is equally troublesome, for the program may in fact be ineffective or harmful, an outcome that could not be detected without a formal program evaluation effort. Again, the result could well be the promotion of such programs because they look or sound good, rather than because they are good.

It appears that what is needed, therefore, is a two-stage evaluation process. The first should determine whether a program is worthy of expense, effort, and legal/ethical/moral controversies and compromises of a long-term followup evaluation effort; the second would be that long-term follow-up itself, in which the enduring effects of the program would be determined. If this is to be done, the program must establish for itself both long-term and short-term objectives. The long-term objectives would involve a specification of just what are anticipated to be the ultimate, enduring effects of the program, such as a reduction in the overall rate of recidivism, a higher income, a more stable family life, and so forth, for those who have been in the program relative to comparable individuals who have not benefited from involvement in the program. The short-term goals are the observable changes in the participants that the program hopes to facilitate, such as increased academic grade level to a certain level, demonstrated mastery of specified vocational skills, enhanced concern for the feelings of others, etc. The short-term goals, then, are the means by which it is anticipated that the long-term goals will be achieved.

Clearly, if a program is not capable of achieving its short-term goals, there is no reason to expect that it will achieve its long-term goals and, consequently, the need for a costly and involved long-term follow-up evaluation is negated, allowing limited resources to be expended in areas that have a greater likelihood of producing positive results. Moreover, monitoring progress towards short-term objectives provides more immediate feedback than does awaiting the results of a long-term evaluation. This, in turn, provides information to the project staff when they can act upon it—namely, while the project is striving to meet its short-term objectives. Information that indicates that progress is not all that had been hoped for allows the staff to make revisions in the design of the program itself, thereby increasing the likelihood that if the program was not capable of meeting its short-term objectives in its initial form it will be capable of so doing as a function of detail improvements revealed as necessary during the program. This, in turn, increases the likelihood that the program will develop into one that is worthy of long-term follow-up evaluation. Such a happening is cause for celebration, for good ideas have been salvaged, the efforts of dedicated workers have not been for naught, and the allocation of scarce financial resources has been justified.

Unfortunately, the ability of a program to achieve its short-term objectives is no guarantee that its long-term objectives will also be realized. Programs stem from our best thinking about the causes and solutions of problems. The helping professions in general, and corrections in particular, have only begun to explore the variables affecting human difficulties and how these difficulties may be remedied. Our knowledge bases are far from complete, and our solutions are only approximations of those that the future holds. Consequently, it should not be surprising that programs that meet short-term objects fail to meet long-term ones, for they are only based upon the best current data and theorizing available. If a program fails to meet long-term objectives after succeeding in meeting short-term objectives, we should be reluctant to brand it a "failure." After all, it has met those objectives that were under its direct control. Instead, we should reexamine the basic data and theorizing that led to the formulation of those short-term objectives.

The failure of a program to meet long-term objectives *after* having met its short-term objectives is more a failure in our understanding of the causes and solutions of the problem than a program failure *per se*. It calls for a rethinking and reanalysis of our conceptualizations of what constitutes the necessary and sufficient ingredients of a program that will positively influence long-term indicators of program "success." These considerations notwithstanding, the evaluation of a program in terms of long-term indicators in the absence of an analysis of the degree to which it first meets short-term objectives runs the risk of wasting financial resources on a program that would quickly be identified as unworthy of a long-term follow-up evaluation. Moreover, a long-term evaluation would provide little information concerning the potential benefit of such a program, for it would not be possible to determine if the failure of the program would be due to a defect in that data base and subsequent theorizing of the causes and solutions of the problem or if the program itself was not successful in achieving short-term goals that are assumed to produce, in turn, changes in those long-term indicators of success.

To date, program evaluation efforts have concentrated on the degree to which programs achieve long-term goals relative to alternate programs and/or control procedures typically involving no programming other than routine treatment. The degree to which programs have achieved short-term objectives has also been examined, albeit to a lesser degree. What is needed, however, is an evaluation technology that allows a determination of whether the specifics of the program produce and are responsible for increases in the ability of a program to achieve the short-term objectives so that a decision on the advisability of subjecting the program to the expense and effort of short-term or long-term *comparative* studies is warranted. Moreover, this technology should facilitate on-line evaluation so that refinements and improvements may be incorporated into the program as it evolves into as effective an intervention regimen as it is capable of becoming. Such an evaluation technology is available (Sidman, 1960b; Hersen & Barlow, 1976) and will be outlined below. This technology provides the basis of the on-line examination of the effectiveness of the offender rehabilitation and management methods that are described in the latter portion of this text.

The most basic of these evaluation procedures is the "reversal" or A–B–A procedure. The assumptions underlying its use are (1) that the level of performance observed prior to the beginning of the program is a function of the naturally occurring conditions in effect then, (2) that the program alters or overcomes them to affect a change in behavior, and (3) that, if the program is suspended or terminated, the reinstatement of those naturally-occurring conditions will influence individuals in such a way that their behavior will return to the old (pre-program) level of performance. The ability to raise and lower performance by instating and suspending the program is taken as evidence that the program is responsible for the improvements in behavior observed, for it is unlikely that chance happenings in the lives of participants would coincide first with that onset of the program to increase performance and then with the suspension of the program to interfere with performance. Although a single A–B–A sequence is taken as an adequate demonstration of the effectiveness of the program, additional reinstatements and resuspensions may be used to strengthen this demonstration. Indeed, it is common practice to reinstate the program following its suspension if the basic A–B–A sequence indicates that the program itself is effective in changing behavior, for the objective of the effort is improvement in behavior. This, in turn, provides the opportunity to test and strengthen the conclusion that the program was responsible for the improvements in behavior observed.

It is obvious, however, that the reversal procedure is not always appropriate, for it requires that the change in behavior that occurred during the program can indeed be "undone," and, equally importantly, that it is ethically permissible to do so. Such is not always the case. When there is reason to believe that the change is, for all general intents and purposes, irreversible or, if the change is reversible but ethical considerations or practical concerns mitigate against so doing, the reversal procedure is rejected and the appropriateness of two alternative procedures is typically considered. These are the "multiple baseline" and "changing criterion" procedures.

In the *multiple baseline* or A-B-B/A-A-B procedure, a program is applied in succession to two or more individuals, behaviors, or settings. If, for example, the multiple baseline were to be employed to validate a program across individuals, the potential program participants would be identified and their baseline levels of performance recorded. Then one would be enrolled in the program, while baseline recording would be continued for the remainder. Once any changes in the behavior of the first individual had been identified, the second individual would be added to the program and any subsequent changes in behavior identified. The procedure would be continued for additional individuals until the effect (or lack thereof) of the program had been shown by the presence (or absence) of changes in behavior of individuals following their enrollment in the program. These changes, coincident with enrollment in the program, would rule out the possibility that chance factors accounted for the effects seen, for it is unlikely that such factors would influence successive individuals at the times of their enrollment in the program. The same logic would apply if the program was applied in succession to different behaviors or in different settings. The successive changes in the different behaviors or different settings as the program was applied to each would demonstrate that the changes were due to the program itself and not to extraneous influences.

The *changing criterion* procedure is the most recently developed of the three evaluation methods. In it, performance of a particular behavior is recorded during baseline and then during an intervention program as in the previous two procedures. The changing criterion procedure differs from the previous two, however, in the manner in which requirements for reinforcement are set. In the previous two, the level of performance expected for a behavior when it is incorporated in a program is constant throughout the evaluation phase. In the changing criterion procedure the *expected* level of performance is increased in a step-wise manner through the evaluation period. If the *observed* level of performance increases in a step-wise manner that parallels what is expected, it may be concluded that the program is responsible for the improvements seen. It is unlikely that nonprogram factors would, by chance, influence behavior at the exact time of each successive program change to produce the anticipated performance increases. Consequently, it must be the program itself, and not extraneous factors, that has produced the changes in behavior observed.

Several additional evaluation procedures have been employed to assess whether intervention programs have achieved their short-term objectives and, if they have, whether these successes may be attributable to the program *per se* or to extraneous, nonprogrammic variables. Most are variations on the themes of the three evaluation procedures outlined above and are described in detail elsewhere (Hersen & Barlow, 1976). In keeping with the assumption that the first issue in the development and refinement of any program revolves around whether the program achieves the short-term objectives that it has established for itself, the work to be reported in the remainder of the text has utilized these evaluation procedures to evaluate its effectiveness. The short-term objectives, which involve remedial education, vocational instruction, and employability-skill training, have been deduced from contemporary views in criminology, sociology, and psychology concerning the economic nature of most criminal activity and the lack, in a majority of offenders, of viable alternatives to criminal activities for economic survival. These ingredients are viewed as *necessary* ingredients in any rehabiliative program for adult offenders. Certainly, supplementary programs, both within and without the institution, are also called for. As has been noted previously, it is only when all these services are provided in a planned and programmed manner that we will approximate a *sufficient* program that would be expected to impact in any significant way upon the accepted indicators of long-term program success. The work to be reported, then, is the beginning of the development of effective correctional rehabilitation and management programs.

CHAPTER

$$\boxed{7}$$

GUIDELINES FOR THE OPERATION OF ETHICAL PROGRAMS IN CORRECTIONAL SETTINGS

The sensitive nature of efforts to affect changes in established policies concerning offender rehabilitation and management is highlighted by the experiences of Geller, Johnson, Hamlin, and Kennedy (1977). Geller et al. were asked to design and operate a structured rehabilitation and management program in two segregation facilities of the Virginia correctional system. From the outset it was clear that the goals of the program were modest, but that it was to come to grips with some of the most common problems experienced in all correctional systems: The program was to encourage "unmanageable" offenders—offenders who repeatedly attacked others, ran prison "rackets," etc.—to acquire the skills necessary to live in the general prison population so that they might avail themselves of the correctional programs available there but not in the segregated facility in which they were placed for the protection of other inmates.

The "Contingency Management Program" (CMP) that they developed was well-designed and humane. It stressed the cooperative involvement of both custody and treatment personnel, stressed rewards for constructive attitudes and behavior, deemphasized punitive procedures, did not deprive participants of amenities routinely available in the segregation facilities in which the program was conducted, was voluntary, and it carefully monitored each participant's progress. Nevertheless, the program came under attack, primarily by the American Civil Liberties Union's National Prison Project. The main focus of the criticisms was whether the goals of the program were in the best interests of the inmates or of the prison officials.

The National Prison Project charged that the real objective of CMP was to "institutionalize" and pacify inmates so that prison administrators would be spared the protests and confrontations of prisoners who were objecting to and rebelling against the inhumanities of the correctional system. Geller et al. acknowledge the many faults of the prison system but point out that the realities of the situation demand that correctional administrators concern themselves with the well-being and protection of inmates in the system as it exists today. They argue that all inmates have the right to be protected in their custody and that this may indeed require special treatment of the few inmates who pose a clear threat to the protected custody of the remainder, as well as to the safety of the correctional staff. Geller et al. also point out that this attack ignored the CMP's emphasis upon education and vocational training, which comprised the bulk of the activities that were encouraged in the program. They argue that a reasonable approach to the problems of corrections must include provisions for *both* rehabilitation and management concerns; to ignore either is to deny the realities involved in facilitating academic and vocational education in all residential settings, be these military installations, university campuses, or correctional institutions.

Related criticisms of CMP revolved around the theoretical basis of the program. CMP was described as a behavior modification program. This was cause for concern on the part of many who were ignorant of the distinction between "behavior modification" as referred to in the popular press and as defined in professional circles. The media and, as a consequence, many lay persons believe that behavior modification involves the use of psychotropic drugs, psychosurgery, and the like. Given this misconception, their adverse reaction is understandable. However, Geller et al. used the term in the professional sense, meaning that their objective was to develop a structured program to encourage inmates to learn new, appropriate ways of dealing with problems so that they could give up their previously-learned, inappropriate modes of behavior. Unfortunately, Geller et al. encountered little success in their attempts to communicate this distinction to either the National Prison Project or the media, perhaps because the confusion made for good politics and good press. In any case, they urge that professionals using learning-based procedures in the design of a project avoid this difficulty by merely *describing* the specifics of the program and refraining from the use of "behavior modification" as a short-hand term to communicate in a general sense what the program is about.

The term "behavior modification" came into use in the early 1960s as a descriptive term applied to psychological procedures that were greatly removed from the mentalistic, medical-model approaches then in vogue. Based on a behavioral-model approach, these procedures were derived from extensive laboratory studies and were found, by the psychologists who first used them with people, to be surprisingly effective. In comparison to the long-term and expensive insight therapies, the behavioral approach to human problems was rapid, economical, and effective.

Because of its proven effectiveness, behavior modification became widely accepted and employed. Unfortunately, the rapid growth of interest in and use of behavior modification led to problems. Everyone wanted to get on the bandwagon of success. Because there was no certification or regulation of the term, many people, some of whom had little or no training in the behavioral approach, began practicing what they too called "behavior modification." It soon became apparent that the general public, and even many professionals, could not distinguish between behavior modifiers who had the skills, training, and background to conduct responsible treatment, and the untrained people who merely borrowed the term "behavior modification" to describe and more often justify the bizarre treatment they were conducting.

In this fashion, behavior modification came to receive a less than admirable reputation. Psychosurgery, the destruction of brain tissue for supposedly therapeutic purposes, had predated behavior modification for at least 25 years. Yet recently, this medical technique has been described as "behavior modification." Chemotherapy, the administration of drugs for their supposed psychological or behavioral effect, has also been labeled "behavior modification." In both of these examples, behavior modification, a psychological term describing a treatment based on experimentally verified procedures of behavior change resulting from environmental changes, has been unjustly borrowed to describe medical treatments which act in sometimes physically irreversible ways upon persons subjected to them. Similarly, old administrative and even therapeutic practices have continued on with only a change in name and not in substance. For example, solitary confinement in "the hole" for protracted periods of time has been dignified with the term "time out." Similarly, Kennedy (1976) pointed out that the punitive use of apomorphine, a drug that produces severe and uncontrollable vomiting, has been described as nothing more than a straightforward and appropriate classical conditioning technique.

Because of these and other excesses, programs described as involving behavior modification are automatically responded to with general disfavor by many professionals and lay persons alike. Even legitimate research and treatment in the area frequently suffer when described as behavior modification. It is, of course, true that as a generic term, behavior modification can be used to describe any procedure or treatment that results in behavior change. Psychosurgery, psychoanalysis, chemotherapy, imprisonment itself, the practice of scientology, religious conversion, physical restraint, Rogerian therapy, army induction, physical paralysis, our system of laws, and even execution could, therefore, be described as behavior modification procedures.

When the term is used as a specific description of certain psychological procedures, behavior modification describes an area of applied psychology that is comprised of a specific set of behavior principles and a specific framework describing the interaction of these principles. Both the principles and the behavioral framework are based on learning theory and are derived from scientific studies in the psychological laboratory with both animals and humans. Critics who have reacted to the practices that have been justified and legitimized by the use of the term "behavior modification" have urged that all practices described as such be terminated and outlawed. In an effort to separate themselves and their procedures from those that have earned the legitimate criticism of the public, many behavior modifiers have suggested that the name "behavior modification" be abandoned and a new term be adopted.

Outlawing the planned and deliberate use of all behavior modification procedures may in itself be unethical since it denies the client and society access to many rehabilitative practices shown to be effective. The prohibition of legitimate behavior modification procedures, indeed, would be analogous to "throwing out the baby with the bathwater." Also, changing the name of the approach to something other than behavior modification may be shortsighted since it does nothing to upgrade the quality of care and rehabilitation. It might be more productive, on the other hand, to consider what features should characterize any program intent on providing effective and humane rehabilitation. Irrespective of theoretical approaches and philosophy of rehabilitation, it would seem that such programs would, at the very least, meet the following two criteria:

1.   The program must maintain or restore human dignity from every possible perspective. People should not be deprived materially, socially, medically, or sensorially. Any treatment that appears, even at face value alone, to detract from a person's freedom, individuality, or dignity must be questioned and justified or abandoned.

2.   The program must incorporate individualized and objective measures of effectiveness. Subjective judgment of effectiveness, while always desirable, cannot stand alone. Procedures must produce measurable changes that are observable to both professionals and the recipients of such treatment.

Both of these criteria must be met. Concern for individual rights and dignity is extremely shallow without demonstrable positive changes derived from the treatment program. But, while all may agree on the effective outcome of a treatment, less than humane means used to achieve such outcome cannot be justified. Although the two criteria provide a general overview of the requirements for a humane and effective program, specific elaboration is needed.

THE HUMANE PROGRAM

A humane program requires that people be treated as individuals, with rights, freedoms, and dignity. Institutions, in which the majority of rehabilitation programs occur, make individualization particularly difficult. It is often tempting to disregard the individual for the larger group. Rather than treating each person receiving rehabilitation as unique, the usual approach is to design treatment to fit the composite individual (patient, inmate, etc.). The usual procedure in such cases is to require all individuals to conform to a standardized treatment. The problem with such an approach is obvious: Treatment may be inappropriate and/or ineffective for some or even many of the individuals. A humane approach should at least tailor the program to if not create a program for each individual. Treatment, therefore, should be designed especially to satisfy individual problems, needs, and skills.

It must never be overlooked that each individual must always retain certain basic human rights. These rights, often compromised in institutional settings, include the right to rehabilitation, the right of social intercourse, privacy, the right to palatable and sufficient food, the right to humane living conditions, and the sometimes conflicting right to freedom from untoward psychological interference.

Professionals must be ever mindful of the conditions they impose upon others in the course of treatment, rehabilitation, or education. They must ask themselves how they would react if placed in a similar position.

THE EFFECTIVE PROGRAM

Concern for the humanistic aspects of treatment is not enough, however. Unless the program results in positive and measurable changes, it is little better than no treatment at all. The demonstration of treatment effectiveness must also be in terms which all can understand. Functionally irrelevant psychological jargon is unacceptable, as is a score on an obscure psychological test. Inmates, for example, do not find themselves in prison as a result of a "psychopathic personality" but as a result of criminal behavior. Treatment that merely results in "ego strengthening" is meaningless in terms of what that individual's appropriate behavior should be. Similarly, a test–retest difference in MMPI profiles does not indicate anything more than the fact that on this particular test, this particular individual answered differently than on the previous occasion. Too often, reliance on such measures has led professionals to prematurely conclude that a program is effective when, in fact, the social and behavioral deficits of the individuals concerned remain largely unaltered.

Therefore, it might be more productive to consider some criteria of general applicability that could be employed to regulate any *correctional program* regardless of its theoretical base. Decisions could be made depending upon where a program falls with respect to the following criteria. Four important criteria are suggested:

1. *The amount of previous validation procedures to be employed.* Validated procedures are those that have been tested in a variety of applied settings, with a variety of populations and have been generally found to be effective in bringing about positive and desirable changes without undesirable side effects. Unvalidated procedures, on the other hand, include both novel and accepted procedures that have not been subjected to empirical scrutiny and that lack documented basis for their justification.

2. *The potential degree of discomfort the individual may experience as a function of the procedures.* The possible degree of discomfort, physical and psychological, derived from a procedure is often difficult to assess. Judgment regarding discomfort should be based upon the combined input of inmates, administrators, and professionals. Most would agree that denying an adult felon a cigarette, even on capricious grounds, is unlikely to cause even minimal physical or emotional discomfort. Similarly, most would agree that employing a cattle prod to awaken inmates in the morning would cause severe physical as well as emotional discomfort.

3. *The level of fundamental changes in the psychological make-up of the individual that may result from the use of the procedure.* Again, judging the anticipated degree of irreversible change in the psychological make-up of the individual as a result of a procedure will often be difficult, requiring a solution such as that suggested previously. Most would agree that teaching an individual the basic arithmetic skills involves little or no fundamental change in psychological make-up while altering an individual's sexual preference would constitute a most fundamental and difficult-to-reverse change.

4. *The degree to which the program may be expected to prepare the individual for a law-abiding and productive community life.* Most would agree that learning to read increases the likelihood of success of obtaining and holding a meaningful job as well as raising the individual's quality of living. On the other hand, most would also agree that having inmates line up and march in lock-step from place to place has no positive effect on postrelease adjustment.

Programs that fall within the intrusive or dehumanizing extremes of any of these four criteria should be subjected to regulations for their implementation in correctional settings. To make clear how programs may be evaluated in terms of these criteria, the use of psychosurgery, psychotherapy, and behavior modification is briefly reviewed.

Psychosurgery

The use of psychosurgery to eliminate aggressive behavior has been soundly criticized (Mitford, 1973). Experts have charged that the use of psychosurgery for this purpose is not a well-validated procedure. Moreover, it is highly likely to produce marked irreversible changes in the client's psychological make-up. However, the procedure apparently does not cause untoward psychological discomfort and if successful in achieving its objective it raises the likelihood of successful community adjustment. Still, psychosurgery falls in the intrusive extreme of two of the criteria outlined previously. Moreover, the whole issue of whether or not to sanction psychosurgery for these purposes is an emotionally charged one that raises visions of mad scientists, authoritarian states, *1984, Brave New World,* and the like in the minds of many. Therefore, it is understandable and appropriate that public outcry against such virtually unregulated efforts brought them to an end.

Psychotherapy

A variety of psychotherapeutic techniques have been used for the last half-century with offenders and have not received the type of criticism that has been directed to psychosurgery. A cursory examination of the practices of psychotherapy in correctional settings in comparison to psychosurgery suggests why this may be so.

First, one might be inclined to believe that the validity of psychotherapy with offenders has been proven whereas the effects of psychosurgery are still in question. Despite the layman's general belief in the effectiveness of psychotherapy, it has not yet been demonstrated with the offender. This, then, may not be the major basis for the absence of criticism regarding psychotherapy.

Second, it might be that psychosurgery subjects individuals to greater degrees of psychological or physical discomfort than does psychotherapy. Certainly, the degree of discomfort associated with psychotherapy is minimal and easily tolerable. Although no firm conclusion can be drawn, as was indicated previously, supporters of psychosurgery claim that it, too, is both psychologically and physically "painless" (i.e. the operation is performed under anesthesia to spare the patient pain). Again, this does not appear to be the strongest basis underlying the different reactions to psychotherapy and psychosurgery.

Third, it might be that psychotherapy is expected to better prepare the individual for community living than does psychosurgery since it deals with feelings, attitudes, motivation, and relationships. Proponents of psychosurgery, however, also argue that their treatment will best prepare the individual for postrelease success by reducing or eliminating chronic aggressive and violent tendencies. As was discussed previously, however, there is little empirical evidence to justify either fervently held belief. This, then, is unlikely to be the basis to explain the different reactions to the two approaches.

Finally, it might be that psychotherapy does not produce the profound and irreversible changes in the individual's psychological make-up that may be produced by psychosurgery. Although we may not be able to predict what the specific effects of psychotherapy will be, we can say with reasonable assurance that damage to the brain produces profound and irreversible changes in the individual's psychological make-up. Such changes have never been attributed to psychotherapy.

Moreover, psychotherapy as a form of treatment enjoys a long tradition, making it desirable in its own right; thus, unlike psychosurgery, it is viewed with approval rather than alarm. Most probably these factors account for the lack of criticism leveled against psychotherapy.

Behavior Modification

A comparison of behavior modification with psychosurgery and psychotherapy reveals similarities and differences. First, a major characteristic that sets behavior modification apart from both psychosurgery and psychotherapy is the degree to which each has been validated. As has been discussed previously, it is generally accepted that the effectiveness of psychosurgery and psychotherapy in the mental health area in general, and in corrections in particular, has not yet been demonstrated. In contrast, a substantial body of literature is available that documents the effectiveness of behavior modification in these areas.

Second, behavior modification and psychotherapy are similar in that neither claims to produce fundamental and irreversible changes in the psychological make-up of the individual in the manner that psychosurgery can. Psychotherapy emphasizes personality change through insight and catharsis while behavior modification strives for behavior change through the teaching of new skills, abilities, and attitudes. Indeed, of the two approaches, behavior modification appears less intrusive than psychotherapy, while both are certainly less intrusive than psychosurgery which strives for permanent psychological change through the irreversible destruction of brain tissue.

Third, the issue of continued community adjustment after successful treatment is one that separates psychosurgery from both psychotherapy and behavior modification. Successful psychosurgery would be expected to have more enduring and trans-situational effects upon behavior and personality than either psychotherapy or behavior modification. The major basis for anticipating transfer of effects from psychosurgery to community life is the irreversible character of the brain alteration itself. While such intrusive and powerful effects cannot be claimed by either psychotherapy or behavior modification, practitioners of both approaches are cognizant of the critical importance of transfer and maintenance of treatment gains to the community. Of the two approaches, however, the behavioral one provides some guidelines on how to accomplish these ends, and some evidence to support such recommendations for treatment.

Taking these three criteria together, it would appear that from the three therapeutic approaches that we can single out a favorable treatment that: *(a)* employs empirically validated procedures; *(b)* effects important behavioral changes which are relevant to postrehabilitative adjustment; and does so *(c)* without untoward intrusion into the individual's basic psychological make-up. That treatment is behavior modification. This conclusion notwithstanding, it is clear that behavior modification is still viewed with apprehension and alarm by professionals and lay persons alike. One reason for this is the popular misconception that for behavior modification to work it must employ coercive procedures which involve physical hardship and psychological discomfort.

This fourth and last criterion, the degree of physical and/or psychological discomfort experienced by an individual, is certainly one of the most important issues in evaluating the pros and cons of these three treatment approaches. Neither the psychosurgical operation nor traditional psychotherapy are likely to provoke untoward physical or psychological discomfort. However, one of the major criticisms of behavior modification is that it causes both. Indeed, it is true some programs that have been called behavioral have subjected participants to unnecessary hardships and deprivation. Such notorious programs are not representative of the tactics followed by behaviorally-trained practitioners in this area since reliance on deprivation and physical discomfort for effecting behavioral change reflects, at best, incompetence and, at worst, malevolence. In conclusion, then, the major objections to behavioral programs are largely unfounded and certainly do not apply to the everyday practice of legitimate behavior modification and behavior therapy. As is discussed in subsequent sections of this book, the most successful behavioral programs are those that rely on positive incentives and eschew the use of deprivation and psychological discomfort in any form.

FOSTERING FREEDOM AND DIGNITY

Perhaps the most pervasive and most difficult question to resolve concerning the use of behavior modification in general, and in corrections in particular, arises from differing philosophical interpretations of the role of behavior modification in a free society. Many object to behavior modification on the grounds that it is contrary to their cherished beliefs regarding freedom and dignity in a democratic society. Nothing could be farther from the truth. Indeed, the behavioral approach insists on extending a full measure of freedom and dignity to those who are seemingly without it. It does so by providing the individual with freedom-enhancing skills in a dignified manner. For example, mental patients and prison inmates are institutionalized because they lack the interpersonal and employment skills that are necessary for effective community living. In effect, they lack the freedom to behave differently. The behavior modification program which emphasizes the teaching of skills that are required by individuals so that they may meet social demands of their environments affords individuals a measure of choice. In so doing, the freedom of these individuals is enhanced.

The procedures that are routinely followed in behavior modification programs are ones that also enhance the individual's dignity. These programs are typically individualized. As such, they recognize the unique abilities, interests, and needs of each person and thereby preserve individuality and personal dignity. Behavioral programs are characterized by their emphasis on personal responsibility. Most mental hospitals treat patients as children who need constant support and guidance because they cannot be held responsible for their actions. Most prisons treat inmates as children who are punished for their misdeeds in the institution by having freely given privileges and favors withdrawn. In contrast, behavioral programs in both settings restore dignity by treating patients and inmates as responsible adults who can earn their way by acquiring new skills and social competencies. The individual's dignity is assured and enhanced when his choices of what to learn and how to learn are respected as in a behavioral program.

To protect the individual from potential psychological or physical discomfort and to insure enhancement of the individual's freedom and dignity, the following program guidelines are recommended. Although they are offered within the context of the behavioral approach in the prison setting, it should be noted that the applicability is considerably broader. Indeed, guidelines such as these would be expected to upgrade and humanize the quality of services provided no matter what the setting or treatment approach employed.

1.   To insure freedom and dignity, the individual should be encouraged to be an active participant of his own treatment and rehabilitation. This may be accomplished by enabling the individual to participate in establishing specific objectives of his treatment, the means to achieve the goals of treatment and, finally, coming to an agreement with the administration regarding the responsibilities and obligations of each to the other for the duration of the treatment.

2.   Short-, intermediate-, and long-range goals should be stated in a clear and unambiguous manner. This will minimize misunderstanding and allow the objective monitoring of progress and completion of treatment by the administration and the inmate himself.

3. The means to achieve objectives should be stated in as clear and unambiguous a manner as the goals themselves. This emphasis on stating explicitly what the goals are and how they may be achieved is basic for informed choice between alternatives and for informed consent itself.

4. Explicit understanding between the administration and the inmates should be reached regarding what individuals can expect in return for their efforts. This agreement can, if desirable, take the form of a written contract. Such an agreement should foster the inmates' becoming responsible for their own choices and conduct.

5. To insure informed consent, the inmate should be made familiar with the characteristics of the treatment programs available. Depending on the specific features of the programs, the inmate may visit, observe directly, and sample some of the actual activities included in the programs under consideration prior to making a decision. In addition, the duration of the training program as well as the behavioral requirements to be met prior to graduation from the program should be explicitly stated to minimize misunderstanding and maximize the inmate's active involvement in reaching the stated objectives.

6. To insure that informed consent is given voluntarily, when daily rewards are involved, the generally impoverished living conditions of most correctional institutions dictate that special precautions be taken. The magnitude of any potential improvement in the quality of life in the prison which might accrue to inmates as a function of their participation in the program must not be reasonably expected to entice them to either enter or continue in a program that they believe may cause them physical or psychological harm. Inmates choosing not to participate in programs should be provided at the very least with basic rights, privileges and amenities as guaranteed by the Constitution, affirmed by recent legal decisions, (e.g., Wyatt vs. Stickney) and required on ethical and humanitarian grounds.

7. To insure that informed consent is given voluntarily, when powerful long-term rewards are involved, additional precautions must be taken because of the likelihood that an inmate's decision to participate in a given program will be easily influenced by such incentives as early release by the parole board and the award of "good time." The most reasonable procedures to follow in such instances is to establish both several alternative criteria for the award of these powerful incentives and several alternative means by which those criteria may be achieved.

8. The most effective means the criminal justice system has of guarding against treatment programs of potential harm to its charges is the careful selection of professional personnel. It is especially important that the professional staff responsible for the design and operation of treatment programs within the criminal justice system be of the highest caliber. Not only must they possess a high degree of technical competence, but also they must adhere to the most stringent of ethical principles and demonstrate the deepest of concerns for the rights and dignity of their fellow humans as they carry out their responsibilities.

9. To further insure the humane treatment of the offender, the criminal justice system must insist that its professional staff routinely submit their treatment programs to the review of their peers throughout the professional community. By so doing, the criminal justice system will further guarantee that these programs are of the highest quality and in the best interests of all concerned. A formal peer review policy not only insures that the professionals within the criminal justice system are abreast with the most advanced thinking in the field but also that their treatment endeavors receive the scrutiny and constructive criticism essential to program refinement and the safeguarding of participants.

10. Although a combination of a thoroughly qualified professional staff and a formal policy of peer review is an effective safeguard for the offender's safety and well-being, it is desirable that the criminal justice system also open its treatment programs to public view and inspection. Not only does the public, as the financial backer of these efforts, deserve to be kept fully informed of their nature and objectives, but an informed public is the most effective means available to the criminal justice system for protecting itself from the polemics, un-informed criticism, and emotional diatribes which, all too often, characterize discussions of its programs, policies, and procedures. Equally important, however, an informed public contributes to the safeguarding of the offender. It better insures the speedy elimination of those programs that either exert an undue hardship upon the offender while under the care of the criminal justice system or have a detrimental effect upon his adjustment once he returns to the community.

11. In addition, the potential contribution of the offenders both to rehabilitation within the criminal justice system and to safeguarding of themselves and their fellow offenders should not be underestimated. The offenders, by dint of their intimate knowledge of the innerworkings of the criminal justice system and the inmate subculture, can provide the professional staff information through advice and counsel that it would otherwise take the staff years to acquire if, indeed, they could, by the nature of their position in the system, acquire at all. The treatment staff that includes ex-offenders among its members will undoubtedly recognize and take into account a number of important considerations that it otherwise would be slow to identify or would overlook altogether. Similarly, the professional staff that makes provisions both to listen to the suggestions and complaints of its target population—the offenders—and then to give weight to these when questions concerning its policies, programs, and procedures are debated will undoubtedly devise more efficient and effective procedures than it would otherwise be capable of developing.

12. Finally, formal reviews of the offender's progress should be scheduled to occur on a regular basis. All those involved in the offender's program (including the offender and his or her representative) should participate. The focus of these reviews should be on the objective indices of the offender's progress, supplemented by the subjective impressions of all involved. The review should not only afford the offender the opportunity to receive feedback from the staff; it should also enable the staff to receive feedback from the offender. Conflicts should be resolved, program adjustments made as required, and the commitment of all to the goals and details of the program renewed. Only by so doing will it be possible to guarantee the highest quality care.

CONCLUSION

The ultimate goal of those working with offenders should be to upgrade the quality of services offered to them and to refine and improve upon routine administrative procedures involving the management of the criminal justice system. Studies are of little value unless the criminal justice system makes use of their findings in its dealings with the offender. Those shortcomings that such studies reveal should be eliminated from the system in general. Similarly, policies and procedures that have been studied and found beneficial should be implemented throughout the system in general. Continued caution must be exercised, however, to insure that the offender is not abused as these policies and procedures are deployed on an increasingly broader scale.

The nature of some policies and procedures will be such that they be incorporated within the criminal justice system as standard operating practices and be applied equally to all those with whom the system has contact. As is discussed in the next chapter, for example, the heavy reliance of corrections upon punishment and aversive control procedures in its dealings with the inmate population appears to contribute to both the unrest in correctional institutions and to the regressive effect a period of imprisonment appears to exert upon the offender. Moreover, the procedures that govern the awarding and withholding of "good time" (that is, time off the length of the sentence) reflect this reliance.

Good time is typically computed and awarded when the inmate enters the correctional system and is then taken away unsystematically as he either violates one or more of the seemingly endless number of ill-defined prohibitions or, for whatever reason, incurs the wrath of one or more of the members of the correctional staff. Recent studies suggest that good time might be better utilized to systematically encourage desirable behavior than to unsystematically discourage undesirable behavior and, by doing so, might contribute to a reduction of both the unrest in our correctional centers and the regressive influence of the institution upon the inmate. If additional studies proved this hypothesis, it would certainly justify a move on the part of corrections to replace its old good-time policies, which stress punishment and aversive control, with alternatives that emphasize positive incentives. Indeed, most would agree that to do otherwise would be both unjust and unethical.

CHAPTER

$$\boxed{8}$$

BEHAVIORAL PROGRAMS IN TWO CORRECTIONAL SETTINGS

OVERVIEW

The National Advisory Commission on Criminal Justice Standards and Goals (1973), acknowledging claims that the American correctional system today appears to offer minimum protection for the public and maximum harm to the offender, has made the following recommendations: (a) that a greater emphasis be placed on community efforts that prevent crime and aid the released offender in readjusting to community life; (b) that corrections adopt a maximum sentence of five years for all offenders, with no statutorily imposed minimum, except for those identified as persistent violators, professional criminals, or dangerous offenders, who would be eligible for sentences ranging up to 25 years; and (c) that there be a 10-year moratorium on the construction of state institutions for adults, except when total system planning shows that the need for them is imperative.

The degree to which the commission has qualified its recommenda-

135

tions and implied the continuation of the traditional correctional apparatus reveals the extent to which prisons are and will continue to be a fact of life in American society for the forseeable future. Considerations such as these gave rise to the following five assumptions, which guided the rehabilitation endeavors described within this report:

1.   Correctional centers, for the foreseeable future, will continue to exist, and men and women will continue to be confined within them.

2.   A greater effort must be made to insure that those who are imprisoned will return to the community no worse for their experiences.

3.   A greater effort must be made to offer imprisoned offenders a full range of programs that have the potential of preparing them to lead more satisfying and productive lives than were available to them prior to their imprisonment.

4.   A greater effort must be made to encourage imprisoned offenders to become productive participants in the program offered in correctional centers.

5.   Such efforts will in no manner impede and will, most probably, contribute to the reforms in correctional thought and practice urged by both the professional community and the concerned citizenry.

SHORTCOMINGS OF THE PUNISHMENT MODEL

The manner in which these assumptions are to be acted upon is less clear than the considerations that have given rise to them. To date, the characteristic treatment philosophy of the criminal justice system has been one that stresses both the threat of punishment to suppress unwanted behavior and to motivate the performance of desired activities. Although these techniques are employed to a greater or lesser degree throughout the criminal justice system, it is in corrections itself that they are most extensively deployed, and it is here that the debilitating effects of this philosophy are most clearly evident (Durkheim, 1947; Glaser, 1971; Milan & McKee, 1974). Even those inmates who are fortunate enough to begin participation in a rehabilitation program immediately upon their admission to the institution soon come under the influence of this form of coercive control and the inmate subculture it breeds. Those who are at first friendly and outgoing turn hostile and sullen. Those who would normally return misplaced items come to steal them instead. Those who are eager to learn in the academic and trade areas, lose interest and malinger. It is apparent that the acknowledged failure of correctional institutions to rehabilitate is due as much, or more, to what is accidentally "taught" the inmate in his free time than to the academic and vocational deficiencies he carries with him when he returns to the community. It is as if the prison itself, with both its social system and its emphasis on obedience, passivity, and punitively oriented control procedures, is a well-designed "teaching machine" (Buehler, Patterson, & Furniss, 1966) that teaches and reinforces lack of initiative, resistance, and adherence to the inmate subculture.

The punitive procedures employed to maintain order and manage inmate behavior in virtually all correctional institutions serve the purpose of controlling behavior. However, their side effects undoubtedly contribute to the unrest which prevails in our prisons and increase, rather than decrease, the likelihood that the released offender will commit additional crimes. Evidence indicates that when punishment is regularly employed to suppress behavior, the punished inmate tends to avoid personal contact with the punishing agents (the correctional staff). It appears, then, that the correctional officers who rely upon punishment to control inmate behavior destroy their ability to interact with the inmate and, ultimately whatever potential credibility they possess as a rehabilitative agent. Of equal importance is the effect of the widespread use of punishment upon the potential for violence within the institution. Evidence also indicates that punishment calls forth from the punished individual aggression that is directed toward the punishing agent and/or peers who are not themselves responsible for the punishment. In addition, and not surprisingly so, evidence shows that individuals actively resist punitive procedures. They work against the system that employs such techniques, and they counterattack, either verbally or physically, both those who represent the system and those who support it. Viewed within this framework, the inmate subculture is an understandable reaction to the extensive use of punitive procedures, for it effectively diminishes the efficiency with which the institutional staff can carry out these procedures. In the end, it is adherence to the inmate subculture rather than commitment to the rehabilitation programs that allows inmates to obtain those things, both tangible and intangible, that they desire.

An additional problem associated with the use of punitive procedures are the accompanying emotional and attitudinal reactions of anxiety, hostility, and resentment. These, in turn, are among the classical features of the juvenile delinquent and the criminal. Combine them with the antisocial predispositions generated by the existent control procedures and fostered by the inmate subculture and it appears that Ramsey Clark (1970) is accurate. Correctional institutions are indeed "factories of crime."

If these regressive effects of imprisonment are to be eliminated and the offender is to be better prepared for full participation in our society, it appears that the institutions themselves must adopt a management system that (*a*) insures order and discipline with only minimal reliance upon the threat of punishment as a control procedure; (*b*) provides for the performance of necessary maintenance tasks and work assignments without primary recourse to the coercive use of punitive procedures (these first two requirements are obviously closely related and, if met, attack what may be the most significant conditions underlying the regressive effects of imprisonment); (*c*) can be administered by appropriately trained and supervised correctional staff, thereby enabling the line correctional officer—the only individual who has daily contact with the inmate—to participate in the rehabilitation program rather than function as an agent of punishment; (*d*) is compatible with and fosters the inmates' participation in formalized rehabilitation programs; and (*e*) approximates, as closely as possible, those conditions that exist in society itself since this strategy would seemingly best prepare the inmate for integration into that society.

THE PROGRAMS

As was noted in Chapter 4, the utility and effectiveness of the behavioral approach has been amply documented in a wide variety of settings with a wide range of diverse groups. The two programs to be described here represent a straightforward elaboration and extension of valid and reliable procedures to the correctional setting. Moreover, as was also noted in Chapter 4, the efforts yet to be described were preceded by similar but less comprehensive endeavors with adult offenders. These endeavors paved the way for the design of more comprehensive programs for the rehabilitation of the institutionalized offenders.

This behavioral approach to rehabilitation of institutionalized adult offenders was first initiated at the Draper Correctional Center, Alabama. Based on its encouraging results, the same behavioral model was extended to encompass an entire prison institution in Buford, Georgia. That a behavioral model of rehabilitation is not dependent upon some idealized physical structure or facility is best revealed by reviewing the features of each project including administration, size of inmate population, and their characteristics. The two programs were conducted in male institutions operated almost exclusively by male staff. This will be reflected in the following chapters by the use of pronouns in the male gender when referring to individual inmates or staff members.

Background and History

THE EXPERIMENTAL MANPOWER LABORATORY FOR CORRECTIONS (EMLC)
PROJECT

The EMLC token economy grew out of a series of projects begun in the early 1960s with inmates at Draper Correctional Center in Elmore, Alabama. A self-instructional school, referred to as the Draper Programmed Learning Project, was established at the prison. The school was the setting for studies conducted to refine motivational and educational management techniques and to perfect the effectiveness of learning systems.

The school employed what, at that time, was a unique approach to academic educational and vocational training. It relied almost entirely upon programmed instruction as the teaching vehicle, with the exception of literacy training and seminars on special topics (e.g., current events, Great Books, and spoken English). Another unusual feature was the Inmate Service Corps, formed to augment the school's staff. Members of the corps served as subject-matter counselors, instructors, clerks, lab technicians, and even programmers. The inmate programmers constructed pre- and post-tests for the commercially developed materials used in the school as well as their own programmed courses in various vocational areas. These courses, now distributed by the University of Alabama, continue to be widely used in high schools, vocational schools, and training projects. College students—the College Corps—also worked in the school on a co-op basis. The College Corpsmen assisted in the classroom observations and data compilation.

The school's programmed instruction approach was effective, as reflected by increased scores on academic achievement tests. Some inmates earned their General Education Diplomas (high school equivalency certificates), and a number subsequently entered college. The academic training provided by the school helped other inmates meet the basic education requirements for vocational training offered by the State Trade School and, later the Manpower Development and Training (MDT) project. Still, it was believed that the best use of programmed instruction had not been determined. Increased emphasis was, therefore, placed on improving the operation of the school itself.

The number of programmed courses offered by the self-instructional school was dramatically increased from the original 5 to nearly 400. The levels of instruction ranged from literacy education to college preparatory. Study carrels were introduced to improve the learning environment, providing privacy and reducing distractions. The process of diagnosing educational deficiencies and prescribing the necessary programmed materials was further refined, allowing the inmate to concentrate on those areas in which his skills were the weakest. The refinement led, in time, to the development of the Individually Prescribed Instructional (IPI) System to be described in detail later. This system is now being used in correctional institutions, secondary schools, and colleges.

Simultaneously, the self-instructional school moved from a service to a demonstration basis. The study designs grew increasingly more sophisticated, and greater emphasis was placed on precise measurement of results. Several of these studies sought to isolate factors influencing inmate motivation, using contingency management to individualize reinforcement and increase academic achievement. In the EMLC's first contingency management study, inmates in the self-instructional school negotiated performance (contingency) contracts in which they agreed to complete certain amounts of programmed material. In exchange, they received break periods to be spent in a "reinforcing event" room, where they could drink coffee, read magazines, listen to music, and so on. Later, the inmates could choose to leave the classroom early instead of taking a break. Under these contingency management conditions, both work efficiency and the amount of work completed increased, and the test performance improved.

The experiences of the self-instructional school and the contingency management studies conducted there provided the foundation for the educational technology and behavioral management techniques used later in several Experimental Manpower Laboratory for Corrections studies. Operation of the self-instructional school overlapped subsequent demonstration projects, providing programmed instruction in basic education and social skills. The projects were operated under contract with the U.S. Department of Labor and the U.S. Office of Education and were also sited at the Draper Correctional Center. Other projects similarly funded were conducted at the federal reformatory in Lorton, Virginia, and the city jail at Rikers Island, New York.

The aim of each project was to test the feasibility of operating Manpower Development and Training Administration (MDTA) programs in these types of correctional institutions: a state institution for adult male offenders, a federal reformatory, and a city jail. Until these projects were begun, manpower training for prison inmates was virtually an unexplored area. Prisoners, because they were unavailable for work, had not been considered a part of the unemployed labor force to which the original MDTA was aimed and were thus not considered eligible for training.

The projects operated by the EMLC provided vocational training in the following areas: auto service station work (mechanic-attendant), barbering, bricklaying, small electrical appliance repair (later changed to air-conditioning and refrigeration repair), combination welding, radio and television repair, technical writing, and sign writing. Courses were dropped and added in response to changing demands for skills in the labor market. Counseling, job development and placement, and follow-up services were provided for all trainees.

These early demonstration projects for prison inmates were successful in accomplishing what they set out to do. They proved that, with considerable modification of guidelines, it was feasible to operate manpower training programs in correctional settings. Many problems were encountered and solved in adapting the structure of MDTA programs to meet the unique needs of prison inmates, a population soon discovered to be a special group among the disadvantaged. The modifications that evolved in these projects helped to structure amendments to the MDTA law (Section 251) that authorized manpower training for a broad number of institutionalized offenders.

As the final demonstration project drew to a close, the Manpower Development and Training Administration authorized the EMLC to conduct, on an ongoing basis a number of studies that would follow up on the knowledge gained thus far, and to indicate the nature of some problems that might require study over an extended period of time. The new objective was to study the needs of the offender, both in the institution and the community, and to develop treatment and intervention strategies that promoted full employment and successful societal adjustment upon release. This effort required an examination of the broad spectrum of behaviors that support adaptive free-world functioning.

The EMLC always maintained a research emphasis in its service orientation and efforts, thereby providing the empirical basis for existing agencies and groups to assist in the rehabilitation of the offender. Thus, the EMLC's involvement with institutional programs, both adult and juvenile, was purposely limited to developing and demonstrating more effective methods of institutional treatment and rehabilitation. Project findings and materials were prepared and disseminated with utilization by other agencies being a primary concern.

Since its inception, the EMLC relied upon the techniques derived in the behavioral science laboratory to assist in more efficiently and effectively achieving its project goals. As such, behavioral principles and techniques were applied to the EMLC's basic education projects, to vocational training, to correctional officer training, and the cellblock token economy. The objective of the EMLC token economy was to change behaviors of inmate participants so as to enable them to benefit from formal rehabilitation programs.

THE MOTIVATING OFFENDER REHABILITATION ENVIRONMENT (MORE) PROJECT

For more than any other southern state, the 1950s and 1960s brought increasing industrialization and urbanization to Georgia. Along with this influx of people and ideals came a growing awareness of the image of the state held by the rest of the country. For political and economic reasons there was a great deal of money and effort spent both by the state government and by the private sector to convince others that Georgia was no longer a backwash area of the nation. The concept of the "New South" was vigorously promoted, with Georgia being billed as the progressive leader in this movement. Efforts were made to attract industry, commerce, tourism and people from the north. To assuage the apprehensions of those skilled and educated people who might fear relocating in the New South due to the region's poor image, Georgia set about making reforms and improvements in many areas: civil rights, the electoral process, public schools, higher education, housing, food processing, social welfare agencies, and so on. Among those areas receiving such attention was the state correctional system.

Even given the generally unfavorable reputation of the state prisons in the South, Georgia still stands out. It has long had, and probably deservingly so, the dubious honor of being stereotyped as the "chain gang capital of the United States." Like more stereotypes, there is a grain of truth (in this case, several grains) to the image this conjures up. Georgia prisons were bad. Many still are. Today, however, most are no worse than similar institutions located throughout the country.

How does one change the image? In the early 1970s, then-Governor Jimmy Carter set about changing Georgia's image by persuading the state legislators to spend more money on improving the correctional system. The MORE research program was a fortuitous outgrowth of Carter's dedication to prison reform. Early in his administration, he had berated Georgia's professional community for an apparent lack of interest in assisting his reform effort in the prisons. Stimulated by this challenge, a proposal to design an effective program of offender rehabilitation was submitted to and approved by the Department of Offender Rehabilitation.

Approval, however, does not always mean implementation. Programs must first be funded, and the state legislature had already allocated more money to the Department of Offender Rehabilitation than ever before. Fortunately, for the future of the MORE project, the Nixon Administration placed a great emphasis on "law and order." The U.S. Department of Justice thus allocated generous funds which, through the Law Enforcement Assistance Administration (L.E.A.A.), were being made available to state and local governments to assist them in improving law enforcement and crime prevention. Politics, of course, played a part in securing this L.E.A.A. funding. It was indeed fortunate that the Nixon Administration was more interested in making friends (not to mention votes) in the South. Although it took a year, L.E.A.A. support was obtained by Georgia for the MORE project.

Thus, having the necessary ideas, money and some political support, all that was needed was a setting in which to implement the project. The requirements for selecting such a setting were many: (a) The prison needed to be small to medium in size so that the new programs and procedures could be designed to apply to the entire inmate population, yet remain manageable; (b) it had to be located near a large metropolitan area so that professional and paraprofessional staff could be more easily recruited; (c) it was, for demonstration purposes, required to have an inmate population reflecting a broad range of criminal offenses; (d) it needed to have ongoing, or at least available, programs of training and rehabilitation; and, most importantly, (e) the setting had to have a superintendent (warden) who would cooperate and support the proposed changes in rehabilitation philosophy and procedure. The Georgia Training and Development Center in Buford, Georgia, just outside of Atlanta, appeared to satisfy most of these requirements.

The treatment and security staff at Buford prison was headed by a superintendent who at the time was one of the youngest wardens in the country. Previously, Georgia prison wardens were political appointees who gained and held their positions through their friendships with influential officials in state government. They were not generally selected for their skills. The Buford superintendent, however, was representative of the changes being made at that time. He was well suited for the new rehabilitation approach since he had earned a B.A. in sociology and was working on his master's degree. He also was experienced and skilled in the security aspects of corrections, having served in this capacity as a Marine Corps officer. He supported the aims of the MORE program and requested that it be located at his prison.

PRISON SETTINGS

THE EMLC PROJECT

The EMLC project was conducted at Draper Correctional Center in Elmore, Alabama. The prison, which opened in 1938, was a maximum-security institution for adult male felons located approximately 35 miles from Montgomery, the nearest urban center. Although it was originally designed to have a maximum of 600 inmates, the population hovered around the 900 mark.

As is typical of southern institutions constructed during that period of time, Draper was designed as a dormitory-style prison. Six two-story dormitories branched from a single main corridor which ran from the prison entrance at one end to the kitchen/dining area at the other. Each dormitory housed between 100 and 150 inmates who slept in two rows of double-deck bunks separated by approximately three feet. Indoor recreation facilities consisted of a single television set located on each floor of each dormitory and an activities area that housed two pool tables and a ping pong table. Outdoor recreational facilities consisted of a large fenced exercise yard containing crudely marked football and baseball playing fields. The visiting facility consisted of a fenced outdoor yard with open sheds as the only protection from the elements. No formal academic or vocational training facilities existed within the prison area itself. Instead, a nearby state trade school served approximately 100 inmates who were bussed the three miles back and forth each morning and evening. The EMLC vocational and educational programs, which at various times served between 50 and 100 additional inmates, were conducted in a converted warehouse located in a third fenced compound adjacent to the prison compound.

The EMLC token economy itself was conducted in the second (top) floor of one of Draper Correctional Center's six two-story wings. Access to the token economy cellblock was from the institution's central recreation area via two sets of stairs that emerged separately into a main corridor. The area was a remodeled dormitory that lent itself well to the project. It was subdivided into various rooms that were used as dormitories, classrooms, study halls, recreational areas, and staff offices. It was adequately lighted and ventilated, and it provided sufficient floor space for both the housing of the inmates and the operation of the project. All support (food, clothing, medical, etc.), general security, and custody-related services (supervision of telephone, mail, and visiting privileges, etc.) were provided by Draper staff. All inmates and project staff members were subject to and followed the general rules, regulations, policies, and procedures of the Alabama Board of Corrections.

THE MORE PROJECT

The site for the MORE project was the Georgia Training and Development Center in Buford, Georgia. This was a medium-security, correctional facility with an inmate population of approximately 200 men, located 45 miles from the nearest urban area, Atlanta.

Formerly known as Rock Quarry Prison, the facility was originally designed for incorrigible offenders. The prison was renamed Georgia Training and Development Center (G.T. & D.C.) when the Manpower Development and Training Act funded vocational training programs. This prison was designated the only institution in the state to receive youthful offenders aged 18 to 26 years. Offenders from all over Georgia were sent to participate in the new training program and the overall goal of the institution became one of providing the offender with functional skills as an alternative to previous criminal activities.

Two large dormitories housed the general population, approximately 60 men in each who slept in double bunks. Each dorm was equipped with one or two ping-pong tables and two television sets. A smaller dorm housed 30 men and was generally used for newly arrived inmates. There were also approximately 25 individual cells for cooks and other workers with unusual hours and for trustees. These individual cells included a barred commons area which served as adequate security such that individual cells were not usually locked. In general, the smaller, more private the living area, the more preferred it was by the inmate. Buildings that housed the prison school, as well as vocational training facilities, kitchen, dining room, and maintenance completed the prison layout. Finally, an inner courtyard was available for sports and general exercise.

The yard included a large basketball court, a volleyball court, and a field for football or softball. In addition, a baseball field located off of the immediate prison grounds, was used for practice and games under the supervision of a security officer who was also the team coach. The officer/inmate ratio ranged from 1 to 20 to 1 to 50 depending upon the shift.

The superintendent had two assistant superintendents, one in charge of the security staff and one in charge of the treatment staff. Medical services consisted of a medical assistant and a part-time physician and dentist. In addition, a full-time director of athletics coordinated sport events and recreational activities for the prison. Religious services were held on Sundays and major religious holidays. Finally, three counselors were available on a regular basis.

SOCIAL CHARACTERISTICS OF PARTICIPANTS

THE EMLC PROJECT

Participants of the EMLC token economy were 56 inmates. The only general prerequisite for participation in this project was that inmates be eligible for either parole or unconditional release within 90 days of the project's termination date. The initial population of the cellblock token economy consisted of 33 inmates. These 33 inmates were selected at random from those who had volunteered for participation in a Manpower Development and Training (MDT) project operated by the EMLC.

The 23 inmates who later joined the token economy cellblock population as replacements for those who left the project were, within the guidelines of the general constraints mentioned previously, selected at random from the general population of the institution. Although the transfer of these 23 inmates to the token economy cellblock was treated as a routine administrative procedure, these inmates, as well as the original 33 volunteers, could discontinue their participation in this project at any time they wished by submitting a standard request for a cellblock transfer to the institution's classification officer. Shortly thereafter (usually between 3 and 5 days), space was found in another cellblock and, if the inmate still desired to discontinue his participation in the cellblock token economy, the transfer was accomplished. The decision to discontinue participation in the project in no way altered the inmate's projected release date or lowered the general quality of his life within the institution relative to the period prior to his enrollment in the project. The average daily census during the course of the 420 days of the project was 22 inmates. The 56 participants (the 33 original inmates plus the 23 who later joined) resided on the token economy cellblock for an average of 99 days, with a range of 10 to 352 days.

The mean age of the 56 inmates at the time of their entrance into the project was 23.6 years, with a range of 16 to 54 years; 42 (75%) were 25 years of age or younger. Thirty–one (55%) were white and 25 (45%) were black. Their mean grade level, as indexed by the Tests of Adult Basic Education (TABE), was 7.4 grades, with a range of 2.9 to 12.3 grades. The mean grade levels for the whites and blacks were 8.4 and 6.1 grades, respectively. Their mean IQ, as measured by either the Otis Test of General Ability or the Wechsler Adult Intelligence Scale (WAIS), was 88.3, with a range of 64 to 112. The mean IQs for the whites and blacks were 92.6 and 82.6, respectively. Of the 56 inmates, 19 (34%) were sentenced from counties with populations greater than 250,000; 7 (13%) from counties with populations between 100,000 and 250,000; 12 (21%) from counties with populations between 50,000 and 100,000; 14 (26%) from counties with populations between 25,000 and 50,000; and 4 (7%) from counties with populations less than 25,000. The representation of the urban and rural portions of the state was, then, approximately equal in the population of the token economy.

Seventeen (30%) of the inmates had been previously incarcerated as adult felons, during which time they served an average of 15.0 months, with a range of 15 days to 120 months. The average length of the sentences that the 56 inmates were serving when they entered the project was 54.6 months, with a range of 12 to 300 months. The distribution of offenses in the token economy cellblock population reflected that of the institution population in general. As Table 1 shows, a large number of inmates had been convicted of multiple offenses. Crimes against property were the most common offenses, with relatively smaller numbers of inmates serving sentences for crimes against persons and for statutory or "victimless" crimes.

Table 1.   Offenses Committed by Residents of the EMLC Token Economy
Cellblock

Offenses	Number[a]	Percent
Crimes against property	55	69.6
Grand larceny	27	34.2
Burglary	17	21.5
Second-degree burglary	6	7.6
Buying, receiving or concealing stolen property	4	5.1
Attempted burglary	1	1.3
Crimes against persons	13	16.5
Robbery	8	10.1
Assault with intent to murder	2	2.5
Child molestation	1	1.3
First-degree manslaughter	1	1.3
Second-degree murder	1	1.3
Statutory or victimless crimes	11	14.0
Escape	2	2.5
Possession of marijuana	2	2.5
Forgery	1	1.3
Perjury	1	1.3
Possession of barbiturates	1	1.3
Possession of LSD	1	1.3
Sale of marijuana	1	1.3
Violation of probation	1	1.3
Violation of state narcotics law	1	1.3

[a] The total number of offenses is greater than the number of residents of the token economy cellblock because a number of the residents were convicted of more than one crime (from Milan & McKee, 1976).

THE MORE PROJECT

The men in the MORE project ranged in age from 18 to 60 years old, their crimes ranged from illegal possession of dangerous drugs to premeditated murder, and their lengths of sentence from one year to life. Half of the men were black, half were white. The average prisoner was approximately 20 years old, had been convicted of a crime involving theft, had 1.5 years remaining to serve on his sentence and had experimented or trafficked in illegal drugs. He had approximately a fifth grade education but functioned at two to three years below that level. Typically, he worked as an unskilled laborer. All inmates had spent some time in one or more prisons prior to coming to the Georgia Training and Development Center at Buford. The prison population represented the urban and rural segments of the state at large.

PRISON ROUTINE

THE EMLC PROJECT

Most inmates were expected to arise at 6 a.m., when the dormitories were unlocked and lights were turned on. They retired for the night at 10 p.m., when they were locked in their dormitories and the lights were turned off. Guards patrolled the main corridor of the institution but, because of their limited number during the night shift, seldom entered the dormitories after the lights-out, even to investigate disturbances. Most work assignments began at 7:45 a.m. and ended at 4:30 p.m. with an hour off for lunch. Inmates were typically assigned to farm work upon their admission to the institution. After they had "proven" themselves, they were considered for reassignment to the kitchen, laundry, clothing room, or janitorial work, all of which were considered more desirable "indoor" jobs than was farm work. A select few, who displayed proficiency in reading, writing, or typing were given the most desirable clerical jobs.

Inmates had free access to most parts of the prison during their free hours on weekends and holidays, although they were required to come in from the yard at dark. Visitation was generally restricted to two to three hours on Sundays. Telephone calls were possible, but in order to do so, an inmate had to justify the call and get a "phone slip" from a prison official. Movies were commonly shown in the dining hall on either Friday or Saturday evening. Counts were taken just before "lights out" and at one or two randomly selected times throughout each day. The institution had an Alcoholics Anonymous and a Junior Chamber of

Commerce chapters, and inmates were encouraged to attend these as well as Sunday morning church services. All in all, Draper was considered a desirable place in which to do time in the Alabama system. In fact, a common solution to disciplinary problems at Draper was to ship "troublemakers" "south"—to one of the larger, more repressive institutions located in the southern portion of the state—as punishment.

THE MORE PROJECT

The work day began at 8:00 a.m. and lasted until 5:00 p.m. for most inmates. Attendance to breakfast (all meals were served in a common cafeteria) was optional after dormitory doors were unlocked at 7:30 a.m. Inmates were required to return to their dormitories for the "count" briefly at noon, and at 5:00 p.m. and then ate lunch and dinner in shifts until 1:00 p.m. and 6:00 p.m., respectively. After the evening meal, inmates were allowed to go out in the prison yard for recreational activities. Inmates returned to their dormitories at dusk and remained there until the 11:00 "lights out."

Saturday, Sunday, and most holidays were reserved for visiting. Each man was assigned a time on weekends to receive visitors for up to two hours. Generally, movies were shown once a week in the prison. Also, because of the prison's proximity to Atlanta, various activities were occasionally available to the inmates such as college extension courses, group psychotherapy experiences, musical concerts and plays, special trips, etc. Other activities such as a chapter of Alcoholics Anonymous and Jaycees, counseling and self-improvement programs were also available to the inmates. Most of these programs were made possible through the efforts of volunteers.

The prison was regarded by inmates as one of the "best" prisons in the state system. Most of the prisoners were young. There was no mandatory road work or other tedious and/or humiliating "hard labor." Of course, for many men, the availability of vocational and academic training was an attractive aspect. In general, because Buford Prison was designed as a training center, inmates with records of violent or aggressive behavior in prison were excluded. While Buford was a "good prison" it was still a prison. Its security rating placed it between medium and maximum security classifications. There were segregation cells for punishment or protection and it was still possible to place a rule-breaker on a "restricted diet." There were double gates to pass through to the main area of the prison. Inmates transferred to or from Buford passed through those gates in manacles and shackles. Although the Central administration attempted to keep the racial composition of the population half black and half white, there were occasional conflicts and usually some tension. But, these racial problems were no better or worse than those experienced in the desegregated urban high schools of Atlanta.

In summary, Buford was a small prison similar to hundreds throughout the country. It represented an institution, functioning as it had for many years past, in need of reorganization and effective methods for motivating its clients.

THE TOKEN ECONOMY PROCEDURES

The EMLC Project

Tokens.   Tokens consisted of "EMLC points" that were acquired and expended through a simulated checkbook banking system. Each inmate was provided with an individualized book of standard checks (see Fig. 1). As inmates completed to-be-reinforced target behaviors or academic assignments, a staff member computed the number of points earned and instructed the inmates to credit those amounts to their accounts. At the same time, the staff member recorded the performance of the task on a master data sheet or, if the points had been earned in the education program, on an education earnings summary sheet. These data were then employed to determine each inmate's total earnings at the end of the day. The use of the simulated banking system and the individualized accounts precluded the exchange of tokens among inmates, thereby reducing the ease with which backup reinforcers could be "bootlegged" (acquired without first engaging in the target behaviors).

Backup Reinforcers. The backup reinforcers were items and activities that could be dispensed and monitored on the token economy cellblock. They consisted of such things as access to various reinforcing event areas (lounge, television viewing room, and poolroom); time in the institution at large (and, by means of this procedure, access to a wide variety of potential backup reinforcers, such as acquaintances not residing on the token economy cellblock, weekend movies, club meetings, and recreational activities available in the remainder of the institution); and small commodities (cigarettes, soft drinks, snacks, etc.) that could be "purchased" in a token economy canteen operated by the project. In addition, Sears' and Penney's catalogs were available for examination from the token economy canteen, and inmates wishing special items not regularly carried by the canteen could order them if they appeared in either of the two catalogs. In order to do so, an inmate was required to deposit in a

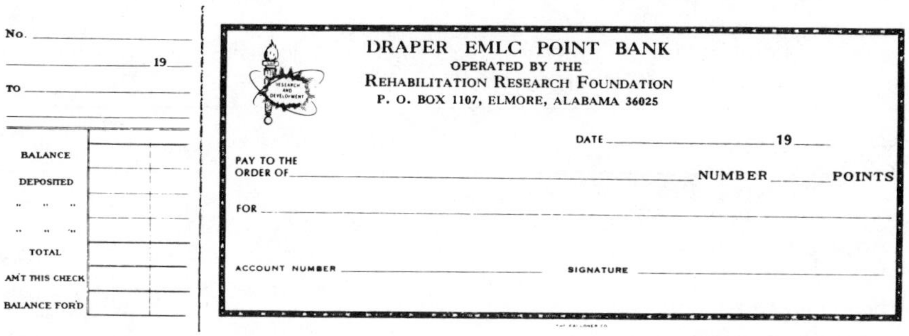

Figure 1. Sample check used by inmates to expand points in the EMLC token economy.

special savings account the point cost of the desired item, with transfers from checking accounts to the saving accounts limited to Sunday evenings. When the required amount had been accumulated in the special savings account, the canteen ordered the item from the catalog sales department of the company. Once the order was placed the inmates were prohibited from withdrawing points from the special savings account or from changing their order.

Target Behaviors. Since target behaviors comprised the subject matter of the studies undertaken in this project, they are described in detail in the body of this report. In general, they consisted of such things as the completion of four routine morning activities, performing of one or more assigned maintenance tasks, and participation and performance in a remedial education program. Typical payoff and cost values, respectively, of representative target behaviors and backup reinforcers are presented in Table 2. It should be noted, however, that these values were subject to change in order to either maintain balance in the token reinforcement system or to answer research questions.

All well-designed token reinforcement systems "balance" target behaviors and backup reinforcers. That is, the relationship between the payoff values of the target behaviors and the cost of the backup reinforcers should be such that, when a participant performs that which is reasonably expected of him, he may, in turn, receive a reasonable number of the backup reinforcers available within the system. Indeed, one of the more difficult tasks involved in the operation of a token reinforcement system is maintaining this balance. As time passes, the seasons change, the population experiences turnover, and so on, the payoff values of the target behaviors and the costs of the backup reinforcers may need adjustment so that the system remains in balance. A

Table 2. Point Values of Representative Target Behaviors and Backup Reinforcers in the EMLC Token Economy

Target Behaviors	Points Awarded
Morning activities	
Arising on time	60
Bed made	60
Living area neat and clean	60
Personal appearance	60
Educational activities[a]	
Student performance	two per min (estimated)
Tutor performance	two per min (estimated)
Assigned maintenance tasks[b]	
Sweep main hall (back half)	60
Empty trash cans in recreation room	60
Mop front steps and landing	120
Dust and arrange furniture in television room	120

Backup Reinforcers	Points Charged
Activities available on the token economy cellblock	
Access to television room	60 per hr
Access to pool room	60 per hr
Access to lounge	60 per hr
Canteen items available[c]	
Cup of coffee	50
Can of soft drink	150
Ham and cheese sandwich	300
Pack of cigarettes	450
Leisure time away from token economy cellblock	one per min

[a] Students were paid on a performance—rather than time—contingent basis. Point values for units of academic material were based on an empirically derived estimated study time per unit and awarded when unit tests were passed.

[b] Although only four are presented here, there was a sufficient number of maintenance tasks to ensure that all residents had the potential of earning 120 points by completing their assignments. Additionally, residents could volunteer for supplementary maintenance tasks to increase their daily point earnings.

[c] Although only four are listed here, a large variety of items was available in the token economy canteen.

(From Milan and McKee, 1976.)

152

well-balanced economy insures that performance of the target behaviors continues at optimal levels.

Operation of the Token Economy. The token reinforcement system was in effect for approximately 7 hours each weekday (from 5:30 to 7:30 a.m. and from 4:30 to 9:30 p.m.) and for 16 hours per day during weekends and holidays (5:30 a.m. to 9:30 p.m.). The hours of exclusion represent those times during which inmates were inolved in other phases of institutional life. For most, this consisted of working on a routine institutional job (such as laboring in a farm squad, assisting in the kitchen, working in the laundry). For the remainder, it involved participation in a formalized rehabilitation program (either the MDTA project or one of the Alabama state vocational school training programs).

The lights in each of the two dormitories were turned on at 5:30 a.m. each weekday. During the following two hours, each inmate could perform his four morning activities and assigned maintenance task(s) and then report having done so to the staff member on duty. The inmate then accompanied the staff member as he checked to insure that the reported performances met the established criteria of acceptability. If one or more did not, the inmate was informed of the deficiencies and encouraged to improve upon his performance. When the performances did meet the established criteria (either when first examined or after correction), the inmate was so informed, praised, and credited with the number of points represented by the completed activities to his point account. At the same time, the staff member recorded the activities completed and points earned on the master data sheet. The procedures followed on weekend and holiday mornings were approximately the same as those followed on weekdays. The major differences involved changes in the time requirements for the completion of target behaviors that allowed inmates to sleep later in the morning.

If an inmate wished to enter a reinforcing event area during the hours the token economy was in effect, he first wrote a check in the required amount and deposited it in a collection box at the entrance to the area. An additional check was required at the beginning of each successive clock hour, from half hour to the half hour (e.g., 4:30 to 5:30). Inmate could leave and reenter the reinforcing event area any number of times during each clock hour. The only requirement, however, was that he had written a check for that clock hour and had deposited it in the appropriate box. Warning bells sounded 10 minutes prior to and at the half hour. Staff members made aperiodic rounds throughout the day to insure that all inmates were abiding by the point expenditure system, to collect all checks near the end of each clock hour, and to prepare the deposit boxes to receive the next hour's expenditures.

Time spent in the remainder of the institution (areas other than the token economy cellblock) during the hours the token economy was in operation was recorded on time cards that inmates punched on a time clock as they left from and returned to the cellblock. These times were then totaled and paid for at the end of each day. The token economy canteen was open one-half hour every evening and one additional half hour in the late morning on weekends and holidays. To obtain items from the canteen inmates wrote checks in the exact amount of the to-be-purchased commodity and exchanged the check with the storekeeper for that item.

Early each morning during the period the token economy was in effect, the point record shown in Figure 2 was completed and posted. On it was an itemized accounting of each resident earnings and expenditures on the previous day and the resultant balance carried forward to the present day. During the hours that the token economy was operating, those with overdrawn accounts were not permitted to purchase commodities from the token economy canteen, to gain access to the various reinforcing event areas on the token economy cellblock, or to spend time in the remainder of the institution except to leave the cellblock with no charge to obtain their meals, receive visitors, and tend to health needs. These restrictions were lifted when a posted point record indicated that they had overcome their point deficits and that their accounts were no longer overdrawn.

Three response cost (fine) procedures were used in the operation of the token economy:

1. Inmates who entered a reinforcing event area without first writing and relinquishing a check were fined the hourly cost of that area and then given the choice of either leaving the area or conforming to the token reinforcement system, i.e., writing a check and placing it in the deposit box.

2. Those who left the token economy cellblock for the remainder of the institution without first punching out on the timeclock were considered to have been off the facility since the last time the staff had evidence they were present (usually the time of the previous attendance check) and were charged for the time between then and their return to the facility.

3. Interest (at the rate of 10% of the overdrawn amount per day) was charged to all those with overdrawn accounts.

(DATE) POINT RECORD NAME	BALANCE BROUGHT FORWARD FROM PREVIOUS RECORD	EARNINGS									TOTAL CREDITS	EXPENDITURES									TOTAL DEBITS	BALANCE TO BE CARRIED FORWARD TO NEXT RECORD
		Arise on Time	Bed Made	House Neat and Clean	Personal Appearance	Education Program	Maintenance Tasks	Bonuses				Fines and Interest	Time Off Unit	Recreation Room #1	Recreation Room #2	Television Room	Lounge	Canteen				

Figure 2. Posted point record on which each inmate's daily earnings and expenditures in the EMLC token economy were reported.

These three specific procedures were employed solely to guarantee adherence to the policies governing access to the backup reinforcers, thereby insuring the integrity of the points and, by extension, the token economy itself.

The More Project

Tokens.   The MORE project used points which could be recorded through the use of a *credit card system.* (A similar system was designed for use in a hospital ward token economy by Lehrer, Schiff, & Kris, 1970). The credit card system produced automatic collection of information (points earned and spent) on each individual transaction.

The credit card system was selected in lieu of a physical currency or token because of the particular population characteristics within this setting. Physical tokens can be counterfeited, lost, or stolen. Within the prison population there are many who are specialists in such tasks. It is imperative that each person receive all the reinforcement he has earned, but that he not be able to obtain incentives by unauthorized means. The credit card system precluded these problems as there was no physical token to become mishandled. In addition, record keeping, a logistical problem with any token economy, was simplified with the credit card system as each transaction produced a set of permanent physical records. Questions regarding payment or nonpayment of points, or the spending or not spending of points, could be quickly resolved by either the inmate or the research staff producing the record of that transaction.

Backup Reinforcers.   Points earned and recorded through the credit card system were exchangeable for an enriched variety of reinforcers. Many items that had previously been available to the inmates only on a cash basis were made additionally accessible through the point system. This system, then, tended to equalize opportunity for access to many basic items for those inmates with limited financial resources. Incentives were of two general types: tangible goods and activities. A large proportion of reinforcers were purchased through the canteen, which stocked a wide variety of items. These goods ranged from consummables such as snacks, drinks, and cigarettes, to such items as leather-making kits and toiletries. The exchange ratio for items in the canteen was $0.02 per point. Inmates could purchase these items with cash, points, or a combination of both. An example of canteen items and their cash and point price is described in Table 3. The bookkeeping activities were carried out by the canteen manager as part of his regular routine, much like any store accepting credit cards.

Table 3.   Monetary and Point Value of Canteen Items in the MORE Program

Items	Cash Price	Point Price
Cigarettes	.40	20
Cigars	.05–.25	3–13
Tobacco	.12–.40	6–20
Pipe filter and cleaners	.09	5
Soft drinks	.15	8
Fruit juice	.15	8
Cakes and cookies	.10	5
Chips, popcorn, peanuts	.10–.15	5–8
Ice cream	.10	5
Gum	.01–.10	1–5
Candy	.01–.59	1–30
Batteries	.25–1.19	13–60
Shoe Polish	.39	20
Shampoo	.49–.79	25–40
Playing cards	.50	25
Baby powder	.59	30
Hand lotion	.50	25
Deodorant	.59–.97	30–49
Shaving products	.49–.98	25–49
Skin care products	.43–.79	23–40
Toothpaste	.69–1.00	35–50
Spray starch	.73	37
Combs	.15–1.00	8–50
Clothing (T-shirts, handkerchiefs, socks)	.20–1.29	10–65
Stationary	.05–.25	3–13
Beverage (coffee, hot chocolate)	.10	5
Sunglasses	1.00–3.00	50–150
Tweezers	.35	18
Nail clippers	.35	18
Razor blades	.89	45
Radio	19.95	998
Sewing needle	.15	8
Polident powder	.59	30

In addition to the tangible goods, a number of special activities were brought into use as incentives. These activities were extremely popular and some inmates spent a large proportion of their point earnings to secure them. The most popular activities consisted of making "special phone calls," mailing "special letters," and securing "special visits."

When an inmate entered this correctional institution, his social contact was limited to a few individuals, specifically his immediate family, to whom he could write and receive letters and from whom he could accept visits. These restrictions, or similar ones, are commonly in force in most prison settings. The special letter and special visit privilege, obtainable only with points, enabled the inmate to ease these restrictions. Of course, this was subject to, in all cases, the approval of the superintendent. Thus, a letter to a friend who was not on the list may have been approved and arranged, but a visit from a former crime partner may not have received the superintendent's approval. After the inmate purchased this privilege from a staff member, the request was then submitted to the superintendent for approval and, as in the case of a special visit, the inmate was notified that the visit could be made. In the case of a denied request, the inmate's points were refunded, with an explanation of the reason for denial. In practice, this rarely occurred during the MORE program.

The list of individuals to whom phone calls could be made was also limited. When calls were permitted, they were directly placed by a correctional officer. Inmates were routinely allowed about one free phone call by rotation every three weeks. A special phone call allowed the inmate to place the call himself (long distance calls had to be made collect) under the supervision of the officer. The inmate could purchase the privilege and schedule an appointment in the phoning area. Because only a total of six calls were allowed each weekday evening a "super phone call" privilege was also available. This service provided for a previously unscheduled phone call to be made any evening selected. However, the point charge for a super phone call was 2.5 times that of a special phone call. Only one super phone call could be placed each evening. This procedure was established when the inmates' demand for special phone calls resulted in advanced scheduling. The super phone call allowed the reinforcer to again be immediate if the inmate so wished.

A number of other special activities were available only with points. These were items that were not previously available in the prison but once introduced, were found to be highly motivating for some inmates.

1.   Polaroid pictures could be purchased with points. The majority of these were sent to friends and relatives outside the institution.

2.   Levis, jean jackets, and other allowable clothing could be ordered through the canteen at the rate of $0.02 per point. Prepayment was required for the order to be filled.

3.   Late week-night television watching, after the time for "lights out" (11:00 p.m.), could be reserved on a rotation basis by dormitory.

4.   Gold Bond trading stamps could be purchased through the point system, at a ratio of 10 stamps per point. An inmate formally registered

for the trading stamp program and the outside recipient he had chosen was notified by mail. Then, each time the inmate purchased stamps, he received a receipt for the points spent and the stamps were mailed directly to the recipient he had named.

The procedure for acquiring these backup reinforcers varied. At the canteen, for example, the inmate could use his credit card directly and charge the items he selected. A list of every inmate's account balance was kept at the canteen on which each transaction (points spent) was tallied. A new updated list was provided three times per week. Each day's cards were tallied and sent to the project office to be recorded on the general ledger where they were posted three times a week. The canteen was open eight hours a day, Monday through Friday.

Other incentives could be purchased only at a specified time during the week. At the time of purchase, the point slip receipt became the voucher of payment which then allowed the inmate access to the reinforcer. For example, a photograph could be purchased on Monday and Friday between 12:30 and 1:00 and between 3:30 and 4:15 on Wednesday, but the pictures themselves were taken only between 9:00 and 10:00 weekdays. Scheduling was necessary to make the most efficient use of personnel and had the added benefit of assisting inmates to follow schedules on their own. Table 4 is a summary of incentive availability both before and during the implementation of the MORE project.

Target Behaviors. The goals of the MORE and the EMLC projects were similar. In general, the target behaviors of the MORE project involved the acquisition of vocational as well as academic skills. For example, mastery of specific mechanical skills and passing tests covering small units of academic instruction were targeted for token reinforcement.

Operation of the Token Economy. In general, the prison credit card system was operated in the same fashion as any credit card system run by a bank, a department store, or a gasoline company. The inmate first filled out an application to obtain a card. Ethically, this application procedure represented further assurance that the individual freely gave his consent to the procedures involved. This procedure amounted to the inmate actively requesting in writing, to participate in the MORE project. Within one to two days, he received his blue plastic card embossed with his name, dormitory assignment, account number and his trade or work assignment. Once the inmate received the card, he was able to earn and spend points in various locations throughout the prison by presenting his card. When he had completed a task for which points could be

Table 4.   Incentives Available Before and During the Token Economy (MORE)
Program

Incentive	*Before* the Token Economy Program	*During* the Token Economy Program
Phone calls	One ten-minute call per 3 weeks	Seven ten-minute calls per 3 weeks
Visits	One two-hour visit per week from *immediate family*	Two two-hour visits per week including *nonimmediate family*
Letters	Unlimited letters to and from *immediate family* only	Unlimited letters to and from immediate and *nonimmediate family*
Recreational activities	Access to music and table games	Access to music and table games as well as pool tables and soccer tables
Television watching	Available until 11:00 p.m. only	Available until 1:30 a.m.
Canteen items	Available for money	Available for money or points
Leather goods	Available for money	Available for money or points
Levis and other clothing	Available for money	Available for money or points
Special order items (radios, greeting cards, etc.)	Available for money	Available for money or points
Movies	One per weekend	2–3 per weekend
Jaycee dues	Payment in cash	Payment in cash or points

Note. The following incentives available for points were not available prior to the token economy program: rap room activities in the Academic School, personal photographs, and Gold Bond stamps.

earned, the inmate merely presented his card to the staff person authorized to record points in that area.

The card was then placed in an imprinting machine, a "points slip" was placed over it, the machine was set to record the appropriate information and the data was imprinted on the slip. Each validated points slip (similar to the receipt the gas station attendant offers a credit card user) was serially numbered and contained the following information: (*a*) the inmate's name; (*b*) his account number; (*c*) his dormitory address; (*d*) his trade assignment; (e) the location code number for that particular machine (e.g., kitchen, school, dormitory A); (f) the date; (g) the amount of points earned; and (h) the earnings code number which identified the task the man had accomplished. In addition, the slip required the inmate's handwritten signature and the staff person's handwritten initials. An area for writing additional comments was also provided for further specifying the accomplished task. Thus, the points slip gave a great deal of information about each earnings transaction for purposes of accounting and data collection.

The serially numbered slips allowed a certain amount of protection from forgery, as did the requirement for inmate and staff signatures. As a further hedge against misuse of the system, many pieces of data could be cross checked; for example, if the transaction code was for academic earnings the location had to be that of the imprinter at the school. Likewise, the staff initials had to be that of the person who had signed out the points slip with that particular serial number.

Each points slip produced an original copy, which was given to the inmate at the time of the transaction, and a carbon copy which was retained by the staff person. The copies were delivered to the program secretary for accounting and data analysis. Three times a week, the secretary recorded all points slips transactions on a general ledger for each man's account. An individual statement sheet, detailing all transactions, much like a monthly checking account statement, was kept for each account and was distributed to the individual inmates every two weeks (see Fig. 3).

Incentives were purchased with points in the same fashion by presenting the card and filling out a points slip. The only difference between an earnings transaction and a spending transaction was the code imprinted on the points slip. A code number of 1 to 49 signified to the secretary that the amount of points should be added to the account, while a code number of 50 to 99 signified that the amount was to be subtracted.

Although men earned points immediately after satisfying the behavioral criteria, spending these points was somewhat delayed to assure that each man was accredited only with earned points and thus could spend no more than that.

When an inmate disputed the point total recorded on the general ledger, he filled out an Account Verification Request form, giving a description of the dispute. These formal complaints were investigated and if the dispute were valid, redress was made immediately. Thus, the codes recorded on the points slips served at any time to give an *exact* accounting of the areas in which all points were actually earned and spent. In practice, these complaints rarely occurred but they allowed the inmate a modicum of protection against unfair treatment.

▬ M ▬ O ▬ R ▬ E ▬

MOTIVATION IN OFFENDER REHABILITATING ENVIRONMENTS PROJECT

NAME   113   John Doe

Georgia Training and Development Center
Buford, Georgia 30518

DATE	NO.	STATION CODE	POINTS EARNED	POINTS SPENT	BALANCE
				BALANCE FWD.	
24 AUG 73	2.0 5	1 4	3.0 0		3.0 0
25 AUG 73	2.0 5	7	.7 5		3.7 5
27 AUG 73	2.0 5	7 0		1.5 0	2.2 5
29 AUG 73	2.0 5	4 8	4.0 0		6.2 5
29 AUG 73	2.0 5	5 1		.3 0	5.9 5
30 AUG 73	2.0 5	6 2		.3 0	5.6 5

NCR Systemedia Division   J 9838

Georgia Training and Development Center
Buford, Georgia 30518

Figure 3. Representative statement reporting an inmate's earnings and expenditures in the MORE token economy.

One of the major problems to be overcome in establishing this program resulted from the special characteristics of the inmate population. Inmates, by definition, are already familiar with illegal ways in which they can obtain what they need. Issues of honesty and fair play, therefore, while they certainly are to be borne in mind, are typically academic in the prison setting.

The following rules were, therefore, established to operate the token economy in a manner that protected the individual and his earnings.

1.   An inmate's credit card could be used only by that inmate. Although he could choose to purchase items and give them to a friend, purchases using the card could be made only by the account holder himself. On occasion, cheating in the form of posing as someone else in order to exchange points for incentives was attempted. In practice, this was detected on three occasions out of literally thousands of transactions. It was possible to determine the frequency with which this occurred because each individual who exchanged the points for items had to sign the point slip. This made it possible to compare this signature with previous signatures made by the account holder. In addition, the most serious cases came about when someone lost his card and another inmate decided to take advantage of the newly found or stolen card to exchange points for items. Again, it was possible to minimize these methods to beat the motivational system because the individual who lost the card would immediately notify the appropriate staff in order to stop payment on the card.

2.   Lost cards were replaced after payment of a 50-point replacement fee. Worn cards were replaced one time at no charge. Additional replacements could be purchased for 50 points. This condition was found to be necessary for two reasons. First, for bookkeeping and accountability, it was desirable that inmates notify the program secretary whenever they lost, misplaced, or had their card stolen. Upon notification, the program issued updated lists of active accounts and the balance of each. This, again, militated against the unauthorized use of someone else's point card. Secondly, this standardized procedure excused the program personnel from being exposed to lengthy explanations as to why a person no longer possessed his card and then being forced to decide whether or not the card should be replaced without penalty. If for any reason a man no longer had his card and wanted a new one, he had to purchase it.

In summary, then, in order to reduce the number of cards lost or stolen, the responsibility for maintaining an individual's card was placed entirely upon each inmate. As a further procedure to safeguard inmate accounts, when a card was reported missing that account number was deleted from the accounts list. The inmate losing the card was issued a new account number, his old balance was transferred to the new account, and the old account number was not reissued for one month or until the missing card was located.

3.   Points were nontransferrable. At no time, whether during his incarceration at the institution or upon departure, could unspent points be transferred from one inmate's account to another. This procedure was enacted to protect inmates from coercion by their peers. It also insured that, to obtain the incentives, each individual would have to actively participate in his own rehabilitation effort. As a part of the pre-release procedure, each inmate who held an account in the motivational program was required to return his card before leaving the prison.

4.   Privileges such as special letters and visits could be purchased by an inmate for himself only. He could not pay the required points to secure these privileges for any other inmate. This rule was another procedure established to protect inmates from peer coercion and to insure as much as possible that each man obtained the incentives only through his own personal efforts. Items such as cigarettes and toiletries were not subject to this control, however, and once purchased, they could be used by the inmate himself or shared among friends.

In general, although there were occasional challenges and complaints, these four basic rules were accepted and welcomed by the inmates. It is important to note that the rules were explained to each man applying for an account before he was issued a card. Exceptions could be made only by the joint written agreement of the assistant program director and the prison superintendent. Such exceptions were rare.

CHAPTER

$\boxed{9}$

REMEDIAL EDUCATION IN PRISON

The academic deficiencies reflected in the populations of both projects are characteristic of inmate populations in general. Some cannot read at all. Of those who can, most can do so only with considerable difficulty. In addition to low reading comprehension, basic mathematical skills are typically impoverished or absent. Programs to remediate these deficiencies should be of the highest priority in all correctional efforts, both in the institution and in the community. Until such programs are universally available, our society will continue in its failure to provide the most basic services to the majority of inmates who pass through the correctional system. Even those who, when released, refrain from criminal activities find themselves limited in our competitive society by the absence of vocational and educational skills. Perhaps, more importantly, for those who are released and who do return to criminal endeavors, it may well be that the sheer absence of free-world options left unremediated by a prison experience void of effective remedial education and vocational training weighed heavily in their repeated offense.

Based upon these considerations, a major objective of both projects was to offer the inmates the opportunity to acquire the educational skills that were found to be deficient. In the EMLC project this took the form

165

of a leisure-time educational program operated on evenings and weekends. In the MORE project this approach was extended to the typical classroom program operated during weekdays. Within the context of both the EMLC and MORE projects, several studies were conducted with the preceding objectives in mind. These studies and their findings are described in this chapter.

INDIVIDUALLY PRESCRIBED PROGRAMMED INSTRUCTION

Programmed instructional materials were used to maximize the achievement of the educational objectives of both projects. The Individually Prescribed Instructional (IPI) System (McKee, 1971) was developed by the EMLC to facilitate the operation of adult basic education programs. This system enables a paraprofessional to diagnose educational deficiencies, to prescribe remedial programmed instructional materials for those deficiencies, and to evaluate student progress throughout the course of the program. The first step in operating the IPI System is to administer the Tests of Adult Basic Education (TABE), a standardized achievement test. The second step is to diagnose the student's academic deficiencies. When the TABE is scored, each incorrect or unanswered question is recorded on a special form called the Modular Analysis of Learning Difficulties (MALD). The completed MALD indicates each area of difficulty and specifies the order in which these difficulties should be remediated.

The MALD also references pages in the IPI Prescribing Catalog that lists instructional modules to remedy each deficiency. An empirically derived Estimated Study Time for completion (EST), usually between 30 and 90 minutes, is also listed for each instructional module. Materials were selected for inclusion in the catalog after an analysis of a wide variety of commercially available programmed instructional materials. One of the criteria for the selection of material was that it be of high interest to the prospective inmate students; that is, it was age, grade, and ethnically appropriate. The catalog is revised as older materials become outdated and/or more effective materials become available.

The IPI System is an approach to basic remedial education in which students study only those discrete mathematic and English skills in which they are deficient. A typical student proceeded in the IPI System in the following manner:

1. He took a 50-item locater test which indicated which *level* of the Test of Adult Basic Education (TABE) had to be administered. Scores were determined as follows: 0–14 correct = Level E ("Easy"), 15–40 correct = Level M ("Medium"), 41–50 correct = Level D ("Difficult").

2. He then took the appropriate TABE level test and a *profile sheet* was drawn from the subtest scores which specified the grade level performance for each subarea.

3. A *modular analysis of learning difficulties* was then developed which determined the areas in which additional study was needed as well as identified appropriate pages in the *prescription catalog* which indicate the remedial materials to be used.

4. The prescribed remedial materials were then written, according to the prescription catalog, into a *study schedule* which listed in order, the particular *modules* of study which were indicated to remediate specific deficits in mathematics and in English. The exact books, pages, and frames were detailed and accompanied by the standardized Estimated Study Time (EST) for that module of work. Two forms of a *module test* were also specified for each module on the study schedules.

5. The inmate then presented his study schedule to his instructor and took one form of the modular test over the first module listed on his study schedule as a *pretest*. Modular tests consisted of from 15–20 written objective-answer questions requiring short written answers or computation. If the inmate passed the pretest, he went on to the pretest for the next module. Passing was determined by standardized criteria set for each modular test and ranged from 80 to 95% correct.

6. If the inmate failed the pretest, he checked out the appropriate textual materials for that module from the clerk, studied them, and conferred with his instructor as necessary.

7. When the student was confident that he was adequately prepared, he took the other form of the Modular Test as a posttest. Passing criteria for the posttest were the same as for the pretest. If he failed the posttest he had to restudy the material and take a second posttest (modular test forms were always alternated such that the inmate did not take the same form twice in succession). If the second posttest was failed, an alternative module covering the material was prescribed from the prescribing catalog and the entire teaching procedure was repeated. Systematic errors in answering test questions were brought to the inmate's attention by the instructor and, in some cases, further remedial material was assigned.

8. When the posttest was passed, the inmate took the pretest over the next module on his study schedule and the procedure was repeated once again.

9. When all modules on one study schedule had been passed, the inmate took the next highest level of the TABE and another study schedule was generated.

10. After completing all D-Level modules, he retook (a different form of) the D-Level TABE test as a final posttest. If the inmate scored at the 11th grade level arrangements were made for him to take the General Educational Development test for high school equivalency.

To summarize, the IPI System emphasizes the remediation of specific educational deficiencies. Rather than noting that a student is "poor" in fractions and then recommending that he "study fractions," the system enables the instructor to identify those portions of the fractions curriculum that the student has failed to master and then allows the instructor to prescribe for the student just those portions (or modules of instruction) necessary to overcome his deficiency. The end-product of the IPI System is an individualized study schedule for each student which prescribes, in order, all the instructional modules needed to bring the student up to the 12th grade level in all areas covered by the TABE.

DEVELOPING ACCEPTANCE OF REWARD PROCEDURES

Despite the availability of educational programs in general and of programmed instruction materials in particular, prison programs attract relatively few inmates and those that are attracted show little academic interest. This state of affairs is typically accepted by institutional staff as characteristic of the inmate population. Although the staff at Buford Prison was not satisfied with the low level of inmate participation, and had from time to time made various efforts to interest the inmates in acquiring academic skills, they had not found any procedure particularly helpful. Despite reports of the encouraging results of the EMLC project, they were skeptical whether any available procedure short of intimidation or coercion would motivate inmate performance in remedial education in their prison. Consequently, initial discussions between the MORE project staff and the institutional staff concerning the potential effectiveness of a behavioral program were met with doubt and general skepticism.

This skepticism was understandable and it was based upon a number of factors. First, the experiences of the teachers and their co-workers with inmates' resistance to traditional motivational efforts were both extensive and generally disappointing. Second, none of the MORE staff had had direct experience working with inmates and were unacquainted with the resistance of this population to academic programs. Third, the procedures that were being proposed stressed the use of positive incentives to encourage inmates to "help themselves." It was this last factor that appeared to run most counter to the philosophy of the criminal justice system. In effect, positive incentives signalled an abandonment of the philosophy that it is the prison's right to demand that inmates perform their assigned tasks and that it is the inmate's duty to cooperate fully with these demands. The introduction of any positive incentive system was seen as undermining this traditional one up, one down relationship. As one of the correctional officers put it: "Today you bribe 'em for passing tests and tomorrow they'll demand $5.00 an hour for cleaning their own cells." Fourth, the use of incentives violated the longstanding practice of helping only those inmates who "wanted to help themselves." Offering positive incentives to individuals who refused to participate voluntarily in their own rehabilitation was seen as wasting the meager resources of the prison on undeserving inmates. Those who required extra incentives to participate in rehabilitation efforts were thought undeserving because they obviously did not have a sincere desire to help themselves go straight and would probably continue their criminal ways regardless of what was done.

Finally, most correctional staff had heard vague anecdotal reports about similar programs conducted elsewhere that had failed, but only after causing considerable disruption within the institution. While no one had specific information on such programs the rumors were so widely circulated that they had achieved "truth" status. Their suspicions were not allayed by a description of successful applications of these procedures in mental hospitals and institutions for the retarded. The success of the EMLC project was regarded as an isolated example confined to one cellblock of a large institution and certainly not applicable to their situation and the program that was being contemplated.

In light of these reservations, the first objective of the MORE project was to gain credibility for the type of methods that could be regarded as helpful to the administrative staff as well as to the inmates. An area that offered such an opportunity, then, was that of academic training. Although the prison training was largely vocationally oriented, the importance of academic training was recognized. Each vocational trainee was assigned a two-hour period each weekday to attend the prison school and, hopefully, learn those basic academic skills necessary for vocational employment. The equivalent of a sixth-grade education was all that the vocational training administration felt trainees needed. Therefore, the general objective of the first efforts made by the MORE staff was to establish the credibility of the approach by developing procedures that maximized the amount of academic skill-learning that occurred in the prison school. Major emphasis was placed on the identification of methods that would systematically and objectively measure academic growth. These efforts are described here because any attempt to implement similar programs in a prison would be expected to encounter such resistance.

Preliminary Procedures

Prior to the initiation of this project, the method of instruction in the academic school did not produce any record of inmate academic performance and progress. School attendance was the only record kept by the instructor.

Shaping–Prompting of Academic Related Behavior

Before a reward system could be successfully implemented, the behavioral requirements for reward had to be defined and suited to the initial level of behavior of the inmates in such a way that immediate and continuous success was guaranteed. In the absence of school records indicating the academic performance of those in attendance, the only behavior that one could build upon was simple attendance. Technically, it would have been possible to reward inmates for attendance, and to then later move on to include academic requirements for the reward. Such a tactic was rejected on the grounds that the long-term consequences would prove to be detrimental to the objectives of the program. Specifically, this procedure could well have built an expectation of an implicit contract between the inmates and the project taking the form that mere school attendance could be exchangeable for rewards.

In an effort to eliminate the grounds for possible misunderstanding and to establish the appropriate relationship between behavioral requirements and rewards, a minimum of academic-related tasks were required from the onset in place of mere attendance. Since such academic requirements had to be observed in the academic classroom, attendance became a necessary but not sufficient condition for rewards.

Method

Initial data collection was begun by providing an incentive procedure for the men to demonstrate academic progress. The incentive consisted of an activity area called the "Rap Room" furnished with comfortable chairs, a game table, a record player, assorted recorded music, and high-interest magazines. At the end of each hour of academic work, the instructor checked the inmates' performance and those whom he judged to have shown satisfactory progress were rewarded with 15-minute access to the "Rap Room." At the end of 15 minutes, the inmates returned to the classroom and once again began their academic work.

Results

Inmate participation in the educational phases of rehabilitation was directly affected by the reward system. Prior to the implementation of this reward system less than 30 inmates out of a possible 175 were participating in an academic program on a regular basis although daily school hours were scheduled for each inmate. Moreover, those attending typically reported to the school and spent their school hours in the library perusing popular magazines. When the motivational system was implemented, however, the number of inmates judged by instructors to have shown some academic progress tripled from an average of 29 to 111 participants per day.

Discussion

Although at this early stage of the project no formal measures of academic performance were available, all instructors were in agreement that the reward procedure had produced a noticeable improvement in the inmates' attitude and academic progress. The results of this study, therefore, encouraged the school teachers to continue the incentive approach. Although their reservations continued they were now willing to explore the potential use of other procedures in the school setting.

USING A LICENSE TO
INCREASE ACADEMIC PERFORMANCE

Casual observations prior to the introduction of the EMLC token economy indicated that inmates were not taking full advantage of the previously described remedial education program. Consequently, one objective of the EMLC project was to explore how different positive incentive procedures would motivate inmates toward participation and achievement in the academic portions of the project. These efforts are described in the following study.

Method

Remedial education was available to all 56 inmates who participated in the EMLC project. Due to transfers, releases, and paroles, the average number of resident inmates on any given day was approximately 22.

Most inmates had access to remedial education five hours per day Monday through Friday, starting between 4:30 and 5:00 p.m. until about 10:00 p.m. In addition, remedial education was available for approximately 13 hours a day on Saturday, Sunday, and holidays.

Indices of Inmates' Academic Progress

Two measures of inmate participation in the education program were selected for examination. The first measure was the percentage of inmates on the token economy cellblock participating in the education program each day. The second measure was the percent of inmates mastering educational material whose Estimated Study Time (EST), based upon the performance of previous students, was equal to or exceeded 500 minutes per week. These data were derived from the information recorded on the study schedule following each module test. This second measure most closely reflected progress in the education program since it was based on an achievement measure: mastery of the material in the instructional modules.

Incentive Conditions

BASELINE 1 — NO TOKENS

This period preceeded the introduction of the token economy. The remedial education program and the importance of the skills that could be acquired through participation were explained and discussed with all inmates. Throughout this condition, inmates were repeatedly encouraged to participate in the program. Moreover, staff members provided special counseling to all inmates who lacked high school diplomas but had tested grade levels that were relatively high (typically at or above the ninth-grade level). During counseling, the staff emphasized to the inmates that intense preparation during the last months prior to their release could prepare them to pass the General Educational Development (GED) test and, thereby, earn the equivalent of a high school diploma. In general, every opportunity was taken to encourage all inmates to partake of the educational curriculum offered them.

TOKENS 1

As in the preceding period, inmates were encouraged to participate in the remedial education program. However, inmates earned points for passing module tests. The number of points earned was equal to twice the number of minutes it was estimated would be taken to complete the module (e.g., if the expected time for completing a certain module was 45 minutes, an inmate was paid 90 points for completing it). The points could then be exchanged for backup reinforcers in the EMLC token economy.

LICENSE

This procedure required that each inmate have an EMLC license to exchange EMLC points for the backup reinforcers available within the token economy cellblock. No exchange was available in the absence of this license. To insure that those who did not participate in the education program would not suffer undue hardship, time off the token economy cellblock continued as a backup reinforcer. However, the cost per minute for time off the cellblock was raised from one to two points per minute for those without the EMLC license. The cost increase was introduced to maintain the value of the points for those who chose not to participate in the education program, thereby insuring that the performance of other activities that earned token reinforcement on the token economy cellblock would continue little affected by the new procedure. By performing the activities that are generally expected of inmates they would earn more than a sufficient number of points to spend their leisure-time hours in other parts of the institution. In so doing, they would be availing themselves of the full range of free-time activities available to other inmates of the same institution, if they so desired.

The EMLC license was earned through achievement in the remedial education program. Points continued to be earned by passing module tests. The first 1000 points earned in the remedial education program each week were credited to the purchase of the following week's license. Any points earned in excess of these 1000 points could be expended within the token economy itself. To assist inmates in their development of academic skills, the license procedure included a shaping component to enable inmates to gradually work up to full participation. A license could be purchased at a progressively reduced cost throughout each week depending upon how many days it would be valid and of use. Once a license was purchased, subsequent point earnings were credited toward the purchase of the following week's license until the required 1000 points were accumulated. Additional earnings in the education program could then be expended in the token economy itself.

Those inmates who purchased a license expended their EMLC points in the same manner that they had prior to the introduction of the license procedure. It was explained that, in most cases, licenses could be earned in less than 10 hours of study, and the hours could be distributed over a week's time in any fashion the inmates wished. The importance of the skill taught with the remedial education program was again emphasized.

It was made clear to the inmates that choosing not to participate in the education program under the new procedure deprived them of nothing to which inmates in the institution at large had access. By performing the routine tasks expected of everyone in the institution, they could continue to enjoy the same privileges as their peers in the remainder of the institution. It was also pointed out that the extra benefits available to the residents of the token economy cellblock were offered in exchange for certain activities on the part of the inmates. The activity that the project staff considered to be of primary importance was self-improvement through education. It was explained that this alone more than justified the new procedure.

TOKENS 2

The license was discontinued during this period and the procedures followed were identical to those during the Tokens 1 condition.

BASELINE 2–NO TOKENS

The conditions in effect during this period were identical to those in effect during Baseline 1.

Results

As Figure 4 reveals, the percent of inmates participating in the educational program increased from a level near zero per day to approximately 17% per day after introduction of the token economy. This effect was not limited to attendance since inmates once in the education program earned points for mastery of academic material. On the average, participants in the program mastered material equivalent to five hours

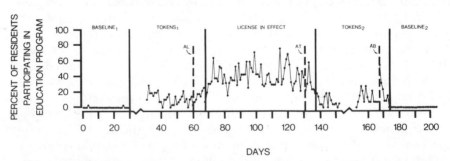

Figure 4.   Percent of inmates studying academic material in the EMLC educational program during the five conditions examined. AL: announce license; AT: announce termination of license; AB: announce baseline 2.

of study each day. Following the introduction of the special license procedure the percent of inmates participating again increased from about 17% per day to 42%. The average amount of academic material mastered by those participating each day was maintained at approximately five hours of study per day.

When the license procedure was discontinued, the attendance dropped from an average of 42% per day to 9% per day. Of those who participated each day, the average amount of academic material mastered remained at approximately five hours per day.

While access to remedial education continued following the termination of the token economy, inmate participation returned to the zero level observed prior to the token economy.

Discussion

The results described previously indicate that the license procedure was an effective means of motivating increased participation in the remedial education program. These data do not, however, fully reflect the high level of involvement that emerged. Although less than half the inmates participated in the program on a typical day during the period in which the license was in effect, considerably higher percentages were involved in the program throughout each week. Differing patterns of participation emerged. Some inmates were active in the program early in the week, others later in the week. Some would work in the program for virtually the whole of one weekend day, while others would work for short periods on each day of the week.

This study also reveals the effectiveness of the token reinforcement procedures employed in motivating performance in the remedial education program. It must be emphasized that the program was conducted during the inmate's leisure time. Most of the residents of the token economy cellblock during the latter third of the project—the period under examination in this study—spent their working hours laboring on the institution farm: picking cotton, hoeing weeds, cutting ditch banks, and the like. Others were on road gangs: cutting grass, striping highways, removing litter, and so on. Still others worked in such places as the institution kitchen or laundry. Only a relatively small number were involved in formalized vocational training programs offered by either the State of Alabama or the federal government through the U.S. Department of Labor's MDT project. Within this context, the performance observed during the token reinforcement procedure in the absence of the licensing condition is encouraging.

It was indeed surprising that virtually none of the residents chose to participate in the remedial education program prior to and following the token economy. Despite the demands of their institutional work assignments, it is difficult to understand why none of the inmates came forward to take advantage of the education program offered to them during their leisure time, especially in light of the special effort the project staff made to encourage them to do so. One would think that some would tire of the dull routine of institutional life and devote some of their evening or weekend hours to the education program to break the monotony, if not to better prepare themselves for the period following their release. Unfortunately, this did not happen. Additional incentives were clearly required to motivate participation.

A COMPARISON OF THREE METHODS OF INSTRUCTION

Skinner (1954) is credited with the development of the widely used teaching machine in which a question or an incomplete sentence is presented prior to a frame which provides the answer. When using a teaching machine, students usually work alone and at their own pace. The procedure involves making a written response to the question frame and then checking this with the correct response in the corresponding answer frame. A second method employs the programmed textbook as the vehicle to present the question and answer frames.

A principal advantage of the teaching machine is that it enforces the requirement that a student respond to a question before going on to the answer frame, thus eliminating the possibility of "cheating" by reading the answer frame before constructing and writing an answer. By so doing, it insures that the student will receive immediate feedback on his actual progress. It also allows the instructor to record the accuracy of the student's performance. It has been suggested that teaching machines may hold the interest of the student longer and provide greater incentive for accuracy than the programmed textbook.

A third material presentation format is also an extension of the concept of the teaching machine. Here individual tutors present the programmed material and explain troublesome points to the students. The technique appears to have all the advantages of the teaching machine, while at the same time providing a high level of individual attention. Some investigation of the use of tutors in programmed courses in higher education dealing with relatively complex concepts has been conducted (Keller, 1969; Johnston & Pennypacker, 1971). It was possible, then, that tutoring by educationally advanced inmates might hold the interest of inmate students even longer than the teaching machine and also stimulate improved performance.

The objective of the study, conducted by the EMLC staff, was to determine which of three formats for the presentation of programmed instructional material would generate the highest levels of student performance during study and testing sessions. This study compared the traditional programmed textbook format to a mechanical presentation procedure (teaching machine) and to material presentation by an individual tutor. The latter format was of particular interest because it explored the feasibility of employing advanced inmates in the education of their peers. If proven efficient, this would underscore the importance of inmate manpower as a valuable resource in correctional education programs.

Procedure

Nine inmates served as students in this study. They were volunteers who had progressed sufficiently far in their IPI prescriptions to make them eligible for the programmed course.

Indices of Academic Progress

The indicators of the effectiveness of the three presentation formats were three performance measures taken (a) during the study session for each chapter, (b) during a performance test scheduled 24 hours after the chapter was studied, and (c) in a performance test scheduled seven days after the chapter was studied. Actual study time and time required to take each of the two performance tests were recorded. Using the study session and performance test times, measures of rate of study (number of question frames completed divided by the study time) and rate of correct responding on performance tests (number of correct test items divided by testing time) were computed.

Academic Materials and Procedure

The same academic material was used in all three instructional conditions. All students studied the commonly used programmed English course, *English 2600* (Harcourt, Brace, and World, 1964). The linearly programmed textbook material was adapted for use in the teaching machine and tutoring formats. The course consists of 69 chapters of approximately equal length (approximately 38 question frames per chapter). The students studied the first 60 of these chapters, with each student using each of the three formats for 20 chapters. The sequences in which the students experienced the three presentation formats were counterbalanced to control for the possibility of order effects.

TEACHING MACHINE

In the teaching machine format, the question and answer frames were cut from the *English 2600* textbook and taped into continuous rolls, one roll for each chapter. A machine was constructed that permitted the student to see one question frame at a time and to write his response. After the student wrote his response, he advanced the roll to see the answer frame and to compare his response to the correct answer. Because the machine would not reverse, he could not change his answer. Students were required to respond to each frame, and their responses were checked subsequent to each study session to record errors and to make certain that they were consistently responding.

TEXTBOOK

In the traditional textbook mode, students were issued an *English 2600* textbook and instructed to study the material and to respond to each question frame before turning to the answer frame. As in the classroom use of programmed materials, there was no way to ascertain whether or not this was done. Students were instructed to go to the staff instructor for assistance if they could not understand a section.

INDIVIDUAL TUTOR

Eight tutors were selected from inmate volunteers who had previously completed the programmed course. For the tutoring mode, the *English 2600* textbook frames were cut apart and pasted on 3" × 5" cards, with the question frame on the front of the card and the answer frame on the back. This allowed the tutor to present the question frame to the student, ask for a verbal response, and then show him the answer frame. Tutors were directed to explain incorrectly answered frames to the student in as much detail as they deemed necessary to ensure that the student understood both why his response was incorrect and what the correct answer was.

Incentives

Both students and tutors received token economy points for their participation under the three methods used in the experiment. One chapter was studied each night until all 60 chapters had been completed. In this experiment, the student and the tutor received 120 points each for the completion of a chapter, independent of study time or test performance.

Results

Data are presented for seven students who completed the course. The collection of data was supervised by project staff members who frequently substituted for the tutors in order to verify the recorded performance of the students. As indicated in Table 5, the analysis of variance revealed that there was a significant difference in the ate of studying programmed material among the three presentation formats. The Duncan Multiple Range Test (Winer, 1962) indicated that the individual tutoring procedure produced higher study rates than either the programmed textbook $(p < .05)$ or teaching machine procedures $(p < .05)$, which did not differ from each other $(p > .05)$.

Analysis of variance of the performance test data failed to reveal any significant differences among the material presentation procedures on either test score or rate of correct responding on performance tests. Students scored significantly higher on the 24-hour retention tests than on the seven-day retention tests $(p < .05)$. There were no significant differences among the rates of correct responding under the three presentation formats, although the individual tutoring condition was somewhat higher than that for the two other presentation formats.

The three materials presentation formats were also compared on the basis of the number of students who had higher rates of correct responding on the majority of module tests. This comparison indicated that a majority of the students had their highest rates of correct responding with the tutoring format. This rate superiority held for both short- and long-term retention tests, with the binomial test revealing statistically

Table 5.   Analysis of Variance for Rate of Studying Programmed Material across Three Presentation Formats

Source	SS	df	ms	F
Total	9.50	20	—	—
Subjects	5.15	6	—	—
Presentation formats	1.90	2	.95	5.28[a]
Error	2.45	12	.18	—

[a] $p < .05$.

significant test rate differences between the tutoring format and the programmed textbook ($p < .05$) and teaching machine formats ($p < .05$). The difference between the latter two formats failed to reach significance.

Discussion

Token reinforcement was used to reward participation in a study designed to evaluate three methods of presenting programmed instructional material. The major finding in this study was that the three methods were roughly equivalent in producing academic performance in rather basic academic material. The choice of which method to adopt in a prison setting should, then, be based on efficiency and cost effectiveness. From the point of view of cost alone, the programmed textbook is to be preferred to the others. In addition, the tutorial method produced slightly faster learning rates than the other methods. However, the hidden costs involved in screening, scheduling, and supervision of tutors might outweigh this slight advantage. This should be considered when choosing such a method of instruction.

MAXIMIZING THE EFFECTIVENESS OF REWARDS

The previous studies demonstrate the effectiveness of token reinforcement procedures in encouraging prison inmates to participate and achieve in remedial education programs. It has also been shown that programmed instructional materials are as effective a format for in-prison education as they are for educational efforts in general. The next series of studies focused upon the refinement of accepted token reinforcement procedures to maximize the effectiveness of rewards.

Study 1: Performance-based vs. Salary-based Pay

It was recognized that awarding tokens on the basis of academic achievement required more staff effort than awarding tokens for participation in the academic program. Consequently, a study was conducted to gain information on the desirability of one form of token payment versus another.

The study took place in the academic classroom of the MORE Project. The room contained individual study carrels. Students studied and took tests at their own levels and speed.

INDICES OF ACADEMIC PROGRESS

The responses measured were the school attendance and test passing in the IPI curriculum (details of this program were described previously).

INCENTIVES

The token point system used is described in detail in Chapter 8. There were two ways of earning points. Performance-based pay was provided for meeting a prescribed academic criteria. Salary-based pay required only that the student be in attendance at school so that he might participate in the educational program.

PROCEDURE

Three men were initially paid on a salary basis. Specifically, these inmates were required to check in with the school clerk when they attended school with the explicit expectation that they would also study for two hours. The pay (12 points) was given to them each day after checking their attendance. This period lasted for 35 days. Next, these same men were advised that the pay would be earned on a performance-based schedule by passing tests. This second period also lasted for 35 days. The EST (estimated study time) for each module of instruction was rounded off to the nearest hour and 12 points per EST hour were awarded when a module test was passed.

RESULTS

Table 6 presents the results of this study. Clearly, performance-based pay is preferable to salary-based pay as a means of promoting high levels of academic performance. These findings were not unexpected and corroborate those obtained with other populations.

The procedure for evaluating the relative effectiveness of salary-based pay on academic performance is sometimes known as the comparison method (or A-B) wherein performance under one condition is compared to that under a subsequent condition. The proper interpretation of the results of such comparisons must take into consideration both the magnitude of the difference between the conditions and the tem-

Table 6.   The Effects of Salary-based and Performance-based Pay on Academic Performance

| | Condition | |
	Salary-based Pay	Performance-based Pay
Mean number of hours[a] of academic material passed per day	2.2	3.6
Total number of hours of academic material passed per period	75.5	127.5

[a] Estimated study time.

poral relationship between the introduction of the second condition and the change in performance. Here, the magnitude of performance change was large and coincident with the introduction of performance-based pay, indicating it was responsible for the inmates' dramatic increase in academic performance.

Study 2: Effects of Modeling Desirable Behavior
Upon Academic Performance

It has been demonstrated conclusively, with other populations and settings, that one of the major sources of social influence involves exposure of individuals to others who model desirable behavior (see Bandura, 1977). This study was designed to extend these findings to include the prison population.

PROCEDURE

Three inmates who did not have experience with incentives were introduced to the academic setting where the inmates of Study 1 were working under performance-based pay. They were paid on a salary-basis and received 12 points each day after checking their attendance to school. This salary-based condition lasted for 70 days.

RESULTS AND DISCUSSION

Inmates under a salary-based pay performed initially at about the same high level as inmates who were paid on a performance basis. However, this initial high performance decreased gradually within the first 30 days and more rapidly by the end of the study for a 43% drop from its initial level (see Table 7).

One interpretation of these results is that, performance under a salary-based pay may be susceptible to social influence. Specifically, when other co-workers appear to be producing at a high level, those around them tend to imitate similar levels of performance. Such a phenomenon has been amply documented in the literature under the term of imitation or vicarious learning (Bandura, 1969). It is to be noted also that such phenomenon is temporary or transitory in the absence of specific contingencies for imitation. For our purposes, it suffices to say that given enough time, imitation alone is an insufficient basis for maintenance of high levels of performance. Again, consistent with previous findings in the literature, performance under salary-based pay decreases in time in the absence of performance-based pay.

Study 3: The Effect of Reinforcement on Inmates' Preferences for Academic Material

One of the major problems in prison rehabilitation programs occurs when there is a conflict between the inmate and the educator regarding what that the content of the rehabilitation program should be. Understandably, some inmates would select for themselves those components from the rehabilitation programs with which they had had previous contact and success, while avoiding those with which they had unfamiliarity or no success. Yet, the very nature of rehabilitation requires that efforts be made to remediate those areas of least familiarity and, hence,

Table 7.   The Effects of High-Performance Models on Academic Performance During Salary-based Pay

	Condition	
	Early	Late
Mean number of hours[a] of academic material passed per day	3.0	1.7
Total number of hours of academic material passed per period	106.5	59.5

[a] Estimated study time.

success. A practical problem arises in attempting to reconcile these opposing interests. If the inmate is forced into programs against his will he will either be indifferent or unresponsive to the training. On the other hand, if he selects programs for himself many of his deficits will continue without remediation. The question then is how to encourage inmates to voluntarily select the range of programs they require to remediate their vocational and academic deficits. To illustrate the flexibility of reinforcement procedures in the resolution of such difficult problems, this study demonstrates the effect of reinforcement on inmates' preferences for academic programs.

SUBJECTS

A group of 70 inmates were engaged in academic activities when this study was begun. By the time the study was completed, however, many inmates had been transferred or released from the institution. Others had not taken at least one English and one math test during the first phase of the study and could not participate in the second phase. Thus, the final number of participants in this study was 22 inmates. Average age was 23.5 years, ranging from 20 to 26 years. Average IQ as measured by the Stanford-Binet for the 22 subjects was 98.9 with a range of 64 to 118. The regular prison classroom, located in the prison school area, was used in this study.

INDICES OF ACADEMIC PROGRESS

The academic response consisted of passing a Material Mastery test at a criterion level of 80% or better in both math and English. Programmed materials were utilized for both subject areas as described previously.

INCENTIVES

Points were earned on a performance-based schedule as described previously (i.e., 12 points per EST hour) for math or English as prescribed by the evaluation design.

Inmates were given the opportunity to engage in math study and/or English study each day and to take Material Mastery tests whenever they had completed the prerequisite assignments. The criteria for passing tests on either material was 80% correct. During one phase of the study, only passing tests in English was reinforced. In another phase, only passing tests in math was reinforced. The procedures were as follows:

Phase 1: (20 days) English—tests passed at 80% or better resulted in reinforcement.
Math—tests passed led to *no* reinforcement.

Phase 2: (20 days) English—tests passed led to *no* reinforcement.
Math—tests passed at 80% or better result in reinforcement.

Under both phases, the students could work on either subject area as they chose.

EVALUATION

A methodological procedure, sometimes referred to as a multiple AB design, was used to assess the effects of reinforcement on inmates' preferences. Separate records of English and math tests passed during Phases 1 and 2 were kept. The number of English tests passed during Phase 1, when only the passing of English tests was reinforced, was compared to the number of English tests passed during Phase 2, when only the passing of math tests was reinforced. A similar comparison was performed for the passing of math tests.

RESULTS

Test passing increased when reinforcement was provided for passing tests. Conversely, test passing decreased when it resulted in *no* reinforcement. When passing English tests resulted in reinforcement, a total of 79 English tests were passed in comparison to only 5 tests when passing English tests did *not* result in reinforcement. Similarly, inmates passed a total of 77 math tests when reinforced for so doing and passed only 23 when *not* reinforced. Taken as a whole, 156 tests were passed with reinforcement while only 28 were passed without reinforcement. Table 8 summarizes the data for both phases and both subject matters.

DISCUSSION

The results indicate that academic test-passing was a function of the contingencies of reinforcement. The number of tests passed in a particular academic subject depended upon whether test passing was reinforced or not reinforced. It may be hypothesized from these results that reinforcement may aid in motivating a trainee to pass tests in an area that he may not favor and at the same time, it may increase test passing in an academic area that is already well liked.

Table 8.   Total Number of Tests Passed in English and Math in the Presence and
Absence of Reinforcement [a]

	Subject Matter	
	English	Math
Phase 1 Reinforcement for English but *not* math	79	23
Phase 2 Reinforcement for math but *not* English	5	77

[a] $N = 22$.

The present study suggests that an analysis of behavior can be performed in an applied setting despite the methodological problems which
such a setting presents. In this study, the procedure of comparing two
dimensions of the same class of behaviors against each other to demonstrate a functional relationship between the variables in question is a
methodological contribution to the applied literature. Because of this
procedural design, one response was always being reinforced and thus
the inmates were always benefiting from the treatment. The study demonstrates again that a systematic analysis of behavior is compatible with a
concern for the individual's human rights and well being. It also represents a systematic replication of similar findings established with other
human populations (e.g., Ayllon & Azrin, 1965).

Study 4: Maximizing the Motivational Effects
of the Incentive System

In the course of the previous studies assessing the relative effectiveness
of incentives on academic progress it was noted that the academic performance for some inmates increased notably in one subject matter or
another but then became stable, suggesting either an intellectual ceiling
had been reached or sufficient motivation was not available. In this
study, a schedule of reinforcement that generated high rates of performance was employed to maximize the motivational effects of the incentive system (for more details, see Kandel, Ayllon, & Roberts, 1976).

SUBJECTS

Two inmates incarcerated for violent crimes and deficient in their
academic work were chosen for the study. One of the inmates, Sanford,

was 22 years old and was functioning at the 6.1 grade level as measured on the California Test of Basic Skills (CTBS) and had an IQ of 65 as measured on the Stanford-Binet. The other inmate, Martin, was functioning at the 7.7 overall grade level and had an IQ of 91. Sanford was known to be rather withdrawn, while Martin had a reputation of being hostile and aggressive, which resulted in his being sent to the "hole" on several occasions. Both inmates had been in prison for approximately a year prior to the initiation of the present study.

INDICES OF ACADEMIC PROGRESS

The target response was passing Material Mastery tests at a criterion level of 80% or better in both math and English. A series of six of these Mastery tests comprised a grade or skill level. Programmed materials were utilized for both subject areas.

PROCEDURE

Points were administered on two different schedules during the first and last condition of the study. During the standard schedule of reinforcement (which served as *baseline*), 20 points were earned by passing each Material Mastery test in a particular academic area. In addition, 120 points were earned for every skill level completed. During the treatment condition, an enriched schedule of reinforcement for passing Material Mastery tests as well as completing grade levels was employed. Under this schedule, the inmates received a greater magnitude of points as the temporal period decreased between tests passed. In short, the faster the inmates passed tests under the rate schedule, the more points they received per test. The slower the inmates passed tests, the fewer points they received. A similar type of rate schedule was used for completing a grade level.

The base level of payment on the enriched schedule was computed by the average number of days it took inmates to pass one test under previous standard conditions. Thus, the average number of days of study it took to earn 20 points under the standard conditions (4 days or more) was the same number of days it took to earn 20 points under the enriched conditions. The inmates could never earn less than 20 points for passing a test; however, the increase in the number of points available for passing each test was considerably more as the number of study days it took them to pass tests decreased. For example, if the individual passed one test in one study day he earned 50 points; but if he passed two tests in one study day he earned 150 points. Ultimately, if he passed six tests in one day he earned 700 points. The number of points available for passing a grade level increased in a similar fashion. If the individual completed one grade level in 16 days he earned 500 points; but if he completed one grade level in one day he earned 4,700 points. Table 9 summarizes the points earning schedules.

The two inmates involved in this study had been participating in a motivational program wherein they received standard amount of reinforcement for three months prior to the investigation of the effects of the enriched reinforcement schedule. Therefore, baseline measures of math and English performance were taken for the two inmates when passing tests was on a standard reinforcement schedule. The rate of academic work in both math and English for Martin and Sanford was fairly stable throughout the three-month standard reinforcement condition; therefore for purposes of parsimony and clarity only the data for the last 20 days for each inmate is presented here.

Measures of math and English performance were taken for Sanford and Martin when passing tests was on an enriched reinforcement schedule. For Sanford, the enrichment phase was 22 days in math and 7 days in English. For Martin, the enrichment phase lasted 14 days in math and 8 days in English. Pre- (before the standard schedule was implemented) and post- (after the enriched schedule was implemented) measures were taken in reading, language, and arithmetic for both inmates on the California Test of Basic Skills.

As Figs. 5 and 6 show, the number of tests passed by the two inmates in math and English was dramatically higher under the enriched schedule of reinforcement than under the standard reinforcement schedule.

Sanford

Math. When Sanford received reinforcement on the standard schedule for math, his performance was stable and relatively high. However, under the enriched schedule of reinforcement, Sanford's rate of performance rose from 11 tests in 20 days to 42 tests in 22 days. Sanford, therefore, passed math tests approximately four times faster under the enriched schedule than under the standard schedule. This increase in rate was related to academic progress. Under the standard schedule of reinforcement, Sanford passed ninth and part of tenth grade algebra. Amazingly, however, in the same period of time, under enriched conditions, he passed and completed tenth, eleventh, and twelfth grade algebra and geometry and began trigonometry.

Table 9.   Enriched Schedules of Reinforcement Designed to Maximize the
Motivational Effects of the Incentive System

Number of Tests Passed	Number of Days Required	Points Earned
1	4 or more	20
1	3	25
1	2	35
1	1	50
2	1	150
3	1	250
4	1	400
5	1	550
6	1	700

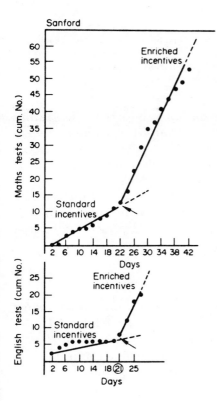

Figure 5.   Cumulative number of math (top of graph) and English (bottom) tests passed for Sanford during two incentive conditions. Standard ncentives were available for passing tests during the first 20 days. The arrow signifies the point where enriched incentives were available for passing tests. Each data point is the total number of tests passed in a two-day period except where the day is circled. (From Kandel, Ayllon & Roberts, 1976).

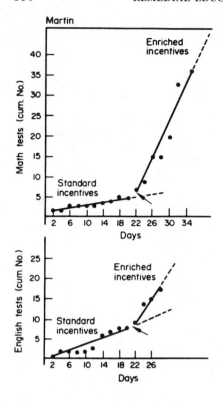

Figure 6.   Cumulative number of math (top of graph) and English (bottom) tests passed for Martin during two incentive conditions. Standard incentives were available for passing tests during the first 20 days. The arrow signifies the point where enriched incentives were available for passing tests. Each data point is the total number of tests passed in a two-day period. (From Kandel, Ayllon & Roberts, 1976).

English.   Under the standard schedule of reinforcement, Sanford passed relatively few English tests. When Sanford was under the enriched schedule he went from six tests in 20 days to 14 tests in seven days. Sanford, therefore, passed English tests over seven times faster under the enriched schedule than under the standard schedule. During the period Sanford was under the standard schedule of reinforcement he completed only ninth grade English; however, in only seven days when the enriched schedule was in effect, Sanford passed tenth, eleventh, and part of twelfth grade English.

Martin

Math.   When Martin received reinforcement on the standard schedule for math his performance was consistently at a low level. Under the enriched schedule conditions his rate rose from five tests in 20 days to 30 tests in only 14 days. Martin, therefore, passed almost nine times as many tests under the enriched schedule as under the standard schedule.

During the period Martin was under the standard schedule he passed eighth grade math; however, in almost half the time when the enriched schedule was in effect he passed ninth through twelfth grade algebra as well as geometry.

English. Under the standard schedule of reinforcement, Martin worked at a relatively stable and moderate rate. Under the enriched schedule of reinforcement he went from eight tests in 20 days to passing nine tests in 8 days. Martin, therefore, passed English tests approximately three times faster under the enriched schedule than under the standard schedule. During the period Martin was under the standard schedule he passed sixth grade English; however, in less than half the time when he was under the enriched schedule he passed seventh and part of eighth grade English.

DISCUSSION

Comparison of California Test of Basic Skills pretest and posttest scores indicated increased achievement for both inmates during the five-month period the motivation system was in effect. Martin increased 1.2 grade levels in reading, 1 grade level in language, and 2.3 grade levels in arithmetic. His overall grade placement increase was 1.5 grade levels. Sanford's increases were even greater: His reading increased 4.9 grade levels, his language increased 6.6 grade levels, and his arithmetic increased 4.6 grade levels. His overall grade placement increase was 5.4 grade levels. Table 10 summarizes these results.

The findings demonstrate that the application of an enriched schedule produced high rates of academic performance with adult criminals who were academically deficient, had a long history of academic failure, were unmotivated to engage in academic work, and who were in an environment that far from encouraged academic achievement. These results expand upon the findings of Lovitt and Esveldt (1970) who found that an enriched schedule of reinforcement resulted in high rates of math performance in elementary school children.

Further, these findings demonstrate that the enriched schedule which Lovitt and Esveldt (1970) found effective on the rate of passing math material already known to the children is useful in facilitating the learning of new materials such as math and reading. For example, the data show that Sanford could progress through ninth grade math to twelfth grade advanced trigonometry when an enriched schedule of reinforcement was available for passing tests. Observations by the prison staff and anecdotal reports of other inmates showed that Sanford and Martin

Table 10.   Pretest and Posttest Scores on the CTBS[a] for Sanford and Martin

	Reading	Language	Arithmetic	Overall Grade Placement
Sanford				
Pretest				
II-Form A	6.3	4.8	8.0	6.1
Posttest				
III-Form B	11.2	11.4	12.6	11.4
Difference	+4.9	+6.6	+4.6	+5.3
Martin				
Pretest				
II-Form A	7.7	7.0	8.3	7.7
Posttest				
III-Form B	8.9	8.0	10.6	9.2
Difference	+1.2	+1.0	+2.3	+1.5

[a] California Test of Basic Skills.
Note. Numbers are in terms of academic grade level.

spent longer periods of time studying for tests as they moved up in levels of difficulty. The instructors reported that the men often studied academics during vocational training periods and recreational periods. Correctional officers and inmates noted that both inmates studied through the night when most other inmates were sleeping. At the same time Sanford and Martin expressed the thought that the work was "bustin' their heads," but that they were "going to get when the gettin' was good."

As one might expect, the two inmates earned a fantastic number of points. This resulted in their purchasing a good deal of canteen items; the point-spending records showed, however, that most of the points were spent on privileges or gifts for their family. The men now had the opportunity to call or write to their family and friends and even have these important people visit them more often. Both Sanford and Martin used the majority of their points to buy Gold Bond stamps with which they purchased goods for their wives and children. These incentives naturally increased the contact of the inmates with their family and friends and gave them an opportunity to enhance relationships. The number of points earned and spent can also be looked at from another point of view. A cost-analysis of the program might show that the enriched schedule speeds up academic learning so considerably that, in the long run, it costs less than a standard schedule which prolongs the rehabilitation effort and thus might result in excessive costs.

In this study standardized tests had placed Sanford at an IQ level of 65 and Martin at a 91 IQ level. While Martin was in the low end of the normal range and Sanford was in the educable mentally retarded range, both inmates were working on twelfth grade algebra and trigonometry by the end of their work in the incentive program, an accomplishment not predictable from their IQ scores. The California Test of Basic skills (CTBS) scores taken before and after the five-month baseline and treatment period indicated that both men made substantial gains in each subtest area and in their overall grade placement. Since the day-to-day measures demonstrate that the major academic gains took place during the enriched schedule conditions, it can be assumed that the change in CTBS scores can be attributed to the brief period of time that the enriched schedule was in effect. That overall gains ranging from 1.5 to 5.3 grade levels were achieved in such a short time suggests that either the IQ measures used for these men inaccurately reflected their intelligence or, in these cases at least, IQ scores do not accurately reflect ability to learn. Because there were only two students involved, and the procedure was presented to the men as a special project, it is possible that the achievement score changes may have been a Hawthorne-type effect (Cook, 1962). It will be recalled that this effect refers to increases in performance due to special attention. Their measured performance, and their actual observable progress through increasingly difficult material, however, suggest that the changes in achievement scores did result from the experimental procedures and were not spurious.

This study clearly indicates the usefulness of an enriched schedule as evidenced in the high levels of performance possible with such schedules. Not only were the men working harder but, as the achievement tests indicated, they were learning a great deal. The most significant finding of this study was that it enabled the staff to properly assess the potential in both the inmates who participated in the study. In so doing, it became clear that Sanford's ability had been grossly underestimated. Clearly too, Sanford himself had come to believe that he had low intellectual capability. Sanford's IQ was tested at 65 when he entered prison the previous year. Yet, it was Sanford who went approximately five to six grades across reading, language, and arithmetic. His performance is obviously unlike that of an individual diagnosed as mentally retarded or one bordering on that diagnostic category. Admittedly, his IQ score is not a valid index of his potential. The question is whether such assessment efforts are worth pursuing. With individuals of known motivational problems, such testing efforts may only serve as a self-fulfilling prophecy for those who expect little from the inmate. It is not unlikely that many individuals such as Sanford may at this very moment be engaged in chores and activities far below the level of their potential. From the point of view of doing justice to the individuals who are to be incarcerated, assessment of their potential must be made with due respect to the motivational level present at the time of testing. These findings also corroborate previous results indicating that when the level of motivation is maximized, even mentally retarded individuals will perform on a higher intellectual level (Ayllon & Kelly, 1973). Also, it is clear that a disservice is being perpetrated on the basis of which some vocational facilities and learning opportunities will be restricted or withheld to fit the obtained IQ score. This study indicates that exposure to learning opportunities and unlimited motivation can lead to great strides in educational growth. This appears far better than sheltering people with limited educational skills from the failure they are expected to but may not experience.

Study 5: Maintaining Performance while Fostering Delay of Gratification

While the results of the preceeding study demonstrate that inmates will perform at unusually high rates under special conditions, these conditions have severe limitations from the viewpoint of the typical resources available to correctional institutions. Specifically, the backup reinforcers that must be employed to maintain the inmates' motivation are typically consumers' goods that would impose an unacceptable burden upon the financial resources of the correctional systems. This limitation could be overcome by incorporating with the exchange system a variety of potential reinforcers such as home furlough, conjugal visitation, graduated release programs, special rehabilitation programs, for example, attendance to college, or vocational schools, parole, and unconditional release.

Another limitation of the procedures employed in Study 4 is that of their indirect effects upon the other behaviors that earn token reinforcement. That is, performance of behaviors to which the rate schedule is *not* applied would be expected to decrease. For example, while one of these individuals earned 1000 points by meeting specific academic criteria, he ceased to make any efforts to earn points in other areas. Consequently, it would be counterproductive to use this procedure with one activity if the objective is to maintain high levels of interest and performance in a variety of activities.

Finally, another limitation of enriched schedules of reward is that they emphasize dependence upon immediate rewards of large magnitude. Superficially, this approach would appear to contribute to what is often claimed to be an undesirable characteristic of offenders, namely that they are unable to postpone or delay gratification. Mordock (1975) for example, maintains that self-control is reflected in the ability to postpone and curb immediate reinforcement in favor of long-term rewards.

The question then is how to maintain motivation to perform a variety of activities while fostering self-control. A procedure to accomplish just such a goal may already be available. It involves linking two or three activities in a sequence so that completion of one activity is *not* followed by a reinforcement but instead allows the individual to work on a second activity, the completion of which earns reward. This procedure appears to be suitable to the area of academic instruction where a major objective of academic programs in general is to encourage academic achievement in a variety of skill areas with minimal dependance on rewards.

Effective academic instruction in one skill area typically required parallel progress in related skill areas. Therefore, the objective of this study was to determine whether such a procedure could be employed to increase academic performance in two subject matters at the same time while holding constant the amount of reward offered. Specifically, the procedure required that the inmate complete an alternating sequence of achievement between English and math to obtain token reinforcement.

SUBJECTS

The same two inmates (Sanford and Martin) who participated in the previous study served as subjects here. The same setting, incentives, and curriculum and materials were used.

PROCEDURES

The procedure required that the inmate pass a test in math and *then* a test in English to earn reinforcement. He earned bonus points for repeating this sequence three times. If he passed two math or two English tests in a row or if he passed an English and then a math test, he did not earn reinforcement.

Because the schedule of payoff emphasized unusually high rates of academic performance, it was anticipated that overall performance would decline under this leaner schedule of reinforcement. However, it was felt that the ultimate gain derived from distributed learning would more than outweigh the short-term advantages of intensive learning limited to one area.

EVALUATION

This study was designed in a multiple-baseline fashion across individuals such that reinforcement for passing both English and math tests was administered to each inmate on different days, after an initial baseline period. The baseline period for each inmate consisted of the last phase of the previous study during which test passing in English was reinforced on a rate schedule and math test passing was not reinforced. The baseline phase began on different days for each inmate and lasted five days for both. The linking procedure was in effect for 10 days for both inmates.

RESULTS

Table 11 shows that administering reinforcement for passing tests linked in a sequence can produce uniform test passing in both English and

Table 11. Comparison of the Average Number of English and Math Tests Passed per Day in the Presence and Absence of a Sequence Requirement for Reinforcement

Phase	Weeks	Math	English
		Average Number Of Tests Passed per Week	
Sanford			
Baseline:			
English: Reinforcement	1	0	12
Math: *No* reinforcement			
Sequence			
Math *then* English: Reinforcement	2	3	3
Martin			
Baseline:			
English: Reinforcement	1	0	6
Math: *No* reinforcement			
Sequence			
Math *then* English: Reinforcement	2	3.5	3

math. Under baseline, when reinforcement was available for English, only English tests were passed. However, when the linking procedure was introduced, test passing occurred in both English and math. As was expected, the average number of math tests passed per week increased under the linking conditions.

Although there was a decrease in tests passed in English, math tests passed increased for Sanford and Martin from a level of zero to an average of three or more tests per week. In addition, the total tests taken per day increased considerably for Sanford and increased slightly for Martin in comparison to the baseline condition.

DISCUSSION

The results demonstrate that reinforcement, when made contingent on performing a linked sequence of academic activities, encouraged these inmates to distribute their efforts between English and math while maintaining their performance. Equally important is that this procedure allowed the offender to experience delay in obtaining reinforcement without disruptive effects on their academic performance or general adjustment in the academic setting. In addition, this procedure recommends itself for use in a variety of practical situations where the major interest is to use the meager resources typically available in the prison setting in the most judicious manner while maintaining acceptable and reasonable levels of performance.

CHAPTER

10

VOCATIONAL TRAINING IN PRISON

Rehabilitation programs have typically emphasized vocational training as a major avenue to prevent the inmate from committing the same criminal acts that eventuated in his incarceration (Fogel, 1977). While the range and type of vocational programs offered to inmates vary widely from state to state and even within the same state, the desirability of equipping inmates with marketable skills is largely agreed upon by criminologists. Paradoxically, these criminologists also agree upon the failure of existing vocational programs to teach most inmates the entry level skills necessary for employment.

To explain such failure, one view that has been advanced emphasizes the inhumanity underlying incarceration and the impossibility of conducting any rehabilitative efforts under such conditions. Another view focuses upon a postulated "criminal personality" and the severe limitations inherent in working with someone who seems to enjoy the excitement of criminal activity and who actively resists any encouragement to change. Rather than accepting these explanations of the failure of vocational efforts and eliminating such programs, the objective of the studies that follow was to upgrade and refine vocational training so that it might have a fair chance to demonstrate its potential worth. This was

198

done through the extension of behavioral procedures found already effective in the prison setting.

The hallmark of a behavioral approach to applied problems is that of specifying objectives that lend themselves to monitoring and quantified evaluation. Meeting this characteristic of behavioral work was perhaps the major problem encountered in the MORE project involving vocational training. In contrast to the relative ease of identification of academic objectives (e.g., raising reading or mathematical skills as measured by a standardized test) the components of vocational training were not formalized in a curriculum as structured as that found in academic education. Complex tasks by and large had not been broken down into smaller component operations. Where this had been done, there was little attempt to arrange the required operations in an orderly and logical sequence. Finally, attempts at establishing criteria to deterimine mastery levels of these operations were minimal. In the absence of these critical features, both teaching and evaluation of mastery were at best arduous and at worst impossible.

Traditionally, vocational training in prisons has been relegated to secondary importance, both in terms of state vocational training programs and institutional priorities. Because the budget for facilities, equipment, and staffing for vocational training is typically minimal, very few training materials are available and these are usually obsolescent or in a state of disrepair. In addition to these obstacles, the ratio of trainees to staff is large and the entry level skills of the trainees vary widely. Some beginning trainees show deficits in following simple instructions, while others lack motor coordination or familiarity with tools.

Finally, the two major methods used to enroll trainees in prison vocational programs also add to the difficulties in implementing a vocational program. Inmates are either assigned to specific trade programs as a routine institutional policy or are given a choice of volunteering for a given vocational program or working on institutional jobs (e.g., farming, laundry room, cleaning details.) In both cases, trainees typically participate in vocational rehabilitation programs not because they wish to master the skills of a trade but because they have been arbitrarily assigned to a trade or because they volunteer in order to escape from an undesirable work assignment.

Admittedly, some inmates are motivated to acquire vocational skills. Unfortunately, these few individuals are quickly discouraged from exerting conscientious efforts in their learning when confronted with the day-to-day difficulties caused by the scarcity and obsolescence of materials as well as the peer pressure not to make other trainees' performance look inadequate. Despite these overwhelming difficulties, there are vocational instructors in every prison who are dedicated to helping these unfortunate young men. Nevertheless, the instructor's efforts are tremendously limited. Even by working overtime, these dedicated instructors are unable on their own to overcome the massive problems which face them daily. As a result, the instructors see their major function as providing as many inmates as possible with the most rudimentary of skills so that the trainee, upon his release from prison, will be able to secure some form of employment in the trade area (carpenter assistant, mechanic's helper, etc.).

Any program designed to assist the beleaguered instructor maximize his use of current resources and justify expenditures for additional teaching materials would have to address itself to the four following areas of concern: First, the vocational curriculum should be divided into smaller instructional modules which can be taught in sequence to facilitate skill acquisition. Second, performance criteria for the mastery of skills taught must be explicitly stated so that achievement of these skills can be evaluated objectively. Third, each trainee's program must be individualized, based on his unique strengths and weaknesses so that he may work at his own rate on those materials he has not yet mastered. Fourth, a motivational system must be established to encourage those individuals who would not otherwise be motivated to acquire vocational skills because of disinterest or peer pressure. Issues such as these have already been addressed and found to be effectively met in the academic educational area.

TEACHING VOCATIONAL SKILLS

The previous series of studies demonstrated that various procedures based on reinforcement theory could influence a wide range of academic performances including participation in an educational program, achievement, study rate, subject matter preference and distribution of academic work.

The question is whether these effects are limited to academic learning or whether incentives would be as effective in the vocational area as they were in the academic one. The present series of studies was designed to answer this question.

Study 1: The Effects of Incentives on Mastery of Auto Mechanics Theory and Skills

The automotive technology trade, a 12-month course designed to produce skills equivalent to those expected of a journeyman automobile mechanic, was selected for study. In general, trainees were expected to obtain two basic component skills: automotive theory and automotive mechanical structure and function. In addition, the men were expected to obtain experience in applying the skills, though little emphasis was placed by the instructor (an experienced auto mechanic who had no formal technical education or teaching experience) in this area. Trainees primarily repaired automobiles and trucks that were either government property or privately owned by prison employees. The instructor assigned trainees to various "jobs," often pairing an experienced trainee with an inexperienced one. He then supervised their work, answered questions, offered advice, and modeled correct procedures. No formal records of trainee progress were kept. Instead, the instructor relied upon his experienced judgment to assess individual progress and competence.

After consulting with the instructors, it was decided that the intervention in this trade would consist of reinforcing the learning of basic component skills while allowing the instructor to conduct his applied training as usual. The instructor agreed that while trainees could demonstrate some knowledge of the basic skills in automotive theory through their applied work, a better assessment could be made through written test. Their performance on theory and structure tests could also provide an initial assessment of ability and competence as well as an objective record of progress.

METHOD

Inmates and setting. There were seven inmate trainees enrolled in automotive training. They had been enrolled in the trade for a mean of five months (range 2 to 12 months). The instructor typically rated each subject's competency as an auto mechanic in a fashion based upon and directly related to their time in the trade. That is, the trainee who had been in the trade for twelve months was "a pretty good mechanic, better than any other inmate here," while the trainees who had just begun "don't know much more than how to change a tire."

Training was conducted in a garage-type building on the prison yard. The building contained complete machining and welding facilities, six hydraulic lifts, a front end alignment rack, a tool room, extensive mechanical and electronic equipment, and a small classroom.

PROCEDURE AND EVALUATION

A series of 20 tests was constructed for automotive theory and also for automotive component structure and function. Tests on *theory* consisted of 20 to 25 objective, multiple-choice items drawn from a textbook available to, but rarely read by, the trainees. *Structure* and function tests consisted of 10 to 25 questions involving the identification of parts of schematic drawings, also derived from the textbook. The texts were designed to assess the trainees' knowledge of parts of the various automotive component assemblies (brake system, electrical system, transmission, etc.). The instructor reviewed each of the 40 tests and answer keys for correctness and comprehension. The tests were then revised based upon suggestions from the instructor.

There were three phases in this study. Phase I consisted of making *theory* and *structure* tests available for one hour daily to trainees, without reinforcement for taking or passing the tests. This period, which lasted 22 days, served to assess the effectiveness of the current vocational practices. The next two phases involved the use of an incentive system. Phase II lasted 11 days during which passing theory tests with 80% or greater correct earned 100 points. Trainees could take either type of test but no points were yet available for passing structure tests. In Phase III, passing only structure tests led to 100 points. While trainees could continue to take theory tests, no points were now available for passing them. This phase lasted 6 days.

RESULTS

Irrespective of the subject matter of the tests, that is, whether they dealt with theory or structure, whenever test passing resulted in reinforcement the average number of tests taken and tests passed increased to a significant degree. Conversely, when reinforcement was discontinued for test passing, inmates rarely took tests.

Under the baseline conditions in Phase I, less than one theory or structure test was passed per week. However, under Phase II (when passing the theory tests at 80% or better led to an earning of 100 points) the average weekly total of theory tests passed increased from 0.9 to 12.25 for the seven inmates. The average weekly number of structure tests passed, which did not lead to any point earning, dropped from 0.25 per week to zero over the first two phases. Table 12 summarizes this data.

When the reinforcement contingencies were reversed, test taking behavior also reversed. In Phase III, when passing structure tests led to reinforcement, both taking and passing structure tests increased to a significant level. On the other hand, the number of theory tests taken fell to zero when reinforcement was withdrawn.

DISCUSSION

The findings in the vocational area extend to those obtained in the academic one. The conclusion from each is strengthened by the other.

Table 12.   The Effects of Incentives on Mastery of Auto Mechanics Material

Phase	Theory Tests		Structure Tests	
	Incentives		No Incentives	
I	Taken	Passed	Taken	Passed
	1.6	0.9	0.25	0.25
	Incentives		No Incentives	
II	Taken	Passed	Taken	Passed
	15	12.25	0	0
	Incentives		No Incentives	
III	Taken	Passed	Taken	Passed
	0	0	19.15	14.15

Specifically, the role of incentives in encouraging the inmates to engage in vocational training was as critical as it was for their academic performance. The traditional approach to rehabilitation emphasizes the influence of the instructor's leadership on the good attitude and general interest on the inmates' self-help efforts. Similarly, it is often assumed that most inmates will want to improve themselves and that the combination of concerned instructors and a motivated inmate will maximize the chances of the inmate's active participation in the rehabilitation program. However, it is known that even with the instructor's dedication and the inmate's good intentions the rehabilitation program will fail unless it includes a structured and well-developed curriculum.

In this study, the instructor acknowledged the importance of each of these factors and, moreover, acted accordingly. They were accessible to inmates as both tutor in a subject matter and unofficial counselor for discussion of the inmates' personal problems. They did everything within their power to encourage the inmates to pursue vocational training conscientiously. In addition, they collaborated with the research staff in the development of a structured training curriculum and a method for evaluating progress. Finally, the inmates themselves expressed the sincere desire to do well in the course and to quickly master the skills of the journeyman auto mechanic.

Despite what would appear to be an optimal basis for success in vocational training, the results of this study indicate that these ingredients, although necessary, are not sufficient to insure high performance in the training situation. An additional and powerful factor seems to be the inclusion of incentives to insure that inmates will work toward and meet the goals specified in the curriculum. In the absence of incentives, it is likely that the combined efforts of the training staff and the inmates will not succeed as shown in the failure of inmates to take and pass tests during the no-incentive conditions in this study.

Study 2: Decreasing the Amount of Errors
in Acquiring Haircutting Skills

The next step in extending the findings from the academic area to vocational training was to incorporate the barber training program into the motivational system. The barbering trade was selected because of the instructor's dissatisfaction with the progress made by inmates in using a special apparatus for teaching barbering skills. The mechanical skill apparatus was designed to train perceptual-motor coordination. On it, a metal stylus is run through several cut out patterns in the apparatus with an error scored each time the boundary is touched. It was the instructor's experience that despite his best efforts, the trainees appeared to make more than what he considered to be an acceptable number of errors and he requested assistance to reduce these errors to a minimum.

METHOD

Inmates and Setting.   There were eight inmates enrolled in a 12-month barbering program. The barbering curriculum was well designed and combined texts; audiovisual materials such as 8 mm films, slides synchronized with cassette tape recordings of barbering procedures and techniques; the skill apparatus; and on-the-job training working as a barber in the prison barbershop under the supervision of the instructor who was himself an experienced barber.

PROCEDURE AND EVALUATION

The trainees in the barbering trade could earn points. Points were awarded on the basis of 2 points per customer and 5 points per day for using the skill apparatus with a bonus of 15 points awarded to the man with the fewest errors each day. In addition, passing written tests at a level of 80% or better correct earned a trainee 5 points. For each additional test passed during a week, the points earned were doubled. Points were recorded each day for a period of one week and were turned in to the MORE office each Monday. Trainees picked up earned points the following day.

The effect of contingent reinforcement was evaluated by performance on the skill apparatus, as defined by the number of errors, as well as by the number of inmates who used the apparatus under no incentive (Phase I) and incentive conditions (Phase II) as previously described.

RESULTS AND DISCUSSION

Contingent reinforcement for low error scores decreased total number of errors on the skill apparatus to less than one-third its original level. The number of trainees using the apparatus showed a slight increase. Table 13 summarizes the data of the study.

The results of this study once again support the general findings with academic performance as well as those involving automotive training. While the previous study showed the importance of incentives in developing theoretical and practical knowledge related to a vocational trade, this study adds a critical component of vocational training, namely the refinement of practical skills.

The inmates' disinterest in matters involving knowledge of the theory and structure of automobile engines might be explained on the grounds that inmates did not see the relevance of such training. It would be expected, however, that the more practical, less theoretical, the training, the less need there would be for artificial incentives to motivate the trainees. Such was not the case. Even a practical skill bearing close and obvious relationship to competence in the trade was not practiced and mastered for its own sake. Only when this vocational training exercise was incorporated within the motivational system did the inmates practice and master the skills involved.

Additional Applications of the
Motivational System in Vocational Training

In an effort to enhance the effectiveness of the entire vocational training, a variety of trade areas were also included within the scope of the

Table 13. Weekly Averages of Number of Errors and Number of Trainees Using Skill Apparatus during Baseline and during the Incentive Period[a]

	Phase I: No Reinforcement	Phase II: Skill Test Reinforcement
Average number of errors	44.5	20.5
Average number of trainees using skill apparatus	5	6

[a] $N = 8$.

MORE motivational system. A brief description of each of these areas now follows:

Building maintenance: Six-month program. It included two months' training in each of three subareas: carpentry, plumbing, and electricity.

Drafting: Twelve-month program. It included drawing, designing, and constructing signs and performing special assignments on the prison grounds.

Masonry: Twelve-month program. It included as typical assignments laying brick walkways or erecting brick walls or siding on prison buildings.

Small engine repairs: Six-month program. It included making repairs of home lawn mowers and equivalent small engines.

Welding: Six-month program. It included periodic opportunities to do "live" welding when such assistance was requested by the prison maintenance.

According to inmates and instructors, the motivational system seemed to help individual trainees in each of these vocational areas. Still, one of the major objectives of the MORE program was not met within the relatively brief funding period for this program. Specifically, a comprehensive behavioral approach to training vocational skills in these areas was not undertaken. In addition to the time constraint mentioned previously, three factors compounded the difficulties encountered in extending behavioral procedures to all vocational areas.

First, the necessity of identifying the various components of the skills involved revealed difficulties in the instructor's ability to identify and describe exactly what was being taught.

Secondly, the daily progress of training efforts depended solely on the impression of the instructors and making their criteria public was not regarded as an important issue. Because an effective motivational system depends upon clear and explicit definition of behavioral requirements and systematic monitoring of progress, it follows that in the absence of these, the instructors could not consistently implement reinforcing procedures.

Thirdly, a few of the instructors in charge of these additional vocational areas were at best indifferent and at worst resistant to the use of the motivational system. Consequently, it was unlikely that even a perfectly designed motivational system would succeed without considerable staff training and attitude change.

This experience underscores the importance of a systematic approach to rehabilitation. Unless all directly involved are committed to the behavioral program and its goals, it will fail to realize its full potential and may, in some instances, prove to be counterproductive.

The previous studies have shown that academic performance and vocational performance as well as preferences for specific academic and vocational content material can be influenced by a systematic incentive program. Up to this point, the stress has been on increasing the likelihood of the inmates engaging in positive rehabilitative activities. However, another use of this incentive program has been aimed at encouraging inmates to develop and practice appropriate personal attributes and skills that will help maximize their potential in the labor market. The manner in which these concerns were addressed is described in detail in the following section.

TEACHING EMPLOYABILITY SKILLS

The preceding studies focused on developing in inmates a wide range of academic and vocational skills. Admittedly, these efforts reflect the major objective pursued in both projects, namely the inmates' rehabilitation.

As important as academic and vocational skills are, they will be of only marginal benefit to the released offender in the absence of appropriate personal habits and employable skills which enable the individual to secure, hold, and advance in a job. Employability skills include personal responsibility and good work habits such as acceptable personal appearance, punctuality, seeking permission before leaving the job, working responsibly under minimal supervision, accepting and acting upon constructive criticism from supervisory personnel and following rules and regulations.

Since these skills are generally accepted as important, both behavioral programs provided systematic experiences to allow inmates to acquire and practice them. Several studies were undertaken to demonstrate the contribution of a positive approach which deemphasized coercive control to develop personal responsibility and employability skills.

I. PERSONAL RESPONSIBILITY

These studies involved activities that are important for daily living, both in an institution, and to a greater or lesser extent in the community. They were: (*a*) getting up on time, (*b*) making their beds, (*c*) cleaning their living area, and (*d*) maintaining an acceptable level of personal hygiene and appearance. These four activities may be subsumed under the rubric of "personal responsibility." It was the objective of this series of studies to investigate various methods of fostering these forms of personal responsibility. In addition, these studies offered the inmates an incentive to practice and strengthen general skills, such as attending to directions, following instructions, accepting constructive criticism, and working toward task completion, that would augment the specific vocational skills taught elsewhere.

One of the first opportunities to give credibility to the positive approach to day-to-day inmate management and employability skill training came when a staff member maintained that inmates lacked discipline and were lackadaisical about doing such expected routines as getting up in the morning and making their beds.

Study 1: A Comparison of Positive Feedback vs. Routine Management Procedures on Personal Responsibility

In the course of studies involving the positive approach to inmate management problems, it was often suggested that the only kind of treatment for such behavior was that based on coercive techniques. This is a widely held view as discussed in Chapter 8. It was not surprising, therefore, that the correctional officer assigned to the cellblock maintained that he could improve inmate performance if given the opportunity to do so. In attempt to compare the positive approach based on feedback and social reinforcement with the officer's best efforts employing coercive techniques, the following study was undertaken. (For more details concerning this and the following two studies, see Milan & McKee, 1976.)

METHOD

Inmates and Setting.   An average of 22 inmates participated in this study each day that it was in effect. These inmates also participated in the subsequent studies to be discussed. All studies took place in the EMLC cellblock.

PROCEDURE AND EVALUATION

The scoring criteria for the four morning activities were explained to each inmate and posted on the token economy cellblock bulletin board. The inmates were informed that they were expected to complete each activity each day and that their performance would be recorded.

Positive Feedback 1.   During this condition, the correctional officer toured the token economy cellblock between 5:30 and 7:30 a.m. on weekdays. He carried data collection forms attached to a clipboard and openly recorded the activities completed by each inmate. The officer also provided feedback, prompts, and social reinforcement to the inmates. No tokens were awarded. Inmates were informed of whether or not their performance of the morning activities met the scoring criteria. If an activity did not meet the performance criterion, the correctional officer instructed the inmate on how to correct his performance and encouraged him to do so. If an activity met the performance criterion, the officer acknowledged and praised the inmate's performance. The correctional officer refrained from the various coercive techniques typically employed to motivate performance in correctional institutions. No intimidation, threats, ultimatums, restrictions, extra work assignments, or disciplinary reports were employed during this condition.

Routine Management. This condition was introduced to evaluate the effect of traditional institutional control procedures upon the performance of the four morning activities. During this condition, the correctional officer employed many of the procedures used in the remainder of the institution to motivate inmate performance—intimidation, threats, ultimatums, curses, and extra work on the token economy cellblock. The correctional officer was not given complete freedom, however, to employ the *full range* of coercive procedures potentially available to him. He was not permitted to write disciplinary reports (for these could result in an inmate's transfer to another cellblock within the institution), or recommend placement in primitive isolation, transfer to another institution within the state system, or the loss of "good time."

Positive Feedback 2. This condition was identical to the *Positive Feedback 1* condition.

RESULTS AND DISCUSSION

Contrary to the officer's expectations, his best efforts had no effect upon the activities subsumed under personal responsibility: to wit, getting up on time, making their beds, cleaning their living areas, and maintaining an acceptable level of personal hygiene and appearance. During the eleven days of the *Positive Feedback 1* condition, the mean percentage of morning activities that met performance criteria was 66.4%. A mean of 63.7% of the four morning activities met criteria during the nine days of the *Routine Management* condition, wherein the correctional officer attempted to insure their performance. This was not significantly different from the previous level of performance.

During the five-day *Positive Feedback 2* condition, the mean percentage of morning activities meeting the performance criteria was 68.6%. This was not significantly different from the level of performance observed under either the *Positive Feedback 1* condition or the *Routine Management* condition.

A possible explanation of the preceding results is that they are to be expected given the barren and impoverished conditions in which prison inmates are forced to live. Indeed, the argument might be made that, rather than increasing the use of coercive methods, a more humane and effective approach to improving personal responsibility might be to reduce the hardship and discomfort of inmates by providing the daily amenities of life.

Study 2: Improving the Quality of Life
and its Effects on Personal Responsibility

It is the presence or absence of such amenities as razor blades, coffee, cigarettes, and snacks that appears to have the greatest impact on the maintenance of human dignity and self-respect (Solshenitzin, 1974). Therefore, it would seem logical that in providing such amenities to inmates, one would increase their motivation to care for and do things for themselves. The goal of this study was to provide such amenities and determine its effects upon personal responsibility.

METHOD

Baseline: No Points.   Because there were no differences in performance across the three phases of the previous study, the data from these three conditions were combined and employed as the overall pre–token economy baseline against which to compare the effects of the various token economy conditions. A mean percentage of 65.9% of the morning activities was completed during the 25 days of this pre–token economy period.

Unconditional Award of Points.   Throughout this condition, 60 EMLC points allotted for each of the four morning activities were awarded on a noncontingent basis (i.e., independent of whether or not the inmate's performance of the activities met the established criteria). The token economy was begun and EMLC points were awarded from the first day of this condition. Beginning on the second day of this condition, inmates could exchange points to obtain the extra amenities which served as the backup reinforcers of the token economy. This procedure greatly increased the quality of life for the inmates residing on the token economy cellblock.

Either the correctional officer assigned to the token economy cellblock or a project staff member toured the cellblock each morning, rated the performance of the morning activities, and provided feedback, prompts, and verbal reinforcement (no intimidations, threats, or ultimatums were allowed). Each inmate was instructed to add 240 points (60 for each of the four morning activities) to his bank account regardless of whether or not he performed the morning activities. The points were then credited to the account of each inmate present on the cellblock that day, and they appeared on the next day's posted point record in the columns allocated to the four morning activities. Inmates not present on the token economy cellblock for one reason or another (e.g., in the infirmary, transferred to a county jail for a court appearance) were not awarded the noncontingent points. In actual practice, this was an infrequent occurrence.

RESULTS AND DISCUSSION

Providing additional amenities on a noncontingent basis did not have an enduring, positive effect on performance. Although the mean percentage of morning activities completed during the 35 days of this condition was higher than the average during the pre–token economy period, there was only an initial improvement in the performance following the introduction of the token economy. This improvement was transitory, with performance during the latter half of the condition (67.0%) being lower than that during the first half (82.0%) and equal to that of the pre–token economy baseline (65.9%).

This study indicates that the introduction of the token economy and the unconditional award of amenities *per se* had a facilitative effect upon the performance of the four morning activities. This improvement was short-lived, with the level of performance gradually returning to that observed during the baseline periods.

Contrary to common notions about overcoming the debilitating effects of imprisonment, raising the quality of the inmates' lives was not accompanied by an increase in personal responsibility. This is not to be taken as an indictment of attempts to improve living conditions within prisons. Indeed, all will agree that at the very least society has the moral responsibility to insure that those whom it incarcerates are treated in a dignified, humane, and responsible way. It merely points out the need to arrange contingent relationships between improvements in living conditions with meaningful work and increased responsibility—as generally exists in a free society.

Study 3: The Conditional Award of Points

The results of the preceding study are not peculiar to the inmate population. Research with other populations, including the mentally ill, indicates that unconditional award of amenities lead to gradual deterioration of the individual's performance (see Ayllon & Azrin, 1968). The question remains of how to both create a humane environment and at the same time foster individual responsibility through other than coercive means. The following study attempted to determine if this twofold objective could be met by the conditional award of amenities.

PROCEDURE AND EVALUATION

Baseline: Unconditional Award of Points.   Since unconditional award of points had only a short-lived effect, baseline for this study was the last portion of the last condition of the previous study.

Conditional Award of Points.   During this condition, 60 EMLC points were awarded on a contingent basis for each of the four morning activities (i.e., only when performance met the established criteria). The correctional officer or staff member on duty each morning toured the token economy cellblock, recorded the performance of the activities, and provided feedback, prompts, and verbal reinforcement. They instructed inmates to add points to their accounts only when the performance of one or more of the activities met the established criteria. When the performance of an inmate was below criterion, the particular deficiencies were indicated and the inmate was encouraged to remedy them. Points were awarded and the activity(ies) recorded as performed if and when an inmate remedied the indicated deficiencies.

RESULTS AND DISCUSSION

When amenities were made conditional on meeting a specific criterion of personal responsibility, the inmates' performance increased from an average of 67.07% during baseline to 86.0% during the performance-contingent period. Moreover, the performance of the activities improved over the course of this condition, with the mean percentage completed during the second half (93.3%) being significantly higher than that of the first half (78.6%). The introduction of the performance-contingent award of tokens appears to have precipitated an improvement in performance, with approximately 90% or more of the activities typically completed during the last 14 days of this condition. This was a level of performance that was markedly higher than that of any previous period.

The findings of this study show that it is indeed possible to create both a humane environment and concurrently foster individual responsibility. This twofold objective was met through the use of conditional amenities. It should be pointed out that these same amenities had been used in the study prior to this one and found ineffective in fostering individual responsibility. The critical difference between these two studies was that the amenities were in one case available unconditionally, and in the other case these were available on a conditional basis. The conditional or unconditional amenities were equally welcomed and enjoyed by all inmates, and they raised the living standards, equally. From the point of view of society's moral responsibility to insure all inmates a humane existence both methods of providing amenities were equally effective. The decision to use one method over another rests on different grounds.

The conditional award of amenities fosters personal responsibility while the unconditional award does not. In addition, the inmate learns to hold himself responsible for the consequences of his own behavior because the relationship between what amenities he enjoys and the activities he chooses to engage in is explicit, straightforward, and experiential.

Finally, the major feature of conditional award of amenities is that it gives the inmate a measure of dignity by allowing him the opportunity to choose what he will and will not do and what amenities he will and will not enjoy. Virtually all inmates choose to maximize the extent of their amenities by choosing to perform all the tasks and activities available to them that earned them those amenities. In providing a situation that allowed for choice, the inmate found that his choices were respected and his dignity as a human being was enhanced.

II. WORK HABITS

An examination of the market place and its employment practices reveals two major reasons for emphasizing the training of work habits. First, the individual lacking good work habits will either be prevented from advancing in his job or, more likely, he will be dismissed no matter how competent his technical skills. Second, individuals with the highest degree of employability skills will not only be retained but probably become candidates for accelerated on-the-job training and advancement often with little reference to their previous technical training. Consistent with this general concern with employability skills, the two research projects (EMLC and MORE) included work habits in their training.

Admittedly, the most desirable context and setting within which to conduct this training would be an actual job outside the prison. Since such a situation was out of the question in these two projects, the projects faced two alternatives: to deny the inmates the potential benefits of such training or to approximate in the prison the major characteristics and requirements of real employment so that employability training could be conducted.

Both projects, independently of one another, opted for the second alternative. The next question to be answered was, how was this training to be done. The EMLC project chose to systematically train supervisory personnel in behavioral principles and rely upon them to develop specific procedures to train inmates. The MORE project, on the other hand, chose to consult with the staff to develop inmate training procedures and then instruct the supervisory personnel on how to carry them out.

Training Supervisory Personnel:
The EMLC Approach to Teaching Good Work Habits

Forward-looking correctional administrators have acknowledged and are beginning to act upon the generally accepted notion that they develop the management and interpersonal skills of their correctional staff so that the correctional officer and other line personnel may more effectively join and contribute to the rehabilitative effort. However, the administrator attempting to implement such a program is forced to choose among a growing variety of treatment philosophies and regimes, each typically offered as the most desirable of all alternatives but lacking anything more than the fervor of its adherents to substantiate its desirability.

The preceding sections of the book have presented evidence that documents the potential contribution of behavioral programming to the rehabilitation of the adult offender. Stemming from the EMLC's work in inmate training programs was an understanding of the key position held by correctional officers in any institutional effort to teach employability skills. The EMLC's Correctional Officer Training project sought to assess the correctional officer's potential to fulfill this role while at the same time demonstrating the value of a behavioral approach to the teaching of good work habits. (For more details see Smith, Milan, Wood, & McKee, 1976.)

There were 40 correctional officers who participated in the 90-hour training program. All were volunteers and most of these officers supervised inmates in prison jobs much as foremen do in real jobs outside the prison. For example, among the officers were men in charge of the kitchen, laundry, clothing room, and farm squads. The officers ranged in age from 23 to 67 years, with a median age of 50 years. The reported education level ranged from the seventh grade to one year of college with the median grade completed being the eleventh. Tested education levels (Tests of Adult Basic Education) indicated a mean grade level of 6.7, with a range of 3.2 to 10.9. Approximately 90% of the officers had lived the greater portion of their lives in Alabama, 65% of those in Elmore County (the location of Draper), and 35% in bordering counties, most of which, like Elmore County, are agrarian communities.

The teaching team, which was composed of a research psychologist, a criminologist, and an information specialist, employed a three-phase approach to training: preplanning session, teaching session, and review session. The preplanning session was designed primarily as a brainstorming period during which possible strategies for each daily presentation were discussed and the teaching program was formalized. The teaching session was conducted on a seminar basis in order to stimulate active discussion. Critical sessions were videotaped for critiquing purposes and to facilitate revisions.

During the initial stages of each cycle of training, the sessions were three hours in duration and were conducted three days per week. Each cycle began with a problem-census of officers so that their special needs and job requirements could be considered along with training topics. These sessions gave the team a vehicle by which to list and recognize officers' concerns, thereby increasing their effectiveness as reinforcing agents. Here too, the officers' fixed attitudes and idealized notions about prison rules were discussed. The remaining sessions were directed toward seminar presentation of behavior modification principles and techniques. The training curriculum covered the following: identifying, defining, observing, recording, and graphing behaviors; positive reinforcement; punishment; timeout; escape; avoidance; extinction; stimulus control; schedules of reinforcement and fading.

Following their formalized classroom participation, the correctional officers embarked upon the practicum phase of training. Here, the group of 15 officers was broken down into five-man groups to meet with the training staff in one-hour sessions, three days per week. During the practicum phase inmates were taught by the participating correctional officers specific employability skills: punctuality, obtaining permission before leaving the job, working responsibility with minimal supervision, and so forth. The practicum phase provided the officers experience in using behavioral techniques within the institution, and allowed the teaching team to assess the officers' effectiveness in employing those techniques under supervised conditions.

PUNCTUALITY

A common problem faced by correctional officers in supervisory positions is that of encouraging inmates to report to work on time. In this case, the officer in charge of the clothing room was faced with this problem. He indicated that nearly half of his men were late for work every day and that the "conventional" methods of encouraging promptness either did not work or were not practical in his situation. Quite often, as a routine policy, a deviant is threatened with transfer to a less desirable job if he does not straighten up, but in this situation the officer was reluctant to follow through with this threat because the men under his care were good workers "once they got started."

Thirteen days of baseline recording revealed that the officer was indeed experiencing a high percentage of tardiness in his workers. The median percent of men on time during these 13 days was only 57%. The correction phase consisted of announcing to the workers that the officer was concerned with all men arriving on time and starting together because each man's job was dependent upon the others, and that if one or two men were not there, it retarded the work of all. He further announced that all men who arrived on time would be let off at the end of the eight-hour shift, and the latecomers would have to report again for the evening shift (an additional two hours). The prompt inmates would, in effect, be able to get off work earlier than they normally would, while latecomers would have to carry the two-hour evening shift with less than a full staff.

The results revealed that the correction procedure initiated on day 14 was highly effective—the median number of men reporting on time increased from 57% to 85%, which the median test indicates is a significant improvement ($X^2 = 12.85$, $df = 1$, $p < .05$).

However, it was impossible at this stage to determine whether it was the officer's emphasis upon promptness and the team work which resulted in the shift in performance, or if it was the contingency earning the privilege of leaving on time with no further work assignment. During the third phase the officer returned to the work schedule in force during the first 13 days of the project; that is, all men were required to be on time and worked the entire eight-hour shift, plus an additional two hours in the evening. The return to the baseline condition resulted in a significant deterioration of promptness as is indicated by the median test ($X^2 = 8.37$, $df = 1$, $p < .05$).

These findings reveal that it was the correction procedure itself and the systematic application of the specified contingencies that gave the correctional officer the power to become a change agent in the institution. Baseline data revealed that, by and large, the officer could identify problem areas but that without the added power provided him through the systematic use of behavior techniques and procedures, he could only maintain the status quo. The level of performance evident during baseline reveals the effect of his "best effort" prior to the applications of the methodology taught in the training project.

LEAVING THE JOB WITHOUT PERMISSION

Another problem was reported by the kitchen steward. He stated that a small number of men left the kitchen area without authorization for varying periods of time. Like the officer in charge of the clothing room, however, he was reluctant to have the men transferred to a less desirable job because they had been through the lengthy training regimen necessary for kitchen work and, hence, were too valuable to lose.

Ten days of baseline indicated that the number of unauthorized absences each eight-hour day ranged from zero to three, with a median of one. The officer indicated that two men were responsible for the majority of the absences, and that, since he only spot checked, he was sure that he was not catching all such absences. The correction phase was initiated on the eleventh day when the officer informed all workers that he expected each man to work a full eight hours. Unless they asked and received permission to leave, any man found missing would be required to make up the time at the end of the shift. In effect, inmates identified as absent without authorization would be kept late for a period of time equal to the time absent as estimated by the steward.

The results indicate that during the 10 days in which the correction procedure was in effect there was a marked drop in the number of unauthorized absences. The median test indicates that this drop was significant ($\chi^2 = 4.54$, $df = 1$, $p < .05$). In addition, the 5 days recorded in the return-to-baseline condition suggests that the 10 days of treatment had a lasting effect, with the differences between the latter two phases not significant ($\chi^2 = .60$, $df = 1$, $p > .05$).

WORKING RESPONSIBLY WITH MINIMAL SUPERVISION

"Fred H. cannot be changed." This was the unanimous opinion of the officers in training. He had been around the institution for years and all efforts to work with him had failed. "Fred is just plain sorry. He's a goldbrick. He won't work. Sent him to the 'dog house,' put him on a good job (the kitchen), put him on a bad job (the farm), and it has no effect. He will not cooperate. All Fred likes to do is sit on his bunk, talk, and play cards." Threats, punitive isolation, sometimes for as long as 21 days, withdrawal of privileges, and so on would not make him a conscientious employee.

Fred's assignment was that of a hall sweeper. His task was to keep the main hall of the institution clean from 6 a.m. until 10 p.m. (a coveted job, for it entailed at most a total of four hours' work and was an "inside job"). The correctional officer who supervised him for a portion of the day indicated that Fred was not performing satisfactorily. The officer said he spent more time looking for Fred to bring him to his job than Fred spent working. Neither sincere "talking to" nor threats yielded any improvements. Seven days of baseline recording of the number of times the officer had to look for Fred produced a median rate of slightly more than once every two hours. Ideally, Fred would "keep an eye" on the hall, clean it when necessary, and thereby comply with the requirements of his assignment.

The correction procedure, which began on the eighth day, stressed "time out" from those things which Fred appeared to enjoy: talking with his friends and playing cards. This was accomplished by finding Fred when necessary, having him sweep the hall, then sitting in the corner of the guard's office for 30 minutes, having him sweep the floor again, and releasing him. The officers were in accord—"this would not work," for long periods of punitive isolation, extra work, and so forth had not. However, the median number of times the officer had to search Fred out during the correction phase dropped to zero, a significant improvement in his behavior as indicated by the median test ($\chi^2 = 10.03$, $df = 1$, $p < .05$). The return to baseline phase produced a slight deterioration in Fred's performance ($\chi^2 = 5.08$, $df = 1$, $p < .05$).

This basic behavior modification procedure appears to have the potential of being as effective in the correctional institution as it has been demonstrated to be in other settings. Moreover, the behavior during the second baseline condition was superior to that during the first baseline, indicating that treatment had a long-lasting effect. Indeed, Fred's improvement resulted in his transfer to one of the most desirable jobs in the institution, where he continued to show the employability skills acquired and practiced as a hall sweeper. Finally, the officer who implemented this program (convinced as he was that it would not work) earned the "prestigious" distinction of being the only man in the institution who could change Fred H.

Staff Consultation:
The MORE Approach to Teaching Good Work Habits

To develop work habits, the MORE project emphasized the instruction of specific procedures, rather than teaching behavioral principles to the supervisory personnel as in the EMLC projects. Two jobs were selected for study; one involved janitorial service and the other kitchen work. These jobs shared many of the same work components that the inmates are likely to encounter in a job situation. There are three major characteristics of a job situation: (a) the individual worker has been assigned a given task and is familiar with his duties, (b) there is supervisory personnel or some one person who is responsible for seeing that the worker's duties are carried out as assigned, and (c) there is a modicum of communication between the worker and the supervisor.

Performance of normal work behaviors by institutionalized persons has often been studied. Ayllon and Azrin (1968a), precisely defined and measured the component behaviors for which each worker was responsible and applied consequences objectively to the satisfactory completion of these behaviors. Ratings of performance represent an alternative method with at least two advantages: (a) Practicality. Supervisors can easily use such a procedure because it would not add to their already overburdened duties. (b) Relevance. A rating procedure duplicates the conditions in "free world" job settings, to which the inmates would eventually be exposed. Most dishwashers, for example, are not paid according to how many dishes they wash, but by how well their supervisor rates their work. This rating procedure, therefore, was selected as a means to evaluate teaching employability skills to inmates indirectly.

METHOD

Inmates and Setting.   Twenty semiskilled and unskilled workers in food service and 15 unskilled workers in the janitorial service area participated in the study five days each week. Inmates ranged in age from 18 to 54 and length of prior imprisonment from two months to 20 years. There was a supervisor for each area: the steward in food service and a correctional officer in the janitorial area.

Ratings of Worker's Attitude and Performance.   Both supervisors made daily ratings of the work performance and attitude of each of their workers. Work performance consisted generally of performing the required duties for that position. Attitude consisted of social behavior and interpersonal interactions which could occur on the job. Ratings were made on a four-point basis: excellent, good, satisfactory, and poor. Attitude and performance were each rated separately. Ratings were based on whatever specifics or generalities the supervisor attended to. No attempt was made to define *a priori* behavioral criteria for each rating, but each supervisor was allowed to use his own judgment and experience in assigning ratings. Thus, criteria were subjectively established by the supervisor as would be the case in the free world.

Points were earned each day according to the rating in each of two categories: work attitude and job performance. Point earnings were as follows:

Rating: Points:
  Excellent   10 points
  Good   5 points
  Satisfactory   2 points
  Poor   0 points

Although daily ratings were not publicly posted, each supervisor gave specific feedback to any inmate who inquired as to his daily evaluation. Points were accumulated daily and entered into the inmate's account three times a week.

The evaluation design in this study was as follows. First, a preincentive period was conducted in both areas during which ratings were taken but no points were earned. Next, points were made contingent upon the daily ratings in food service and janitorial area, respectively. During the period in which men could earn points, performance sampling checks were taken periodically on each of 10 consecutive working days by the staff in order to assess the relationship between ratings and observed work performance. Performance sampling was monitored by randomly observing the work performance of half of the men in each area. There were two different measurement procedures. In the janitorial maintenance area, the specific duties for which each of these workers was responsible were obtained from their supervisor. Each of these men was observed for three consecutive minutes from 4 to 10 times daily and scored as being "on-task" or "off-task." A percentage of time on-task behavior was computed for each man and a mean percentage of time on-task behavior for the group was thus computed. In food service, because job responsibilities sometimes overlapped, a different procedure was used to measure work performance. The job hours for each worker were obtained from the supervisor and each worker was similarly rated as "on-task" or "off-task," depending on whether or not he was present in his work area at any time during the three-minute observation period. Observations were conducted from 4 to 10 times daily. Again, a percentage of time on-task behavior for each man and a mean percentage of time on-task behavior for the group was computed.

RESULTS

When points were made contingent upon the level of ratings, the number of "excellent" ratings for both groups, cooks and janitors, increased substantially and almost immediately. During baseline, none of the 15 janitors received a rating of excellent in performance or work attitude. When incentives were available only to those who met criteria, every one of the 15 janitors received ratings of excellent in both performance and attitude.

On the other hand, during baseline, 5 of 15 food service workers received excellent ratings for their attitude and performance. In food service, where there were some skilled jobs (e.g., cooks, butchers, and bakers), there was a great deal of variability in the percentage of the workers who received excellent ratings during the "no points" condition. This ranged from 0 to 52%. When points were made available, however, all 15 food service trainees received excellent ratings.

Supervisors only once or twice made distinctions between job performance and on-the-job attitude. Generally, excellent ratings in work attitude were accompanied with excellent ratings in performance. The performance samples taken by the staff showed that a high-percentage of the behavior of the inmates was on-task, thus supporting the suggestion that ratings given by the supervisors closely reflected actual work performance.

DISCUSSION

The availability of points resulted in more satisfactory job performance and in an apparently improved attitude for institutional maintenance workers. In addition, the extent to which the performance samples closely followed the ratings suggests that such a procedure may be a practical and valid alternative to more rigorous and time-consuming measurement.

Comments from supervisors and inmate workers were sought via interviews. This information indicated that supervisors viewed, as the major benefit of the motivational system, the resultant improvement in inmates' attitudes. As one explained, "I could always get them to do their work (through threat, punishment, etc.), but now they do it without back talk, or trying to avoid it. They usually do it right the first time, too." It is of interest to note that this particular supervisor, who was a correctional officer, had been the subject of many inmate complaints concerning his attitude toward them. The frequency of such complaints was drastically reduced when he began to rate performance and give points to his workers. The interviews also indicated that no supervisor wished to discontinue giving points. In fact, in some cases, the supervisors requested that they be allowed to increase the amount of points they could give out.

The inmates' interview responses were similar to the supervisors' in that the workers unanimously appreciated the motivational system and wanted it to continue. Most importantly, they felt that the point system improved their interpersonal relationship with their supervisors.

The results of this study also indicated that there was about 80% correspondence between the actual performance of the job and the rating given by the supervisor. This should not be surprising since a rating is a reflection of a general impression of what the individual has done. This, of course, is largely the method used to give feedback in the free world because it is both practical and inexpensive.

Following Rules and Regulations

This study conducted in the EMLC cellblock paralleled the one conducted by the MORE program in that the token economy system was used to foster improved work habits. A time clock and timecard rack were located adjacent to the entrance/exit of the EMLC token economy cellblock. Inmates were expected to record the times at which they left and returned to the token economy cellblock throughout the day, in much the same way as an employee is expected to record the time he leaves and returns to the job in industry. At the end of each day, the number of minutes each inmate had spent off the cellblock during the hours of operation of the token economy were computed and charged to his checking account.

A staff member made aperiodic rounds of the cellblock, recorded the names of the inmates present, and checked them against the timecards. If an inmate was identified as having left the token economy cellblock without recording his departure time, the staff member entered the last time the inmate could be identified as being present. The time was either the time of the preceding attendance check or the last time the inmate had recorded his return to the cellblock, whichever was the most recent. The interval between then and the time of his return was included in the total time charged to him for being away from the cellblock. This procedure invariably resulted in the expenditure of more points for each detected violation than if the established procedure had been followed.

The time clock violations described previously appeared, in general, to be acts of commission rather than acts of omission. When confronted, the violators typically offered no excuse. When pressed, they explained that the staff failed to detect the majority of their violations and that, in the long run, the violators were coming out ahead of those who followed the prescribed procedure. That is, by slipping off the token economy cellblock for short periods of time without punching out, they were saving more points than were being charged to their accounts when their violations were detected. Indeed, the entire matter took on the characteristics of a game between the inmates and staff. The inmates attempted to judge whether or not an attendance check was imminent and the staff attempted to increase their unpredictability in order to detect as many violations as possible.

A number of procedures were considered to reduce the number of time clock violations. The simplest was to increase the frequency of attendance checks. This would detect a greater portion of the violations and, hopefully, make repeated violations more costly than following the established procedures. This procedure was not feasible, however, for the staff had additional duties that would suffer if it was followed. A second possibility was to leave the frequency of attendance checks unchanged but to increase the costs of detected violations. This alternative was not adopted either, primarily due to the staff's general preference for a positive reinforcement strategy rather than a punitively oriented response cost procedure. Rather than examining the effect of increasing the response cost for violations of the time clock rule, it was decided to assess the feasibility of reducing the number of violations by employing the same reinforcer that was assumed to be maintaining the rule violations, namely free time off the cellblock.

METHOD

The definition of the time clock violation was unchanged: Any inmate who was identified during an attendance check as having left the token economy cellblock without punching the departure time on his card during the hours the token economy was in operation was charged with a violation. An inmate could accumulate any number of violations each day. The total number of violations detected was determined for each day. This value was then converted to a rate measure by dividing it by the number of inmates on the token economy cellblock census that day and then dividing the resultant value by the number of hours the token economy was in effect for that day. This transformation compensated for fluctuations in daily census and allowed comparisons between weekdays, during which the token economy was in operation for seven hours per day, and weekends and holidays, during which the token economy was in operation sixteen hours per day.

Inmates and Setting.   The setting was the EMLC cellblock and the subjects were all inmates residing on the cellblock each day.

Prior to this study, the instructions to staff concerning the performance of attendance checks stated only that they were to perform an unannounced check on the average of every 30 to 45 minutes. In order to both insure that checks were made and to increase their unpredictability, the attendance check procedure was formalized in this study. An interval timer was made available and each of the seven 10-minute increment values between 0 and 60 minutes, inclusive, was recorded on a separate card. At the start of the shift, the staff member responsible for the token economy cellblock was to perform an attendance check, record the violations detected, shuffle the seven cards, select one, and set the interval timer to the value prescribed by the selected card. The ringing of the timer signified another check was due, and the procedure was repeated. If the card bearing the zero value was selected, a check was performed immediately. This procedure insured that attendance checks were virtually unpredictable by the inmates, were systematically conducted by all staff members, and performed, on the average, every 30 minutes throughout each shift.

Baseline 1: Formal Attendance Check.   The formalized data collection procedures described previously were implemented on the first day of this condition and continued through the entire second phase and half of the third phase of the experiment. The steps followed when an inmate was detected in violation of the policy concerning leaving the token economy cellblock were unchanged. As was described previously, when an inmate was identified as having left the cellblock without recording the departure time on the timecard provided for this purpose, the staff member detecting the time clock violation entered the latest time the inmate could be identified as having been present on the unit. The inmate was then charged, at the standard rate of one point per minute, for the time between then and the time at which he returned. At the end of each day, the total number of points each inmate expended to gain access to the remainder of the institution was deducted from his checking account balance.

Reinforcement for Following Rules.   The same method of dealing with detected violations and the same data collection procedures were used in this period as were used in the preceding condition. However, a procedure that provided reinforcement to those who regularly recorded their departure times was introduced. Reinforcement consisted of time off the token economy cellblock at no charge, the same activity that was assumed to be maintaining rule violations. Beginning on each Sunday and continuing through the following Saturday, inmates earned one-half hour of free time off the cellblock each day that they recorded all their departure times. These half hours were accumulated and could be used as the inmates wished on the following Sunday. The attendance checks determined who did and did not earn the half hour of free time each day. Those who went the entire day without accruing a time clock violation were considered to have recorded all their departure times that day. Those who were identified as having left the cellblock one or more times on a particular day failed to earn that day's free half-hour. A record was posted on the cellblock bulletin board, and a cumulative total of the free time earned was maintained throughout the week for each inmate.

Baseline 2: Formal Attendance Check. The procedures followed during the first 14 days of this condition were identical to those followed during the *Baseline 1* condition. Beginning on the fifteenth day, the formalized recording procedure utilizing the interval timer and randomly selected intervals between attendance checks was discontinued. The project staff was instructed to return to the original procedure and again perform attendance checks on the average of every 30 to 45 minutes, as they saw fit. Follow-up was conducted on days 21, 26, and 34 of this condition, during which the formalized data collection procedure of the reinforcement condition was again employed in order to obtain an estimate of the longer-term effect of the reinforcement procedure.

RESULTS AND DISCUSSION

Table 14 shows that there were approximately four violations per day during the baseline period. This number was reduced drastically to approximately one violation every two days during the reinforcement condition and it remained at the same level even during the reinstatment of baseline conditions. The number of violations per day returned to approximately three during follow-up.

In contrast to previous studies, this study illustrates the kind of problem that often results with punitive behavior control measures.Specifically, when an individual appears to defy or actively seek to circumvent explicit and agreed upon regulations, the characteristic reaction in prison, for example, is to mete out punishment in the form of elimination of privileges. An alternative to these conventional methods would be to provide consistent positive supervision once the individual has acquired the desired skills so that they will be maintained. In the absence of

Table 14. Total Number of Rule Violations per Day

Phase	Number of Days	Total Number of Rule Violations	Rate
Baseline 1	14	55	3.9
Correction	21	13	.6
Baseline 2	14	10	.7
Follow-up	3	8	2.7

consistent management, the behavior of individuals, both in prison and in the market place, will gradually deteriorate and eventually become unacceptable once again.

GENERAL DISCUSSION

The series of studies concerning the acquisition of vocational skills emphasized three major characteristics of the behavioral approach: (a) the importance of breaking down the content of the vocational training into manageable units of learning; (b) the need for an explicit understanding between the instructors and the inmates regarding the instructor's expectations of what the inmates were to do and the inmates' anticipation of the rewards available for meeting such expectations; (c) the development of an instructional system that related the inmates' accomplishments to the instructor's rewards in a fair and consistent manner. Taken together, the results obtained from these series of studies indicate that inmates are interested in and responsive to vocational opportunities when these are undertaken in a climate of positive regard and reinforcement.

The preceding findings were not limited to content areas, such as auto mechanics and barbering. The same approach was found to be highly effective when complex social habits such as employability skills were taught. Indeed, studies concerning the teaching of employability skills indicate that inmates, like other workers, can learn and will practice critical work habits, such as punctuality, working conscientiously with minimal supervision, and satisfying supervisor's expectations. A work setting that employs positive incentives will foster these activities.

CHAPTER

11

SUPPLEMENTARY EVALUATIONS OF THE TWO BEHAVIORAL PROGRAMS

Ideally, the evaluation of a program should include objective and subjective indices of its effects. In practice this is seldom achieved. Yet the importance of doing so cannot be overestimated. Indeed, a program that is effective in meeting therapeutic objectives but in the process generates widespread feelings of hostility, resentment, and antagonism will have little, if any, long-term value. Similarly, a program that produces positive feelings of cooperation and self-regard but fails to teach important skills and competencies will also have little, if any, long-term value.

The preceding chapters have documented the utility of the behavioral approach in the teaching of critical skills and competencies. This chapter completes the evaluation of these behavioral programs by examining other equally important indices of program impact. The evaluation conducted by the EMLC program will be reported first.

THE EMLC PROGRAM

As will be recalled from the previous chapter, a major effort was the deployment of behavior modification principles within the institution through the training of supervisory personnel. A number of procedures were employed to assess the impact of this effort. The officers' mastery of the principles and techniques of behavior modification was assessed through (a) direct observation of their performance on practicum exercrises, and (b) a comparison of the pre- and posttest performance on training material.

A third indicator of the effects of training was the behavioral observation index, which was an instrument specially designed to provide behavioral descriptions of officers' performance in the job setting. In addition, officers were asked their opinions and attitudes of the usefulness of training. Finally, inmates evaluated the officers' ability to work with them.

Assessment Procedures

PRACTICUM EXERCISES

The practicum exercises provided the opportunity to assess the ability of the first two groups of officers to apply the principles of behavior analysis in on-the-job situations. Two members of the project staff visited each officer on the job in order to observe potential behaviors with which the officer might work. After the project staff and the officers agreed upon a behavior, the officers then collected baseline data. The data were discussed in small groups and the officers were assisted in developing treatment procedures. Each checkpoint in their practicum exercises— observing, graphing, correction (treatment), and so on—was correlated with the training material presented.

BOOKLET TESTS

The booklet tests that were administered to the third group of officers before and after each programmed booklet consisted of multiple-choice questions keyed to the content of each booklet. Two measures of performance were maintained for the group of officers who completed the booklets: (a) average score on pre- and posttests and (b) the amount of time required to complete each booklet.

BEHAVIORAL OBSERVATION INDEX

The Behavioral Observation Index (BOI) developed by Witherspoon (1971) was used in the training project to obtain empirical data concerning the officers' behavior on the job. The original BOI included nine behavior indices that measured the effects of training on the officers' interactions with inmates. During the course of the training, the BOI was modified to focus exclusively on officer/inmate interactions. Seventeen trained officers and 15 controls were observed using the modified BOI that included the following items: (a) total number of interactions with inmates, both personal and job related, (b) percent of personal interactions with inmates, (c) percent personal interactions with inmates initiated by the officer, (d) verbal contact score (content and tone of interaction), and (e) behavioral response score (percent of positive reinforcement used by officer in interaction with inmates).

OFFICER EVALUATION OF THE BEHAVIORAL APPROACH

A posttraining questionnaire was administered approximately four months following training. The questionnaire was developed to provide information in two general areas: (a) training effectiveness and (b) correctional officers' reactions to the training. Officers were also asked to evaluate the training curriculum and to suggest institutional changes that would facilitate the training.

Inmate evaluation of officers. An inmate evaluation of the entire officer population at Draper was conducted before and after training. A total of 56 randomly selected inmates evaluated the officers along four dimensions: (a) general caliber, (b) punitiveness, (c) concern with inmates' welfare, and (d) fairness. The names of all officers were typed on index cards and the inmates ranked each of them from 1 (best) to 5 (worst).

Results

PRACTICUM EXERCISES

Twenty-six of the 30 original trainees initiated practicum exercises by recording baseline data. Six of these officers (23%) did not begin the treatment phases of their practicum. Reasons ranged from job changes to a baseline indication of low occurrence of the behavior. Of the 20 officers who began treatment phases, 13 (65%) completed this phase and 9 of the 13 (45%) returned to baseline conditions following treatment.

The practicum exercises demonstrated that the officers were capable of employing the techniques and principles learned in training to the real-life job situation. The 13 officers who had completed the treatment phase of their individual projects reported satisfaction with the effects of their treatment regimen. In each case, the officer had produced a behavior change in the desired direction.

BOOKLET TESTS

Analysis of the booklet test data for the 10 booklets used in the training revealed that all officers increased from pre- to posttraining on all booklets. The range of scores was quite wide, from 0 to 91% correct on the pretests and from 20 to 100% correct on the posttests. The smallest average gain was 12% and the largest, 80%, indicating that the officers' knowledge of behavior modification techniques and the history of corrections had increased. The average study time per booklet was 34 minutes, with a range of 24 to 42 minutes.

BEHAVIORAL OBSERVATION INDEX

Observations using the Behavioral Observation Index indicated that more trained officers (35%) increased the total frequency of their interactions with inmates than did nontrained officers (7%). In addition, more trained officers (76%) increased their use of positive reinforcement in interactions with inmates than did nontrained officers (43%). No differences were observed in the three remaining indices.

OFFICER EVALUATION OF THE BEHAVIORAL APPROACH

The posttraining questionnaire administered to the 40 officers approximately four months after training showed that the officer trainees responded favorably to the training situation and to their individual projects. In an overall evaluation of the training project, a significant majority of the officers (70%) responded that the most valuable aspect of training was learning new ways of dealing with inmates. Other responses included: learning techniques to use at home, gaining an understanding of why people behave as they do, and encouragement to continue what they had always done. Three officers reported having gained nothing from training. Officers also reported the need for some changes to be made within the institution, most of which would facilitate the use of behavioral techniques in the institution. Included among them were more time to work with inmates, more training, more authority for line staff, more administrative support, improved facilities, and more personnel. Four of the officers saw no need for change.

INMATE EVALUATION OF OFFICERS

Both the trained and the nontrained officers showed improvement when the pre- and posttraining evaluations were compared. However, greater improvement was shown by the trained officers. For instance, 10 of the 16 trained officers (65%) were seen by the inmates as increasing in their general effectiveness in working with the inmate population while 7 of the 14 nontrained officers (50%) increased in effectiveness. Twelve of the 16 trained officers (75%) were seen as decreasing in punitive behavior as compared with only 8 of the 14 nontrained officers (57%). In their interpersonal interactions with inmates, the inmates considered 11 of the 16 trained officers (69%) to be more concerned with the inmates' welfare in contrast to 7 of 14 (50%) of the nontrained officers. It was only in the last category, fairness in dealing with the inmates, that the nontrained officers tended towards a greater positive change than did the trained officers. Nine of the 14 nontrained officers (64%) gained, as compared with 9 of the 16 trained officers (56%). Anecdotal observations indicated that the basis of this lies in the trained officers' new concern with consistency. The trained officers applied rules equally to all inmates while the nontrained officers continued to accept excuses and allow exceptions, thereby appearing "fairer."

Overview

In summary, the correctional officer training project met its major objectives. The trained officers demonstrated the acquisition of knowledge of the basic principles of behavior modification as well as the ability to apply them in the institution. In addition, the officers described the training project as beneficial both to the performance of their duties and in their everyday lives. Finally, the trained officers were rated by project staff and inmates as engaging in more frequent, more positive, and more concerned interactions with inmates, a result, incidentally, which the previously described alternative training programs often depict as their *primary* objective.

The training was not conducted without some difficulties, however. For example, the question of custody versus treatment and rehabilitation concerns grew gradually more sensitive as the training proceeded. To clarify the complementary relationship of custody and treatment concerns, the training team explained that the training was designed to expand the officers' roles by providing them with new techniques of behavior management that would lessen their reliance on punishment and help them fulfill their security functions. Additionally, the past experience of one trainer in military corrections gave the officers confidence that the team was aware of the daily requirements of the job and could relate the training to these requirements. Two of the trainers also regularly visited the officers on duty to observe on-the-job situations and familiarize themselves with the security problems involved. At the same time, these visits gave the trainers cues to certain behaviors of inmates which could be treated in the officers' practicum exercises. This contact and demonstration of interest allayed the officers' doubts and encouraged their continued participation in the training.

While such difficulties as these could be overcome through the training team's increased efforts, major problems stemmed from a single cause that is common to most institutions—the reluctance to change. Perhaps this reluctance is due in part to the traditional attitudes of the region or to the nature of the correctional institution. For whatever reason, the total commitment to the necessary change was missing. As the training proceeded and as it became increasingly apparent that the techniques taught in class called for institutional change, the interest of the institution administration waned.

Three major problems resulted from the absence of the administration's total commitment to the training: (a) the lack of an institutionwide setting (or a portion of the institution) keyed to the behavioral approach; (b) the absence of systematic reinforcement for officer trainees from key administrative personnel; and (c) the unintentional interference with the practicum exercises that were conducted. The first of these problems severely limited the opportunities for the trained officers to begin and complete practicum exercises or to continue applying behavioral techniques after training, both of which were considered critical to maintaining their new skills. Although an EMLC token economy was operating in one cellblock of the institution, a shortage of line personnel to carry out the routine security measures made it impossible for the trainees to conduct their practicums there.

Secondly, the trainees were not reinforced by the administration or their peer officers for their participation in the training. In fact, since the training often contradicted the usual institutional approach to such matters as discipline and correctional procedures, the officers were subjected to occasional ridicule and sometimes received direct orders that countermanded their attempts to use their newly acquired skills with their inmate charges. It would be expected that the trainees would come to view the training as useless, for they could see that they would not be encouraged or allowed to practice what they were learning. It was somewhat surprising, therefore, to discover that in their evaluation of the training most officers responded that training had been of value to them in their work and in their home situations. It is also to the officers' credit that they continued in training, for the participation required extra hours with no compensation from the institution.

The third problem, that of indirect interference with the practicum exercises, was obviously related to the two previous problems. Many of the reasons given by the officers for not completing practicum exercises revolved around institutional job reassignments and inmate transfers. While several of the practicum exercises might have taken as long as three months to complete, much of the interruption of these exercises probably could have been avoided if the institution administration had been more committed to the training.

The Staff Training Program in the Behavioral Approach

As a result of the EMLC's experiences in training officers, certain recommendations in regard to planning a similar program can be made:

1. Review the training goals with the department of corrections as well as the institution administration. This should be done early in the planning stages and should include an overview of the behavior modification approach and a detailed description of what the training is designed to accomplish. The review should emphasize that the training is incompatible with a punitive approach to the management of inmate behavior, thus dispelling any expectations by the administration that the trainees will become "super custodians."

2. Involve the institution administration as much and as directly as possible in the training. Ideally, the training should be conducted by supervisory-level institution staff. If this is not possible, their active participation in the training sessions is essential. For example, administrative and supervisory staff should read the training booklets, attend discussion sessions, help plan practicum exercises, and frequently verbalize their support for the new orientation and skills being taught.

3. Schedule practicum exercises to allow for their completion. Since the practicum exercise is perhaps the most accurate means of evaluating the effectiveness of the training and provides an opportunity for the monitored use of new skills, each trainee should have the opportunity to complete at least one practicum exercise. Transfer of his inmates or his reassignment to another job should be avoided whenever feasible. In some cases it may be possible to have other trained officers assist in data collection if the trainee must be absent.

4. Encourage the trained correctional officers to continue to use their new skills in the institution. The institution administration should make detailed plans of how the trained officers will function after their training. These plans involve committing one wing of the institution, or the entire institution, to a behavioral model. Whenever plans are devised, they should give each officer frequent opportunity to make use of what he has learned in the training.

5. Reinforcement should be made available for the officer trainees. Reinforcement should be primarily the responsibility of the institution and should realistically take the form of salary increases and job promotions. Other reinforcers may also be employed, including desirable duty assignments, compensatory time off, a special citation from the trainee's immediate supervisor, or a certificate of recognition at the completion of training. A simple display of interest (e.g., asking how a practicum exercise is going) by key administrative staff would also be expected to be reinforcing to the trainees. However, all reinforcements must be scheduled and delivered on a systematic basis to be maximally effective.

6. If the training is conducted by personnel from outside the institution, they should familiarize themselves with the requirements of the trainees' jobs. This process should involve spending a reasonable amount of time with each trainee on his job. Examples used in the training could then be addressed to particular situations to help the officers in applying the techniques, and plans for practicum exercises could be better evaluated and designed. The trainees would also feel some assurance that the trainers were aware of the nature of the officers' jobs and that this had been considered in presenting the behavioral management techniques. The development of positive relationships between the trainers and the trainees—"getting to know one another"— appears to be a key component of effective training.

7. The administration must be committed to a formal rehabilitation program. Whether correctional officers who are equipped with new behavior management techniques can apply them will depend upon administrative permission and facilitation. The EMLC correctional officer training project was not designed to demonstrate that behavior modification was in fact a rehabilitation tool. However, a good case can be made for its having the potential of being a significant rehabilitation technique. The administration must go beyond its use for a smoother operation of the institution (e.g., getting inmates to work on time, keeping the place clean, etc.) and seek to engineer the institution in such a way that rehabilitation-oriented programs constitute its chief mission. If such a situation can evolve, then the correctional officer can indeed apply his new skills. Without this transformation of the prison, no amount of training will lead to the sustained and productive application of these positive techniques of behavior management.

THE MORE PROGRAM

Although the intent of the MORE program was to enhance the inmates' opportunities for rehabilitation, the possibility existed that many, if not all of the inmates, thought that the program was undesirable. Clearly, ethical considerations are paramount in institutional settings in general and particularly in prisons (see Chapter 7). Three different efforts were made to evaluate this aspect of the program: Two consisted of surveys of the inmates' impressions and the third one of a review of inmate case histories.

The Inmates' Questionnaire

Much to the surprise of the program staff, a survey was being circulated on these very questions at the same time the staff was trying to compose a similar survey. Apparently, the inmate who had been assisting the staff in the school, had constructed two questionnaires, Form A, which asked questions concerning the changes brought about by the program and Form B, which asked questions concerning the inmate's attitudes toward it. The inmate assistant distributed the questionnaires by placing the forms on each inmate's bunk on a Monday. Although he did not collect the forms until a week later, 27 inmates had their anonymously completed questionnaire ready to be picked up.

Form A listed 10 areas of concern and requested that inmates indicate the changes resulting from the program by selecting a response from five possible answers: [There has been] (a) much positive change, (b) some positive change, (c) no change, (d) some negative change, or (e) much negative change. Form B was distributed at the same time as Form A. This questionnaire asked the men to rate the program as either: (a) excellent, as good as it could possibly be, (b) good, needs only minor improvement, (c) fair, would do as well without it, (d) poor, is hindering progress.

RESULTS

Form A.   As Table 15 indicates, on 9 of the 10 questions, over 50% of the responding inmates indicated that the program had resulted in some

Table 15.   Inmate Responses to Surveys on Change Brought About by the Program (Form A) and Overall Perception of the Program (Form B)

Form A: Change Area	% of Inmates[a]		
	Positive Change	No Change	Negative Change
Attitudes between inmates and administration	74	4	23[b]
Attitudes between inmates and correctional officers	60	25	16
Attitudes between inmates and other inmates	70	29	0
Work habits of inmates	67	30	4
Overall conduct of inmates	67	25	8
Your feelings toward education	78	22	0
Language used by inmates around the institution	23	67	11
Manner of dress among inmates	59	30	11
Recreational scene at this institution	55	37	8
Personal feelings about being in prison	55	37	8

Form B: Overall Rating	Excellent	Good	Fair	Poor
Rating of entire incentive project	33	55	3	0

[a] N = 27.
[b] Rounded to nearest percent. Totals may vary from 99 to 101%.

or much positive change. On no question did more than 23% of the 27 inmates indicate negative changes.

Form B.   Of the 27 inmates responding, 24 (88%) rated the project "excellent," or "good," three (12%) rated it "fair" and *no one* rated the program as "poor."

The responses on Forms A and B indicated that inmates reported a preponderance of favorable changes resulting from the program. Further, nearly all of the respondents rated it as ranging from good to excellent. The most gratifying finding was that not one single respondent regarded the program as offensive or as a hindrance to his rehabilitation. In these times of increasing concern over civil and basic human rights, it is reassuring that the program pleased 88% of the inmates. (Perhaps this was because every attempt was made to recognize the worth of each individual inmate.) Finally, it was gratifying to know that an inmate who had assisted in carrying out the program was concerned enough about his fellow inmates to compile a questionnaire that would allow them to express their feelings. Even more encouraging was that the inmate-assistant, without reservation, shared this feedback with the program staff.

The Staff's Evaluation

A more intensive and systematic evaluation procedure was carried out by the staff at the completion of the program. A 56-item survey concerning various aspects of prison life was given to a sample of 30 inmates (20%) randomly selected from the population (Roberts, unpublished). The survey canvassed opinions in many different areas. All questions were posed to the sample of 30 inmates. Analysis of the survey is discussed on the basis of 19 questions covering four categories of concern: attitudes toward rewards, punishment, and academic and vocational training.

CATEGORY 1: INMATES AND REWARDS (5 QUESTIONS)

Over 80% of the inmates agreed that rewards should be contingent upon good behavior and task completion. Less than one-fourth of the inmates felt that rewards adversely affected respect for authority or the goals of rehabilitation.

CATEGORY 2: DOES TRAINING HELP? (4 QUESTIONS)

The inmates (over 80%) were largely in favor of academic and vocational training after they had experienced it under the motivational program.

CATEGORY 3: INMATE BEHAVIOR AND "GOOD TIME" (5 QUESTIONS)

Inmates overwhelmingly (over 90%) maintained that "good time" earned should be maintained as a reward for good behavior. About half, however, felt that "good time" should be withdrawn as a punishment for bad behavior as well.

CATEGORY 4: PHILOSOPHY OF PUNISHMENT AND REHABILITATION (5 QUESTIONS)

Most inmates (90%) agreed with the statement that alternatives to punishment should be considered when a man continuously breaks rules. Further, 90% of the inmates disagreed that "most inmates are just plain sorry," and therefore rehabilitation is useless.

The results from the questionnaire composed by the program staff paralleled those from the questionnaire administered by the inmate as-sistant. Both surveys show that inmates are overwhelmingly in favor of taking part in a behavioral rehabilitation program. The staff question-naire showed that the inmates felt that the academic and vocational training under the behavioral program helped them. More importantly, the questionnaire revealed that inmates viewed the philosophy of re-warding inmates for progress as the only philosophy acceptable to them.

Case Histories of Inmates

The MORE Program had demonstrable rehabilitation effectiveness and from all the surveys it was apparent that the inmates welcomed it. The program was an integral part of the inmates' lives while imprisoned. Just what were the effects of this program in the everyday life of the inmate? The surveys give only a surface indication of how it affected the inmates' lives. The following cases are presented to give some indication of the scope and personal meaning of the program from the inmate's point of veiw. While each case is based on actual inmates who participated in the program, the names have been changed to insure privacy.

LEROY FLOYD

Leroy was the oldest inmate at the prison. He had been in and out of prisons since 1947 when he was convicted of murdering a man in a barroom fight. Leroy had been sentenced to life but had previously been paroled twice. Each time he had been released, his inability to stay away from drinking had gotten him into some kind of trouble which resulted in reincarceration. When first imprisoned he had been a troublemaker. He had, in fact, done time at the prison when it had been the Rock Quarry Prison, designed to "break" such incorrigibles as he was then. The years had mellowed Leroy, however. Now he was the editor of the prison newspaper and fairly well trusted and respected by the prison administrators. Perhaps they feared him a little too, as he was reputed to be the "boss man" or unelected leader of the inmates. Although Leroy was much older than most of the inmates, his experience, intelligence, and leadership characteristics commanded a great deal of respect from the younger men.

He had completed school before ever coming to prison and over the years had been a formal and informal instructor in many prison schools. Leroy was well read in many fields and the monthly newspaper he put together reflected this. When the staff of the program first came to the prison, Leroy introduced himself and requested reading material which would help him understand "where you folks are coming from." He poured over the various textbooks given to him, making copious notes and suggestions in the margins which the staff later found very insightful and helpful. A few weeks later Leroy presented a 10-page typed manuscript which included a plan for a point system listing the amount of points to be earned for each rehabilitation task and possible incentive activities complete with their cost in points. Some of his ideas were eventually incorporated into the actual incentive system developed.

Leroy's insight to the future effectiveness of the program was uncanny. A point he made over and over was that prisons are designed to teach men what not to do within the prison environment, resulting in inactivity and maintenance of the *status quo*. He was encouraged by the proposed program because it was, he said, "the first time I've seen something in a prison really designed to teach men to learn, to achieve, and to be responsible." Leroy had, however, one basic disagreement with the plans of the program, regarding the proposed involvement of guards in the rehabilitation effort. He had developed over the years, a deep and all-pervading distrust for "security." Over and over Leroy warned against allowing guards any participation in the program. He attributed the mistrust he held for guards to their usual lack of education, and vested interest in maintaining the *status quo*. He was aware that the guards' power was only to punish "bad" behavior rather than to "reward" good behavior. He put it this way, "While every officer has the fullest measure of power to deny, to deprive, to punish, there is no positive power to give, permit, or pardon, except in the hands of the warden. While any correctional officer has full freedom to seize anything any inmate owns, that same inmate must see a warden to get a toothbrush." This keen observation was helpful in shaping the scope of incentives to be made available to all inmates.

Leroy was well on the way to his own rehabilitation before the program was started. He had mastered many skills that he could put to good use once he was released. He had joined Alcoholics Anonymous and thought he could now handle his drinking problem. In general, he probably did more for the program than the program did to help him. Through his prison newspaper job, he had previously been in a position to take photographs of inmates on the sly and either give or sell them a print since he developed the film himself. When the program started, he agreed to take and process photographs only when the inmates had paid points for this activity. The program paid Leroy for his photographic services in points. Leroy's greatest contribution, however, was in terms of the public relations work for the program he did among the other inmates. He supported all the various procedures of the program, encouraged new inmates to apply for a credit card immediately and gave the program staff feedback on the effectiveness of various procedures, incentives, and so on. For this contribution, Leroy was *not* paid. He talked up the program because he believed in it. He said he had seen many programs come and go in prisons and he thought this one was something special which would really help inmates and potentially change "for the first time in 100 years" the way prisons operate.

The program was able to help Leroy in some ways. The points he earned by taking photographs, contracting to do jobs, and by publishing the newspaper on time each month (he had previously had a habit of being late quite often), were later put to good use. As Leroy's date for parole consideration again came up, he used the points he had earned to make a lot of special phone calls and send special letters. In this way he contacted a daughter he had not seen in 18 years and made some arrangements for a job should he gain parole.

Later Leroy was paroled. He now works in a small print shop and is saving money to start his own business. He has stayed away from alcohol and is an officer in an AA chapter on the outside. We still hear from Leroy from time to time and he has maintained his interest in rehabilitation. He still believes the program was a good thing and is not shy about telling people whom he meets about it.

EUGENE SCOTT

Gene was from a large family who lived in a ghetto in the Atlanta inner city. He had dropped out of school between junior high and high school but never learned to read beyond the second grade reader. He was fairly good in math, perhaps because math skills were useful in his business as one of the biggest heroin dealers on the near west side of the city. Gene was quite successful in business until, like many people, he began using drugs himself. High-grade "coke" got to be expensive, and Gene became careless. Ultimately, he was convicted of selling five dime bags to an undercover policeman and, at the age of 18, was sent to prison.

Gene did not trust "honkies" and since all the administrative and security staff at the prison were white, as were most of the program staff, he was not one to immediately run down and apply for a credit card as soon as he arrived. It took him a while to "feel out" the program, talk to the "brothers," and so forth, before he was ready to participate. Everything has its angles and catches after all, and if there was anything Gene mistrusted more than honkies, it was a "do-gooder," white or black. Eventually, he could not find any inmates who seemed to be getting "ripped off" or used in any way by the program, so he decided to check it out himself. When the program staff told Gene the whole purpose was to get inmates to work harder and learn more skills, he was surprised that they would be so open about it. He still figured that there was probably a catch somewhere, but decided that he "sure could use some of those good things the other dudes were getting with these points."

Gene was placed in the brick masonry grade. He was not thrilled about learning this skill but some inmates he knew had told him at the Diagnostic and Classification Center to try to get into masonry if he could. The story was that this trade course was only six months long whereas most of the others were 12 months. This meant that a man could complete the course and look good on paper sooner for parole consideration. Gene was not really interested in remedial academics either. Every experience he had previously with school seemed bad. The only good thing he could remember was that school was a good place to meet girls. The prison school, however, did not even have this going for it. But, if he wanted to get points he had to go where the points were. While Gene earned points for learning his vocational trade skills, he still needed more points and the school seemed like the next easiest way to earn them.

At first Gene came to remedial academics two hours per day, five days a week. Although he did not see the need for more schooling than he already had (he had after all been a successful "businessman" on the street), he took the placement tests and began to work in English and reading. As he often told the staff, "I don't give a damn for this jive school, I'm only here to get your points." After a while, however, Gene's attitude began to change. He saw that this school was different from the schools that he had attended on the outside. In the first place, there were no grades or classes. Every man was working on material at his own level and as fast or as slow as he wanted. In addition, "they did not just give you a 200 page book and say do every page." Each inmate had assignments that covered only the things that he did not know. Gene found that in math, during the first month, he had done assignments in five different books, from third to ninth grade level. The teachers in the school were also different from those he had known before. They did not "bug" him about doing his work or paying attention or about how dumb he was. Still, the teachers were available if he wanted them when he had difficulty working through his programmed material and needed help understanding something. The only time he *had* to see a teacher was when he did not pass a test over his assigned material, which occurred rarely, or when he had an advanced oral reading test which had to be taken with one of the teachers. Strangely enough, Gene found himself *wanting* to talk to one of the teachers sometimes. This usually happened when he passed a more difficult test. Gene said it was because "I just wanted the dude to see that I was really gettin' the stuff, man."

Gene ended up actually liking academic learning and was selected for one of the special accelerated learning procedures. After two months in his masonry trade, Gene decided he just did not care to do that kind of work. He said he was "born to use my head, not my back, to earn my bread." So, he applied to the vocational training placement officer to request a transfer to drafting, even though it was a 12-month course. Unfortunately, his application was denied, because the drafting trade required trainees to achieve academically on at least the seventh grade level prior to starting the course. Gene, always a talker, did not take this lying down. He begged and pleaded and finally persuaded the warden to let him drop masonry and go to remedial academics full-time, until he was up to the achievement level needed for drafting. This took about 5 months but Gene finally made it. Even after he got into drafting, he continued to work on his academics and eventually earned his General Education Diploma.

Gene was denied parole the first time he became eligible—most inmates convicted of drug pushing were—but it did not seem to bother him as much as everyone thought it would. He was just getting started in drafting, and was doing a little tutoring work in the school. He said he had not expected to make it the first time and sort of wanted to complete the drafting course to "have something decent to fall back on if I can't get into something really good."

He was, of course, earning a lot of points during this time. Most of his points were spent at the canteen. Gene had a thing about Dr. Pepper. He always seemed to have a Dr. Pepper in his hand. He also had a penchant for panatelas, preferring the most expensive cigar carried by the canteen. He said that "only low-class dudes" smoked anything but good cigars. Gene also made extensive use of special phone calls and visits, usually from old girl friends. After a while he began to special order some very strange goods through the canteen manager. He had observed one of the program staff often doing needlepoint on her breaks. He asked her if she also knew how to crochet. When he found that she did, he asked her if she would teach him how. Although it seemed an unusual request coming from Gene (or any other inmate for that matter), she did teach him the basics of crocheting. The root of all this was discovered later, when he started talking to the canteen manager. Gene, always a "businessman" had noticed how many of the black inmates were acquiring small crocheted caps and how popular this fashion was becoming. Gene decided this was a chance to make some extra money. They all laughed at him and made a few smart remarks about his masculinity when he first started crocheting in his cell. But, he was soon taking orders for his caps with delivery dates far in advance of his production schedule.

As this is written, Gene is again up for parole. He has almost finished his drafting class and is really hoping to make it this time. The other day Gene was reminiscing with one of the staff members about how he felt regarding the program when he first started earning points. "I thought I was really conning you dudes and rippin' you off for points because I didn't give a damn about learnin' anythin'; just about gettin' points. Later, I figured out that I was the one gettin' conned because you had it all set up so's the only way I could get them points was to learn to read. Once I learned readin', I had it, and it felt good, man."

JAY TUCKER

Pride was the one word description for Jay. Born and raised in the North Georgia mountains, he learned that pride was the one thing even a poor dirt farmer could always call his own. Jay had quit the county consolidated high school the day he turned 16 and gone to work on his "daddy's" farm. His father did not believe in welfare, food stamps, or any "such thing," and Jay felt the same way. He believed such things were for the "coloreds and hippies and other low-life types." Even when the land was poor and the crops were bad, his father had always figured out some way of getting by even if it meant "not eatin' good" during the winter. Country pride does not allow asking strangers for help. That same country pride (some people call it a "wonderful sense of independence" while others call it "damn, pig-headed stubbornness") helped Jay get into trouble with the law. One night he and a friend had gotten a little drunk at a road house tavern and decided they wanted to drive down to Atlanta to see the sights. The only problem was that they had run out of money and "everyone knows you can't have no fun in 'Atlantr' without no money." At the time, the best idea they could come up with was to dip into the cash register at Ike's service station. While Jay was inside prying open the register, Ike drove in the back way and surprised his friend who was outside on lookout. His friend got scared, grabbed a coke bottle from the rack and hit Ike with it. Thinking Ike was just knocked out, Jay and his friend went on down to Atlanta and spent the $143.85, "seeing the sights." When Jay drove home the next afternoon, the sheriff was waiting for him with an arrest warrant. It seems that someone had seen his father's pick-up "scratching off down the highway" near Ike's and gave a description of it to the sheriff when they found Ike lying dead. Jay told them what had happened, but refused to identify his friend. Jay said that since he got caught he would "take my medicine like a man," figuring that he would probably go to jail for a while because of the burglary since he was not the one who actually hit Ike. Instead, the sheriff charged him with murder, and the judge "threw the book at me" because he still refused to identify his friend.

Jay had already served seven years of his life sentence and had been turned down for parole once by the time he was transferred to our prison. He felt that he did not need any special training or trade because he already had one in farming. Jay had a good record while in prison. He had not gotten into any scrapes but was considered something of a loner, preferring his own company or that of just a few other "country boys" he had met while in prison. He was assigned to the position of prison sewage-treatment plant operator. This was a lonely job but it did involve some measure of training and responsibility. Every day Jay would go out to the little shack by the skimmer and settling ponds in back of the prison to spend his time. The job was mostly routine but someone was needed to check pressures, take water samples, and make sure nothing got through the pipes to clog the machinery.

It was several months before Jay applied for a program credit card. That old country pride of his told him he did not need any handouts from anybody, nor did he need to ask anybody for anything. It was thought that his friend, Johnny, who was the inmate assistant in the canteen, finally convinced him that getting a credit card was not begging and, in fact, that he had the points coming to him for the work he was doing. Jay seemed to be a little ashamed of himself but admitted he could certainly use some points to get a few things at the canteen, which he lacked the cash to purchase. He was told that he was due some recognition for his hard work. The correctional officer who was responsible for running the sewage treatment plant was asked to start rating Jay's work performance and attitude so that he could earn points.

All worked well for a while. Jay got high ratings, showed up weekly to collect his points, and spent them at the canteen. Then one week when Jay showed up at payment time, the officer had forgotten to submit a weekly rating sheet on him. It was the usual policy of the program to ask the inmates in such situations to remind the work supervisor about his ratings rather than having staff talk to him. In so doing, this provided another chance to increase inmate–supervisor interactions. For Jay, however, this was not a good policy. To him, reminding the officer seemed like begging or admitting to someone else that he needed something from them. This was something that his old country pride would not allow him to do. The next week when Jay showed up for his pay, the officer had again failed to turn in a rating and it was the last straw for

Jay. He threw down his credit card, said he was all through with that "damn crap," and said he had been foolish to go along with it as long as he had. He said he would just keep on doing his work and "keep my mouth shet from nigh on!" The program staff became quite upset at this development, realizing that through their error of not being sensitive enough to this inmate's individuality they might have discouraged him from participating in any further rehabilitation programs. The officer responsible for rating Jay's work was contacted and he, too, shared our concern for Jay. He said he would make it right with Jay since he knew how to talk to him "being's I'm just an ol' country boy myself." The next day Jay asked if he could have his card back as he and Mr. Grey had "talked things out and decided one of us is forgetful while the other's stubborn." From now on, Jay related, they had decided to help each other out to avoid such misunderstandings as this from happening again. This agreement seemed to work. From then on Mr. Grey usually turned in Jay's ratings on time and when he did forget, Jay did not get angry. Rather, he just went and reminded Mr. Grey and within a day or so the officer turned in the rating sheet, reminding the staff that Jay should get two week's worth of points next payday.

After a few months, Jay came around to the remedial academic school one day and asked how much trouble it would be if he could borrow a book to study out at the sewage treatment plant during his spare time. With much encouragement and reassurance, Jay was convinced to take a placement test and get a listing of the specific skills and the assignments he needed to study to complete his education. Finally, his supervisor told Jay that he could take two hours per day off his job to go to the school and get some help from the teachers on his academic work.

It was later learned from his friend, Johnny, that Jay had always wanted to "get more book 'learnin'," but had not approached anybody about it until he started needing more points than he had been earning for his work performance. It seemed that Jay found out that his father had come on to hard times again and needed some help for which he would not ask anybody outside the family. Jay decided the one way he could help out was by buying Gold Bond Stamps with his points. He could then use the stamps to obtain some of the clothing and tools that his father needed.

At about the same time, it was learned from the prison medical technician that the dentist had been trying to fix Jay's teeth for a long time. Jay had never been seen by a dentist before, had never learned good dental hygiene habits, and consequently had very poor teeth. The dentist knew that the teeth were causing Jay a considerable amount of pain, and it was obvious to everyone that Jay was ashamed of their appearance. But, that pride which did not allow him to accept charity, plus a good measure of dentist phobia, kept Jay from consenting to have the bad teeth extracted and getting a set of false teeth. Even the warden had talked to Jay in an effort to persuade him to consent to the badly needed dental work, but he had no more success than anyone else.

Finally, knowing his current need for more points, everyone involved worked out a plan to get Jay to accept this dental help. He was told that one substantial aspect of rehabilitation, in addition to academics, vocational, and work training, involved helping the inmate resolve his physical problems. We would, therefore, offer him additional points for allowing the dentist to repair his teeth. Jay was informed of how many points he would earn per each extraction and the total number of points he would earn when the entire procedure, including prosthesis, was complete. This approach was successful. While months of pleading, threatening, and ordering Jay to accept dental help were useless in convincing him, offering a positive incentive for making this choice was the solution. While getting his teeth fixed was certainly not the "key" to Jay's rehabilitation, it did solve some of his problems with self-consciousness and did alleviate some of his pain, without the use of coercion or violation of his self-respect.

Jay is still the sewage treatment plant operator and still wants only to return to his farm when he is released. He is making good progress in his remedial academics program, and has made an arrangement with one of the guards, who has a farm, to obtain some books and magazines about modern farming methods. Jay seems to be getting some new ideas from his reading and says that he is trying to tell his father about them on visiting day. But, he tells us, his father is "pretty set in his ways" and is not likely to change by himself. The MORE staff believes that, when Jay is eventually released, he will return to his father's mountain farm and the correctional system will probably never hear from him again.

SANFORD CARUTHERS AND MARTIN GREEN

A common belief in prison rehabilitation (and in education, mental health, vocational rehabilitation, and many other fields) is that many people are lacking in skills and accomplishments because of their early experiences and opportunities. There are, of course, a few diehards, however, who insist that some people are just born "dumb" or "bad." Those holding this view insist that the main ingredient in all adult accomplishment is "intelligence" which, they maintain, is genetically determined at conception. This point of view, which places so much emphasis on irreversible IQ scores, has led to many disagreements among professionals and nonprofessionals alike. These disagreements, and sometimes full-fledged battles, usually revolve around the question of whether some particular testing material or procedure is appropriate for any given group of individuals. There seems to be no way to resolve these disagreements to everyone's satisfaction, much to the amusement of those who value experience and opportunity over test scores. If it can be shown that persons who are "failures" or have inferior IQs can learn and perform as well as persons with "normal" characteristics, then the high value placed on intelligence scores must be seriously questioned. The program resulted in many such demonstrations.

Sanford Caruthers was a "life-long failure." He came from Birmingham, Alabama, where "school quit him" when he was in the fifth grade. Although he had previously been sent to the principal's office many times for many different offenses, the last time was a little unusual. When he left the classroom as the teacher ordered, he picked up a rock outside and threw it back into the room, aiming at her but narrowly missing another student's head. Sanford says that he really wasn't trying to hit anyone, but just trying to "get back at that old bag." The outcome of this incident was that Sanford was placed on "home bound" status, meaning that he could no longer attend school with the other students. Instead, the visiting teacher would pay periodic visits to his home to insure his continuing education. This lasted a total of one visit. After that, Sanford had no further contact with the Birmingham Public School System. Sanford, of course, had to find something to do with his time and most of these activities contributed to his acquiring a thick file with the juvenile court. At age 18, Sanford was finally arrested in a Norcross, Georgia breakup of a large interstate car theft ring. After spending seven months in the county jail awaiting trial, he was convicted of grand auto theft and sent to prison. The routine assessment procedures at the prison Diagnostic and Classification Center revealed that Sanford had an IQ of 65 and was functioning academically at the 6.1 grade level. The report did indicate that Sanford had good "fine-motor coordination" and therefore he was placed in the welding trade.

Martin Green was a "classical" high school dropout. In Macon, Georgia, his hometown, he had attended school regularly through the tenth grade. Unlike Sanford, Martin was not a "behavior problem" in school. Through the ninth grade he went to the "colored" schools. The year that Martin entered tenth grade, however, the high schools were desegregated and he found himself placed in the "vocation track" which consisted predominantly of black students like himself. Martin actually enjoyed his shop classes and got along well with the instructors and the other students. The academic classes were different, however. He stated that "the teachers in English and math were out to show us black kids just how dumb we really were. I guess compared to the kids from the white schools we were a little behind." According to Martin, the teachers made no allowances for the differences in previous educational background, but assigned all the work at a level which, while appropriate for most of the white students, was beyond the achievement of all but a very few black students. Martin tried going to his shop classes while cutting his English, social studies, and mathematics classes. The school would not, however, accept that kind of attendance and Martin was told to start attending all his classes. Martin quit school in December. "When I went to class I just didn't even try to do the work. But that got me into just as many hassles as when I skipped, so I said to hell with it all."

Martin worked for the sanitation department, picked pecans for a while, and finally landed a construction job. He was making some money and "doing all right" for about a year until the highway was completed and the job ran out. About the same time he took an interest in a woman who happened to be married. Because he had no job and could not find anything else, it worked out that he could spend time with this woman during the day when her husband was away. One day, however, they were discovered when the husband came home sick. "Not only did that big ugly bear beat the hell out of me but the fox started screaming rape." Even though it was a "jive charge," the woman's husband was a teacher and had some influence in the community, so Martin was convicted of sexual assault and sent to prison. Martin was very bitter about the whole thing but noted that at least it was a "good thing that fox was black cause if'n she'd been white I'd be daid." The routine diagnostic assessment of Martin indicated that he had an IQ of 97 and was functioning at the 7.7 grade level. He was transferred to the prison and assigned to the barbering trade.

Both Sanford and Martin participated in the program procedures in their respective trades and made good progress toward mastering vocational skills. Both of them also participated in the incentive earning procedures in the academic school. While their progress in their academic learning was good, it was not anything exceptional, until they were among the first inmates chosen to participate in the special accelerated learning procedure. As described previously, the regular incentive procedure for academics provided incentives based on the number of tests passed and the number of grade levels progressed. Each time an inmate passed a test or completed all the tests in a grade level, he earned points. The special accelerated procedure continued this relationship between learning and incentives but included one additional, critical element in the procedure: time. The amount of points an inmate earned for passing tests and grade levels was dependent upon the amount of time he took to do so. The faster he progressed, that is, the less time between passing test, the more points he earned (the details of the special accelerated learning procedure are described in Kandel, Ayllon, & Roberts, 1976). The procedure was described to Sanford and Martin and both expressed their interest in participating.

The impact of this new procedure on these inmates was truly amazing. In a three-month period, Sanford progressed 5.3 grade levels and Martin 1.5 grade levels. Such progress was not easy for them, however. At first, they were understandably skeptical. Because this was a new and untried procedure, only a few inmates were offered the opportunity to participate in it and they were asked not to tell their friends about it, at least until we had a chance to evaluate the procedure and decide whether to continue it. Sanford asked if he could quit the new procedure if he did not like it. He was assured that he could go back to the regular incentive system any time he desired. Martin wanted to know what the long-range consequences of his participation would be: "If I don't go along with y'all on this will the whole board hear about it?" He was assured that the parole board would never know if he participated or chose not to and that the decision was entirely his to make.

Both men, of course, did give it a try, but sometimes, certainly, considered withdrawing. They soon learned that once they started studying and passing tests, there was a lot of built-in pressure to study harder and harder and to pass tests faster and faster. Some of this pressure began to show. Martin complained that "this stuff is really bustin' my head man, it's all I think about." Sanford got into an argument with the inmate clerk: "Come on man, hurry up and get that test for me. Got to have it now! I ain't got time to fool wit' you." We found out that the men were studying in their dorms late at night even sometimes after "lights out." They took every opportunity to spend as much time as possible in the academic school. Finally, their vocational instructors had to become very firm with Martin and Sanford in order to limit their time in the school and make sure they kept up with their trade assignments. The men were constantly reminded, however, that if the pressure got to be too much for them or if they got too tired of their academics, they could stop participating in the special procedure or, at least, slow down a little if they chose to. The choice was always up to them. Occasionally they did "take a little vacation" but only for a few days at a time, usually only after passing a grade level. But, as Sanford said, "Once you pass on test, man, that only makes you want to go harder. 'Cause you see that time clickin' off and you know you gotter get goin' if'n you want to get into them heavy points."

It was not easy for the staff either. The inmate clerk had to work harder to keep up with the men. They demanded that he score their tests quickly and that he not make any mistakes in grading them, either. When they came to particularly difficult material they demanded help with it immediately. However, at the same time, they did not want any unsolicited assistance. Martin summed it up this way, "When I'm gettin' the stuff on my own from the book, I don't need nobody to come 'round slowing me down. When I get stuck on something I ask Mis Jan (one of the instructors) to help me; as soon as I get it, I go back to workin' on my own. I can learn better doin' mysel'." After Sanford and Martin had been working in the accelerated program in math another problem occurred to the staff. They were studying material that was difficult for the teacher. Even though the teachers were college graduates and had certainly known their plane geometry well once, they were a little "rusty." When correcting the inmates' tests, they found that if a geometry proof deviated from the answer given in the teacher's manual, it was not necessarily wrong as there are several ways to solve such problems. In order to adequately instruct the men and to evaluate their work fairly, it was necessary for the teachers to read and study some of these advance materials to "brush up" on their own academic skills.

The special accelerated learning procedures helped Martin and Sanford make substantial gains in academic achievement in a relatively short time. The procedure motivated the inmates to work diligently, probably harder than they had ever worked before. Because the inmates worked so hard, the staff was required to increase their efforts just to keep up with the progress of the men. Was all this extra work worth it? Certainly from the staff's point of view it was. The academic gains made by these men in this relatively short period of time were of the order any teacher would take great satisfaction in seeing his student accomplish. Few schools, even expensive prep schools, can raise their students 1.5 to 5.3 grade levels in overall achievement in three months. Yes, the instructional staff and the staff of the program were pleased with Martin and Sanford's progress and felt the extra effort was worth it.

What about Martin and Sanford? Did they feel that all the hard work was worth it? The answer was an unqualified "yes." As indicated previously, their continued participation was voluntary. The choice to continue working in the accelerated learning procedure was theirs. In fact, they did not stop working until they had completed all the high school level curriculum material available. Not until the staff discontinued the procedure, did Martin and Sanford discontinue their extra efforts. At that time the men elected to study the advanced academic material previously described. Martin said that now, "I kind of dig school, you know. It's something I'm really good at." When the staff asked them for their suggestions or comments on the procedure after they were finished, both men reiterated how hard it had been but both felt it was worth it. They agreed that their major suggestion to the program was that we should "give some of the other dudes here the same chance you gave us."

At first we thought they meant that we should put other inmates into the accelerated learning procedure. Maybe that is what they meant. Perhaps, however, they meant more than that. Both of these men had not really received a good chance to show how well they could achieve academically in their previous educational situations. We gave them a chance to show what they were capable of achieving. Perhaps they also meant we gave them a chance to show that they were not actually as "dumb" or "slow" as others had previously labeled them. Martin, for example, had an IQ of only 97, while Sanford's 65 IQ placed him in the retarded category. Who would expect such learning from these IQ scores? A better question is, who would even give men with such scores the opportunity to show that they could do algebra and geometry? This is not the place to join the argument over intelligence scores but three questions come immediately to mind: (a) Were the IQ scores given for Martin and Sanford inaccurate? (b) Are IQ scores irrelevant in terms of relating to or predicting the inmates' achievement capabilities? (c) Should learning opportunities be denied on the basis of such low IQ scores?

In actuality, we do not know what will happen to Martin and Sanford after they are released. We do know that both men now have their general education diplomas and perhaps have some self confidence that they did not have before. Martin is continuing in his barbering trade and planning to go to barber's school when he is out to gain some additional training in men's hair styling not available at the prison. He is also taking a night course offered at the prison in small business management, because he wants to run his own shop one day. Sanford, on the other hand, finished his welding trade but does not plan to make it his career. He has been trying to get into a college in Atlanta. Should he be accepted (several staff members have written letters of recommendation for him), he will apply for the educational release program. He does not know for sure what course of study he will pursue but he says he now knows that college is the place for him. We give both Martin and Sanford a good chance of succeeding in reaching their new goals.

DISCUSSION

The supplementary evaluations of the two programs indicate that they both were well received by the inmates. The results from the EMLC program indicate that officers who used behavioral techniques were generally regarded by inmates as showing greater competence and concern. These impressions were corroborated by independent indices which indicated that these officers interacted more frequently and more positively with inmates. The results of the MORE program confirm those of the EMLC. Briefly, the questionnaires and case histories show consistency with respect to the inmates' favorable judgment of the behavioral program. It can be said, then, that both behavioral programs not only achieved their objective rehabilitative goals but at the same time fostered inmates' positive feelings toward the programs and the employees who implemented them.

Despite these positive findings, there are several legitimate questions regarding the use of rewards in a prison setting that requires answers. The usual doubts expressed by prison officials and employees are illustrated in the following dialogue:

Question: Aren't you bribing inmates and compounding the prison's problem?

ANSWER: An incentive program should make rewards available only when the individual has met a particular performance or criterion. Bribery consists of giving someone incentives with the full expectation that the individual who receives them is obliged to do what he is asked, typically something dishonest or illegal. Bribery is generally associated with a sub-rosa type of activity wherein the individual is given incentives but the understanding is not made public and therefore not easily monitored by others. An incentive program should be public and therefore allow inmates to serve as witnesses to the fact that the individual being rewarded has met specific and publicly recognized expectations, and that the incentive was of the correct amount and for the specified and publicly agreed upon performance.

Question: Aren't incentive programs spoiling the inmate to expect incentives for everything he does?

ANSWER: First, an incentive program should not pay inmates for everything they do. The major tactic is to pay the inmate only to gain his active participation in his own rehabilitation. When an inmate develops academic, vocational and social skills, they enable him to interact with his environment more effectively. At such time these skills become the natural rewards for the individual and incentive systems become secondary if not superfluous. An incentive system in a rehabilitation or therapeutic environment may be viewed as a prosthetic device. As such it is useful to bridge the gap between lacking certain skills and having them. An everyday example may illustrate this point. A person wearing crutches after a skiing accident does not regard his crutches as a permanent item but rather as a help in the transition between being unable to walk and resumption of his walking without them. Similarly, a child who wears braces to correct his teeth does not wear them for life but rather as a temporary device that facilitates a certain outcome.

Question: How do you decide how much to pay an inmate in a point system?

ANSWER: The major guideline for the value attached to specific performance on the job or in the academic area follows from a supply and demand type of consideration. This means that if academic instructors feel that more people should be having greater exposure to English, the incentives could be increased for English as contrasted to the incentives available for some other subject matter, such as math. Similarly, when the institution requires for its smooth functioning the assistance of a specific maintenance man, e.g., a plumber, electrician, etc., an appropriate incentive(s) might be offered to the individual whose specific skills are needed at that time. This tactic would be consistent with the intent of a complex motivational system, namely, to duplicate insofar as possible the characteristics that obtain in the free world.

Question: How do you convince the line staff that they have problems that could be handled more effectively through a reward system?

ANSWER: In our experience, we have found that most of the individuals who are asked to describe whether they have problems do not admit to having them. Perhaps this is because problems often go undetected, are regarded as unsoluble, and hence people adjust to them or, at worst, keep them from public scrutiny. Therefore, one way of introducing a new system into the prison is to select the most competent and best regarded staff member and solicit his assistance in trying out new practices. Once he experiences success, and other staff members become aware of it, he functions as a model for others and his new practices legitimize the approach.

Question: Our staff knows and will readily admit to having problems. However, what happens if they don't believe rewards could work with inmates?

ANSWER: An approach based on rewards appears to some to be coddling inmates. Therefore, the employees' typical reaction is one of skepticism or even total disbelief. For this reason, it is best to avoid time-consuming discussions and instead select a small area where there is a problem, the solution to which will enhance the credibility of the program. An illustration of this type of tactic involved the prison school in which the academic instructors had a severe problem with inmates coming late. Although school started at 8:00 in the morning, there were many inmates who did not arrive until 8:30. A procedure was introduced to minimize lateness: men who were in the classroom at 8:00 a.m. were allowed, at 8:45, to take a 15-minute break in an adjacent room in which there were high-interest magazines, a record player, and playing cards. Inmates who were late for class were asked to remain in the classroom to make up the time they had missed. Within one week, this simple procedure had effectively eliminated arriving late to class, and provided an effective demonstration to the academic instructors that such arrangements could be very useful to them. In this case, once the inmates were on time, it was discovered that their performance during the academic program was largely deficient or nonexistent. Since the inmates now were in attendance, the instructors could much more easily recognize a more serious problem: the inmates' severe deficiency in academic performance. Again, the tactic used here was to simply meet the demands of instructors. After the instructors got used to everyone appearing on time, they raised the level of expectations and focused on academic performance. Similarly, as the instructors found that free time as an incentive was limited, they were ready to move into more complex but effective incentives. This tactic, again, allowed the instructors to gain experience with the effectiveness of each of the procedures before going on. In short, seeing rewards work is believing.

Question: In our setting we are interested in introducing incentive programs but our major problem is to teach the employees as well as the instructors and counselors this approach. Is there a workshop or a training package to help us do this?

ANSWER: Training packages for prison personnel are already available and are effective in terms of their having been utilized by those who work in prisons. Training packages, in general, are rather expensive. An alternative to a didactic, formal training basis is that based on experience on the job or in-service training. This particular orientation relies heavily on modeling, peer coaching, and on-the-job assistance. This orientation is particularly suited to the correctional and custodial staff. In our experience, we have found that with individuals with college backgrounds, it was both effective and less time-consuming to expose them to the effectiveness of a procedure that was tried out in a specific area and within a limited period of time. Having had the opportunity of sampling the effectiveness of the newly introduced procedures, the college-educated employee may now be in the best position to acquire further, more complex information on a more didactic and formal basis. Workshops for such individuals would then become not only timely but much greater in overall effectiveness. That is not the case for individuals who have had, at most, a high school education. The emphasis here is to not only expose the individual to the experience of using the procedure, but limiting the training to a cookbook orientation. This allows individuals who typically are not verbally oriented to feel comfortable about employing procedures rather than principles because in their experience implementing procedures defines their work. Hence, from a practical point of view, the training should be specifically oriented toward resolution of problems within the context of the prison.

CHAPTER

$$\boxed{12}$$

CONCLUSION

The objective of the series of studies described in this report was to examine the effects of systematically deploying the behavioral model to aid in the understanding and solution of the problems confronting those charged with the care and rehabilitation of the institutionalized male felon. This objective grew from an analysis of various aspects of the correctional process and the inescapable conclusions to which it gave rise. These conclusions and considerations, as described earlier in Chapter 8 were: (a) Correctional institutions will continue to exist and continue to confine men and women offenders; (b) the minimum necessary objective for all correctional institutions is to assure that offenders return to society no worse for their prison experience; (c) those concerned with corrections have a responsibility to make available to incarcerated offenders programs that, at the least, have the potential of increasing their chances of success upon release; (d) correctional workers must also encourage offenders to participate in rehabilitative programs, in addition to simply making them available; and (e) such efforts will not retard but instead hasten the reforms in correctional practice which are so urgently needed.

Additionally, this objective of employing a behavioral model was also generated from an examination of existing policies and procedures practiced by correctional centers vis-à-vis the care and rehabilitative services provided to the institutionalized offender. These policies and procedures often stress the use of punitively oriented practices to suppress unwanted actions and the use of aversive control procedures to motivate the performance of required activities. In addition, the bulk of both the undesired and desired activities are only vaguely defined, creating a situation that cannot help but foster inconsistency and arbitrariness on the part of both line and supervisory correctional staff. All too often, the inmate, who is never able to predict with complete certainty what is expected of him or how the administration will react to what he does, concludes that the staff is, at best, whimsical or, at worst, discriminatory and vindictive in their dealings with him and his fellow inmates. Not only do such conditions negate effective rehabilitation programs, they undoubtedly contribute in large measure to the unrest festering in today's correctional institutions, not to mention its contribution to the generally regressive effects imprisonment has upon the released offender's ability to adjust to community life.

It is apparent that the conditions that have evolved in the correctional institution encourages the inmate, albeit unintentionally, to isolate himself from the institution staff and bulk of the inmate population. He does only those things that are required of him and rarely volunteers for additional work. He establishes a small circle of confidants and spends his leisure time with them or by himself. He attempts to maintain a clean record, make no enemies among either the institution staff or the inmate population, and counts off the days remaining until he is either to appear before the parole board or to be released, either the short way (with "good time") or the long way (without "good time"). Unfortunately, such a course of action leaves the inmate no better prepared for life in the community than he was prior to his apprehension, conviction, and imprisonment.

Finally, an essential consideration in formulating this objective was the evaluative research assessing the effectiveness of a variety of approaches for solving problems in corrections and closely allied fields. An examination of the evaluative research data indicated that behavior modification has enjoyed considerable success in the health-related fields and also with predelinquent youths and juvenile offenders in the criminal justice system. This research suggests that the behavioral model holds significant potential for better understanding and remediating the behavior of the adult offender, yet it was concluded that a clear demonstration of its applicability to the adult offender population was seriously lacking.

The behavioral strategy adopted here provided the opportunity to demonstrate that procedures that stress incentives and positive reinforcement for academic performance and vocational accomplishment are equally or more effective in achieving institutional training and re-habilitation objectives than those that stress punishment and aversive control for infractions and nonperformance. It appears that the policies and procedures that the correctional institutions now employ to govern inmate life undoubtedly contribute in large measure to both the unrest in correctional institutions and the regressive effect of imprisonment. It is as if the correctional institution, with its emphases upon obedience, passivity, punishment, and aversive control procedures, is "well de-signed," albeit unintentionally, to instill dependence, helplessness, lack of initiative, resentment, and aggression—traits that most would agree are maladaptive both within the institution and broader context of soci-ety. Indeed, it is difficult to conceive of how any environment could be better engineered to achieve these unfortunate ends.

Obviously, then, the objective of the behavioral programs reported here was to reengineer the environment, substituting contingencies of positive reinforcement for the already-existing contingencies of punishment and aversive control. In focusing on the development of a management system based on positive reinforcement, the behavioral programs minimized reliance on the use of punishment and aversive control procedures. In this, the behavioral programs confronted what may be the two most significant conditions underlying the regressive effects of imprisonment upon the released offender's readjustment in the community.

Each of the studies conducted by the behavioral programs sought to assess the manner in which selected target behaviors were affected by rearranging, in one manner or another, conditions existent in either the correctional institution at large or the token economy itself. These studies clearly demonstrated that the same principles of behavior that have been validated and refined in a variety of different areas are no less applicable to the adult offender than they are to other nosological groupings. Perhaps even more importantly, these studies demonstrated that it is feasible to deemphasize punishment and aversive control pro-cedures in correctional institutions if care is taken to replace them with appropriately designed and monitored contingencies of positive rein-forcement. Within this context, the behavioral programs also demon-strated that these new procedures may be effectively employed by the line correctional officer. Of course, he must be provided with the neces-sary training and be made part of an accountability system such as that which is an integral part of any other well-designed token economy or behavior modification endeavor.

It is also again apparent that the remediation of educational and voca-tional deficiencies will not take the form of introducing contingencies where none existed before. Instead, the remediation will involve supplanting contingencies that foster nonparticipation in rehabilitation programs with those that encourage the inmate to avail himself of the services offered within the institution. One strategy that has gained considerable popularity is to make the offerings themselves more appealing: Operate the program in an appealing environment, provide services that the inmate can readily identify as meaningful, employ academic and vocational training materials with which the inmate is comfortable, utilize staff members who have the potential of establishing rapport with the inmate, and so on.

Unfortunately, making remedial, academic, and vocational training intrinsically appealing has had little, if any, impact upon the inmates' participation or performance in it. At best, such efforts made the task of the motivational system less difficult, in that it is likely that greater magnitude of reinforcement would otherwise have been required to reach the performance levels achieved. What is most apparent in these studies is that the engineering of contingencies—in this case in the form of a token economy—was clearly the element necessary to gain inmate's voluntary participation in the educational and vocational programs. This strategy will probably prove to be equally important in other rehabilitation programs in other institutions.

The role of systematic evaluation, such as that described herein, is an important one in the evolution of correctional programming. The criminal justice system is now in the position that the mental health field found itself a half-century ago: Both professionals and the informed public alike recognize the inadequacies of current practices and urge the search for more effective alternatives. As the criminal justice system develops both an analytic orientation and capability, it will, as the mental health field has, begin the difficult task of identifying shortcomings and validating effective strategies. Only through empirical study will the criminal justice system come to determine with any certainty which of its procedures, either established or proposed, are beneficial and worth retaining, and which are harmful and to be eliminated. To block or unnecessarily restrict such research is to freeze our state of knowledge and quality of programming at its present impoverished level.

SUCCESSFUL TRANSITION FROM INSTITUTION TO COMMUNITY

An enduring concern of behavior modification centers upon the degree to which changes in behavior achieved in one setting or under one set of conditions will be continued in other settings or under other sets of conditions. A common criticism of this particular approach to the understanding and remediation of human problems is that behavior change induced by artificial means in the remedial education classroom, mental hospital, or correctional institution is of little utility because it is unlikely that the behavior change will be maintained once the individual leaves the controlled setting and returns to the natural environment. Moreover, many of the findings reported herein indicated that behavior changes correlated with changes in environmental contingencies were short-lived once changes in environmental contingencies were reversed or removed. Such findings are often interpreted as supporting this argument. Critics who construct such an argument, however, have not yet grasped either the complexities of this approach to the understanding of human behavior or the subtleties involved in its application to the solution of human problems. Indeed, such critics might be genuinely surprised by the degree to which applied behavior analysts would support them in this argument, insofar as it goes.

Most behavioral applications operate under the assumption that modified behavior will *not* generalize from one situation to another if the transition is rapid or the two situations are markedly different. Similarly, they also assume that behavior maintained by certain contingencies will not be maintained by others if the change is sudden or the contingencies are greatly dissimilar. These assumptions do not, however, represent critical weaknesses within this approach to human behavior. Such assumptions, instead, are among its more important strengths, for they formalize the now generally accepted premise that all intervention programs—no matter what their theoretical basis—must provide continuity of care and treatment if they are to maximize the likelihood that they will yield enduring effects. An important advantage of the behavioral model is that it offers the practitioner detailed information and specific technical procedures to more effectively provide this continuity.

Two general procedures are employed to help insure that behavior changes produced in a particular setting or under a particular set of contingencies will generalize to another setting or be maintained under another set of contingencies. One is *fading,* in which distinguishing characteristics of the training environment are changed in a gradual and progressive fashion until they approximate or are indistinguishable from those of the setting in which the behavior is to be continued. The second procedure entails the *attenuation of reinforcing consequences.* Here, the focus of attention is upon differences between the contingencies of reinforcement programmed in the training situation and those occurring naturally in the environment in which the behavior is to be maintained. Typically, the contingencies programmed in training situations

employ different types of consequences, greater quantities of reinforcers, and richer schedules of reinforcement than those of the natural
environment. In the attenuation of reinforcing consequences, these differences are also eliminated in a gradual and progressive fashion until
the contingencies of reinforcement operative in the training situation
come to approximate or are indistinguishable from those of the natural
environment in which the newly acquired behavior is to be continued.

Although fading and the attenuation of reinforcing consequences
contribute greatly to the generalization and continuance of intervention
effects, they succeed only when the conditions of the natural environment are such that they do, in fact, support the behavior change once the
artificial support of the training setting is fully withdrawn. All treatment
endeavors, regardless of their theoretical orientation, acknowledge this
requirement for an enduring effect of intervention. Based upon an
analysis of the environment, the practitioner must be prepared to deal
with two general possibilities: (1) that no contingencies exist in the
natural environment to support the behavior change or (2) that the
naturally occurring contigencies are such that they will actively foster
older, inappropriate forms of behavior at the expense of the newly established alternatives.

To overcome these difficulties, more and more behavior therapists
either precede or accompany individuals as they return to the environment in which new behavior is to be maintained. The emphasis of their
endeavors has been upon rearranging naturally occurring contingencies
and reeducating significant others in the lives of these individuals so that
the natural environment can support changed behavior. Indeed, most
behavior therapists working in the natural environment have redefined
the practitioner–client relationship. No longer is the individual who is
the original focus of the therapeutic process looked upon as the sole or
primary client. Instead, clients are defined as those people who, for one
reason or another, are the significant others in the lives of these individuals. These are the agents who can support changed behavior once
the individual does return from the training setting. Clearly, then, the
behavioral model dictates that it not be assumed that behavior change
accomplished under one set of contingencies in the training environment will transfer to and continue under other sets of contigencies in the
natural environment. It is equally clear, however, that the careful utilization of appropriate behavioral procedures can maximize the likelihood
that the rehabilitative services provided in the training environment will
be effective in changing behavior and that this change will generalize to
and be maintained in the natural environment.

The token economy programs reported upon herein are typical of most "prosthetic environments." Artificial contingencies were employed to encourage inmates to remediate deficiencies that they would not otherwise seek to overcome and to acquire skills that they would otherwise be incapable of mastering. Some skills, such as the ability to read or to repair a small motor, are easily generalized to and maintained in the natural environment. However, the preceding discussion has emphasized that it would be unreasonable to expect that other skills, such as employability and interpersonal skills, will generalize to and be maintained in the natural environment unless there is a programmed transitional effort to both insure that this will occur and to teach additional community-living skills that cannot be approximated in the institution setting. Institutions, through prosthetic programming and intensified behavioral training, can remediate deficiencies and expand skill repertoires, thereby providing the released offender with more options than he possessed prior to his imprisonment. There is little, if anything, the staff in the institution can do to guarantee that the contingencies of the natural environment will either permit or encourage the offender to exercise these options following his release. Clearly, a behavioral approach to the development of continuity in care and rehabilitation will prove to be as critical for the success of programming within each division of the criminal justice system as it has been in the education and mental health professions.

REFERENCES

Adams, S. A. (1961). Interactions between individual interview therapy and treatment amenability in older youth authority wards. *California State Board of Corrections Monograph, 2,* 27–44.

Anastasi, A. (1954). *Psychological testing.* New York: Macmillan.

Argyle, M. (1961). A new approach to the classification of delinquents with implications for treatment. *Board of Corrections Monograph Number Two.* Sacramento: State of California Printing Division, Documents Section.

Atthowe, J. and Krasner, L. (1968). Preliminary report on the application of contingent reinforcement procedures (token economy) in a "chronic" psychiatric ward. *Journal of Abnormal Psychology, 73,* 37–43.

Ayllon, T. and Azrin, N. H. (1965). The measurement and reinforcement of behavior of psychotics. *Journal of the Experimental Analysis of Behavior, 8,* 357–383.

Ayllon, T. and Azrin, N. H. (1968a). *The token economy: A motivational system for therapy and rehabilitation.* New York: Appleton-Century-Crofts.

Ayllon, T. and Azrin, N. H. (1968b). Reinforcer sampling: A technique for increasing the behavior of mental patients. *Journal of Applied Behavior Analysis, 1,* 13–20.

Ayllon, T. and Haughton, E. (1962). Control of the behavior of schizophrenic patients by food. *Journal of Applied Behavior Analysis, 5,* 343–352.

Ayllon, T. and Kelly, K. (1972). Effects of reinforcement in standardized test performance. *Journal of Applied Behavior Analysis, 5,* 477–484.

Ayllon, T. and Michael, J. (1959). The psychiatric nurse as a behavioral engineer. *Journal of Applied Behavior Analysis, 2,* 323–334.

Ayllon, T. and Roberts, M. D. (1966). The token economy: Now. In W. S. Agras (Ed.), *Behavior modification: Principles and clinical applications.* Boston: Little, Brown.

Azrin, N., Naster, B., and Jones, R. (1973). Reciprocity counseling: A rapid learning-based procedure for marital counseling. *Behavior Research and Therapy, 11,* 365–382.

Bailey, J. S., Timbers, G., Phillips, E. L., and Wolf, M. M. (1971). Modification of articulation errors of pre-delinquents by their peers. *Journal of Applied Behavior Analysis, 4,* 265–281.

Bailey, J. S., Wolf, M. M., and Phillips, E. L. (1970). Home-based reinforcement and the modification of pre-delinquents by their peers. *Journal of Applied Behavior Analysis, 3,* 29–38.

Baker, R. (1971). The use of operant conditioning to reinstate speech in mute schizophrenics. *Behavior Research and Therapy, 9,* 329–336.

Bandura, A. (1969). *Principles of behavior modification.* New York: Holt, Rinehart, and Winston.

Bandura, A. (1977). *Social learning theory.* Englewood Cliffs, New Jersey: Prentice-Hall.

Bannister, D., Salmon, P., and Lieberman, D. M. (1964). Diagnosis–treatment relationships in psychiatry: A statistical analysis. *British Journal of Psychiatry, 110,* 726–732.

Barron, F. (1953). An ego-strength scale which predicts response to psychotherapy. *Journal of Consulting Psychology, 17,* 327–333.

Barron, F. and Leary, T. F. (1955). Changes in psychoneurotic patients with and without psychotherapy. *Journal of Consulting Psychology, 19,* 239–245.

Beck, A. T., Ward, C. H., Mendleson, M., Mock, J. E., and Erbaugh, J. K. (1962). Reliability of psychiatric diagnosis: A study of consistency of clinical judgement and ratings. Journal of Applied Psychology, 119, 351–357.

Bergin, A. C. (1971). The evaluation of therapeutic outcomes. In A. E. Bergin and S. L. Garfield (Eds.), *Handbook of psychotherapy and behavior change.* New York: Wiley.

Birkey, H. J., Chamblis, J. E., and Wasden, R. A. (1971). A comparison of residents discharged from a token economy and two traditional psychiatric programs. *Behavior Therapy, 2,* 46–51.

Boren, J. J. and Coleman, A. D. (1970). Some experiments on reinforcement principles within a psychiatric ward for delinquent soldiers. *Journal of Applied Behavior Analysis, 3,* 29–37.

Brill, N. Q. and Beebe, G. W. (1955). A follow-up study of war neuroses. Washington, D.C.: Department of Medicine and Surgery, Veterans Administration.

Brown, D. G. (1971). Behavior analysis and intervention in counseling and psychotherapy. In H. C. Rickard (Ed.), *Behavioral intervention in human problems.* New York: Pergamon.

Buehler, R. E., Patterson, G. R., and Furniss, J. M. (1966). The reinforcement of behavior in institutional settings. *Behavior Research and Therapy, 4,* 157–167.

Burns, V. M. and Stern, L. W. (1967). The prevention of juvenile delinquency. In *The President's Commission on Law Enforcement and Administration of Justice, Task Force Report: Juvenile Delinquency.*

Chute, C. L., (1923). Juvenile probation. *Annals of the American Academy of Political and Social Sciences, 105,* 223–228.

Clark, R. (1970). *Crime in America.* New York: Simon and Schuster.

Clements, C. B. and McKee, J. M. (1968). Programmed instruction for institutional offenders: Contingency management and performance contracts. *Psychological Reports, 22,* 957–964.

Cohen, H. L. and Filipczak, J. (1971). *A new learning environment.* San Francisco: Jossey-Bass.

Cohen, H. L., Filipczak, J. and Bis J. (1967). *A study of contingencies applicable to special education: Case I.* Silver Springs, Maryland: Educational Facility Press-IBR.

Cohen, S. I., Keyworth, J. M., Kleiner, R. I., and Brown, W. L. (1974). Effective behavior change at the Anne Arvandel Learning Center through minimum contact interventions. In R. Ulrich, T. Stachnik, and J. Mabry (Eds.), *Control of human behavior: Behavior modification in education.* Glenview, Ill.: Scott, Foresman.,

Colman, A. D. and Baker, S. L. (1969). Utilization of an operant conditioning model for the treatment of character and behavior disorders in a military setting. *American Journal of Psychiatry, 125,* 101–109.

Colman, A. D. and Boren, J. J. (1969). An information system for measuring behavior and its use by staff. *Journal of Applied Behavior Analysis, 2,* 207–214.

Conrad, J. P. (1971). *What should society expect of corrections?* Paper presented at the National Conference on Correction, Williamsburg, Virginia, December.

Costello, C. C. (Ed.). (1970). *Symptoms of psychopathology: A handbook.* New York: Wiley, p. 364.

Craighead, W. E., Kazdin, A., and Mahoney, M. J. (1976). *Behavior modification: Principles, issues, and applications.* Boston: Houghton-Mifflin.

Crowther, C. (1969). Crimes, penalties, and legislatures. *Annals of the American Academy of Political and Social Sciences, 381,* 147–158.

Durkheim, E. (1947). *The division of labor in society,* p. 89. Cited by Toby, J. (1970). Is punishment necessary? In N. Johnston, L. Savitz and M. E. Wolfgang (Eds.), *The sociology of punishment and correction.* New York: Wiley.

Eisler, R., Hersen, M., and Miller, P. (1973). Effects of modeling on components of assertive behavior. *Journal of Behavior Therapy and Experimental Psychiatry, 4,* 1–6.

Epstein, L. H. and Hersen, M. (1974). A multiple baseline analysis of covariant control. *Journal of Behavior Therapy and Experimental Psychiatry, 5,* 7–12.

Eysenck, H. J. (1952). The effects of psychotherapy: An evaluation. *Journal of Consulting Psychology, 16,* 319–324.

Eysenck, H. J. (1961). Classification and the problem of diagnosis. In H. J. Eysenck (Ed.) *Handbook of abnormal psychology.* New York: Basic Books.

Eysenck, H. J. (1966). *The effects of psychotherapy.* New York: International Science Press.

Fairweather, G. W., Sanders, D. H., Maynard, H., and Cressler, A. L. (1969). *Community life for the mentally ill: An alternative to institutional care.* Chicago: Aldene.

Federal Bureau of Prisons. (1948). *Annual report.* Washington, D.C.: United States Government Printing Office.

Federal Bureau of Prisons. (1964). *Rational innovation.* Washington, D.C.: Bureau of Prisons.

Filipczak, J. and Cohen, M. L. (1972). *The case II contingency management system and where it is going.* Paper presented at the 80th Annual Convention of the American Psychological Association, Honolulu, September.

Fixsen, D. L., Phillips, G. L., and Wolf, M. M. (1973). Achievement place: Experiments in self-government with pre-delinquents. *Journal of Applied Behavior Analysis, 6,* 31–47.

Fogel, D. (1977). The justice perspective in corrections. *Quarterly Journal of Corrections, 1,* 14–29.

Ford, D. H. and Urban, H. B. (1963). *Systems of psychotherapy: A comparative study.* New York: Wiley.

Franks, C. M. (1969). *Behavior therapy: Appraisal and status.* New York: McGraw-Hill.

Freudenberg, R. K. and Robertson, J. P. S. (1956). Symptoms in relation to psychiatric diagnosis and treatment. *Archives of Neurology and Psychiatry, 76,* 14–22.

Geller, E. S., Johnson, D. F., Hamlin, P. H., and Kennedy, T. D. (1977). Behavior modification in prisons: Issues, problems, and compromises. *Criminal Justice and Behavior, 4,* 11–43.

Ghiselli, E. E. (1964). *Theory of psychological measurement.* New York: McGraw-Hill.

Glaser, D. (1964). *The effectiveness of a prison and parole system.* New York: Bobbs-Merrill.

Goldsmith, J. B. and McFall, R. M. (1975). Developing and evaluation of an interpersonal skill-training program for psychiatric inpatients. *Journal of Abnormal Psychology, 84,* 51–58.

Grant, J. D. and Grant, M. (1959). A group dynamic approach to the treatment of nonconformity in the Navy. *Annals of the American Academy of Political and Social Sciences, 322,* 126–135.

Graziano, A. M. (1969). Clinical innovation and the mental health power structure: A social case history. *American Psychologist, 24,* 10–18.

Greenson, R. R. (1967). *The techniques and practice of psychoanalysis* (Vol. 1). New York: International Universities Press.

Gripp, R. F. and Magaro, P. A. (1971). A token economy program evaluation with untreated control ward comparisons. *Behavior Research and Therapy, 9,* 137–149.

Harcourt, Brace, and World. (1964). *English 2600.*

Harrison, S. I. and Carek, D. J. (1966). *A guide to psychotherapy.* Boston: Little, Brown.

Hersen, M. and Barlow, D. (1976). *Single case experimental designs: Strategies for studying behavior change.* New York: Pergamon Press.

Hersen, M., Eisler, R., Miller, P., Johnson, M., and Pinkston, S. (1973). Effects of practice, instructions, and modeling on components of assertive behavior. *Behavior Research and Therapy, 11,* 443–451.

Hoover, J. D. (1970). Prison reform has come a long way, still more to do. Cited by Robert Betts in *The Montgomery Advertiser,* February 27, p. 3.

Isaacs, W., Thomas, J., and Goldiamond, I. (1960). Application of operant conditioning to reinstate verbal behavior in psychotics. *Journal of Speech and Hearing Disorders, 25,* 8–12.

Jenkins, R. L., Bemiss, E. L., Jr., and Lorr, M. (1953). Duration of hospitalization, readmission rate, and stability of diagnosis in veterans hospitalized with neuropsychiatric diagnoses. *Psychiatric Quarterly, 27,* 59–72.

Jenkins, R. L. and Hewitt, L. (1944). Types of personality structure encountered in child guidance clinics. *American Journal of Orthopsychiatry, 14,* 84–95.

Jesness, C. F. (1969). *The Jesness inventory manual.* Palo Alto, Calif.: Consulting Psychologist Press.

Jesness, C. F. (1970). The Preston topology study. *California Youth Authority Quarterly, 23,* 26–28.

Jesness, C. F. and DeRisi, W. J. (1973). Some variations on techniques of contingency management in a school for delinquents. In J. S. Stumphauser (Ed.), *Behavior therapy with delinquents.* Springfield, Ill.: Charles C Thomas.

Johnston, J. M. and Pennypacker, H. S. (1971). A behavioral approach to college teaching. *American Psychologist, 26,* 219–244.

Journal of Applied Behavior Analysis. (1968–   ). Ann Arbor, Mich.: Society for the Experimental Analysis of Behavior.

Journal of the Experimental Analysis of Behavior. (1958–   ). Bloomington, Ind.: Society for the Experimental Analysis of Behavior, January.

Kaebling, H. J. and Volpe, P. A., II. (1963). Constancy of psychiatric diagnosis in readmissions. *Comprehensive Psychiatry, 4*(1), 29–39.

Kandel, H., Ayllon, T., and Roberts, M. D. (1976). Rapid educational rehabilitation for prison inmates. *Behavior Research and Therapy, 14,* 323–331.

Kanfer, F. H. and Saslow, G. (1969). Behavioral diagnosis. In C. M. Franks (Ed.), *Behavior therapy: Appraisal and status.* New York: McGraw-Hill.

Karacki, L. and Levinson, R. B. (1970). A token economy in a correctional institution for youthful offenders. *The Howard Journal of Penology and Crime Prevention, 13,* 20–30.

Kazdin, A. E. (1975). *Behavior modification in applied settings.* Homewood, Ill.: Dorsey.

Keller, F. S. (1969). A programmed system of instruction. *Educational Technology Monographs, 2,* 1–26.

Kennedy, R. E. (1976). Behavior modification in prisons. In W. E. Craighead, A. E. Kazdin, and M. J. Mahoney (Eds.), *Behavior modification: Principles, issues, and applications.* Boston: Houghton-Mifflin.

Krasner, L. (1968). Assessment of token economy programmes in psychatric hospitals. In N. H. Miller and R. Porter (Eds.), *Learning theory and psychotherapy.* London: CIBA Foundation.

Krasner, L., and Ullman, L. P. (Eds.). (1965). *Research in behavior modification.* New York: Holt, Rinehart, and Winston.

Kreitman, N. (1961). The reliability of psychiatric diagnosis. *Journal of Mental Science, 107,* 876–886.

Kreitman, N., Sainsbury, P. P., Morrisey, J., Towers, J., and Scrivener, J. (1961). The reliability of psychiatric assessment: An analysis. *Journal of Mental Science, 107,* 887–908.

Lehrer, P., Schiff, L., and Kriss, A. (1970). The use of a credit card in a token economy. *Journal of Applied Behavior Analysis, 3,* 289–291.

Lemert, E. M. (1971). *Instead of court: Diversion in juvenile justice.* Washington, D.C.: United States Government Printing Office.

Lerman, P. (1968). Evaluative studies of institutions for delinquents. *Social Work, 13,* 55–64.

Levine, J. and Zigler, E. (1973). The essential-reactive distinction in alcoholism: A developmental approach. *Journal of Abnormal Psychology, 81,* 242–249.

Levinson, R. B., Ingram, G. L., and Azcarate, E. (1968). Aversive group therapy: Sometimes good medicine tastes bad. *Crime and Delinquency, 15,* 336–339.

Levinson, S. H. (1970). The language of involuntary mental hospitalization: A study in sound and fury. *Journal of Law Reform, 4,* 195–214.

Liberman, R. P., Ferris, C., Salgado, P., and Salgado, J. (1975). Replication of the Achievement Place model in California. *Journal of Applied Behavior Analysis, 8,* 287–300.

Libet, J. M. and Lewinsohn, P. M. (1973). Concept of social skill with special reference to the behavior of depressed persons. *Journal of Consulting and Clinical Psychology, 40,* 304–312.

Lindsley, O. and Skinner, B. F. (1954). A method for the experimental analysis of the behavior of psychotic patients. *American Psychologist, 9,* 419–420.

Lloyd, K. E. and Abel, L. (1970). Performance on a token economy psychiatric ward: A two year summary. *Behavior Research and Therapy, 8,* 1–9.

Lorr, M., Klett, C. J., and McNair, D. M. (1963). *Syndromes of psychosis*. New York: Macmillan.

Lovitt, T. C. and Esveldt, K. A. (1970). The relative effects on math performance of single vs. multiple-ratio schedules: A case study. *Journal of Applied Behavior Analysis, 3,* 261–270.

Maley, R. F., Feldman, G. L., and Ruskin, R. S. (1973). Evaluation of patient improvement in a token economy treatment program. *Journal of Abnormal Psychology, 82,* 141–144.

McCord, W., McCord, J., and Zola, I. K. (1959). *Origins of crime: A new evaluation of the Cambridge-Somerville youth study*. New York: Columbia University.

McKee, J. M. (1971). Contingency management in a correctional institution. *Educational Technology, 2*(4), 51–54.

McKee, J. M. and Clements, C. B. (1971). A behavioral approach to learning: The Draper model. In H. C. Rickard (Ed.), *Behavioral intervention in human problems*. New York: Pergamon.

McKee, J. M., Jenkins, W. O., and Milan, M. A. (1977). The effect of contingency management procedures on the rate of learning. *Quarterly Journal of Corrections, 1,* 42–44.

McReynolds, W. T. and Coleman, J. (1972). Token economy: Patient and staff changes. *Behavior Research and Therapy, 10,* 29–34.

Meehl, P. C. (1955). Psychotherapy. *Annual Review of Psychology, 6,* 357–378.

Meichenbaum, D. and Cameron, E. (1973). Training schizophrenics to talk to themselves: A means of developing attentional controls. *Behavior Therapy, 4,* 515–534.

Menninger, R. (1968). *The crime of punishment*. New York: Viking.

Meyer, H. J., Borgatta, C. F., and Jones, W. C. (1970). The Girls' Vocational High study. In W. Johnston, L. Savitz and M. E. Wolfgang (Eds.), *The sociology of punishment and correction*. New York: Wiley.

Michael, J. and Meyerson, L. (1962). A behavioral approach to counseling and guidance. *Harvard Educational Review, 32,* 382–401.

Milan, M. A. and McKee, J. M. (1974). Behavior modification: Principles and applications in corrections. In Glaser (Ed.), *Handbook of criminology*. Chicago: Rand McNally.

Milan, M. A. and McKee, J. M. (1976). The cellblock token economy: Token reinforcement procedures in a maximum security correctional institution for adult male felons. *Journal of Applied Behavior Analysis, 3,* 253–275.

Miller, W. B. (1970). The midcity delinquency control project. In N. Johnston, L. Savitz and M. E. Wolfgang (Eds.), *The sociology of punishment and correction*. New York: Wiley, pp. 635–656.

Mitford, J. (1973). *Kind and usual punishment: The prison business*. New York: Knopf.

Mordock, J. B. (1974). *The other children: An introduction to exceptionality*. New York: Harper and Row.

Morris, N. and Hawkins, G. (1970). *The honest politicians guide to crime control*. Chicago: University of Chicago.

Murphy, P. V. (1972). Address to the Bar Association of the City of New York, December 20, 1971. Cited in "Courts to easy on crime? Police chiefs speak out." *U.S. News and World Report,* January 31, 52–53.

National Advisory Commission on Criminal Justice Standards and Goals. (1973). *Report on corrections*. Washington, D. C.: United States Government Printing Office.

Nunnally, J. C. (1967). *Psychometric theory*. New York: McGraw-Hill.

Palmer, T. B. (1970). An evaluation of differental treatment for delinquents. *Community treatment project report series* (No. 2). Sacramento: California Youth Authority.

Palmer, T. B. (1971). California's community treatment program for delinquent adolescents. *Journal of Research in Crime and Delinquency, 8,* 74–92.

Pasamanick, B., Dinitz, S., and Lefton, M. (1959). Psychiatric orientation and its relation to diagnosis and treatment in a mental hospital. *American Journal of Psychiatry, 116,* 127–132.

Patterson, G. R., Cobb, J. A., and Ray, R. S. (1973). A social engineering technology for retraining the families of aggressive boys. In H. E. Adams and I. P. Unikel (Eds.), *Issues and trends in behavior therapy.* Springfield, Ill.: Charles C Thomas.

Patterson, G. R. and Reed, J. B. (1970). Reciprocity and coercion: Two facets of social systems. In C. Neuringer and J. L. Michael (Eds.), *Behavior modification in clinical psychology.* New York: Appleton-Century-Crofts.

Phillips, E. L. (1968). Achievement place: Token reinforcement procedures in a home-style rehabilitation setting for pre-delinquent boys. *Journal of Applied Behavior Analysis, 2,* 213–223.

Phillips, E. L., Phillips, E. A., Fixsen, D. L., and Wolf, M. M. (1971). Achievement place: Modification of the behaviors of pre-delinquent boys within a token economy. *Journal of Applied Behavior Analysis, 4,* 45–49.

Phillips, E. L., Phillips, E. A., Fixsen, D. L., & Wolf, M. M. (1973). Behavior shaping for delinquents. *Psychology Today, 7* (June), 74–79.

Phillips, L. and Draguns, J. G. (1971). Classification of the behavior disorders. *Annual Review of Psychology, 22,* 447–482.

Powers, E. and Witner, H. (1951). *An experiment in the prevention of delinquency: the Cambridge-Somerville youth study.* New York: Columbia University.

Quay, H. C. (1964). Personality dimensions in delinquent males as inferred from the factor analysis of behavior ratings. *Journal of Research in Crime and Delinquency, 1,* 33–37.

Quay, H. C. and Parsons, L. B. (undated). *The differential behavioral classification of the juvenile offender.* Morgantown, W.V.: Robert F. Kennedy Youth Center, monograph.

Rachman, S. (1971). *The effects of psychotherapy.* New York: Pergamon.

Raimy, V. C. (1950). *Training in clinical psychology.* New York: Prentice-Hall.

Ramp, C. A. and Hopkins, B. L. (1971). *A new direction for education: Behavior analysis.* Lawrence, Kansas: University of Kansas.

Reckless, W. C. (1961). *The crime problem.* New York: Appleton-Century-Crofts.

Reiss, A. J., Jr. (1952). Social correlates of psychological types of delinquency. *American Sociological Revue, 17,* 710–718.

Reynolds, G. S. (1968). *A primer of operant conditioning.* Glenview, Ill.: Scott, Foresman.

Rimm, D. C. and Masters, J. C. (1974). *Behavior therapy: Techniques and empirical findings.* New York: Academic.

Rutner, I. T. and Bugle, C. (1969). An experimental procedure for the modification of psychotic behavior. *Journal of Clinical and Counseling Psychology, 33,* 651–653.

Sandifer, M. G., Pettus, C., and Quade, D. (1964). A study of psychiatric diagnosis. *Journal of Nervous Disease, 139,* 350–356.

Schaefer, H. H. and Martin, P. L. (1966). Behavioral therapy for "apathy" of hospitalized schizophrenics. *Psychological Reports, 19,* 1147–1158.

Schaefer, H. H. and Martin, P. L. (1969). *Behavioral therapy.* New York: McGraw-Hill.

Schmidt, H. O. and Fonda, C. P. (1956). The reliability of psychiatric diagnosis: A new look. *Journal of Abnormal and Social Psychology, 52*, 262–267.

Schwitzgebel, R. K. (1964). *Streetcorner research: An experimental approach to the juvenile delinquent.* Cambridge, Mass.: Harvard.

Schwitzgebel, R. K. and Kolb, D. A. (1964). Inducing behavior change in adolescent delinquents. *Behavior Research and Therapy, 2,* 217–304.

Shah, S. A. (1971). A behavioral approach to out-patient treatment of offenders. In H. C. Rickard (Ed.), *Behavioral intervention in human problems.* New York: Pergamon.

Sherman, J. A. (1965). Use of reinforcement and imitation to reinstate verbal behavior in mute psychotics. *Journal of Abnormal and Social Psychology, 70,* 155–164.

Sidman, M. (1960a). Normal sources of pathological behavior. *Science, 132,* 61–68.

Sidman, M. (1960b). *Tactics of scientific research.* New York: Basic Books, Inc.

Skinner, B. F. (1954). The science of learning and the art of teaching. *Harvard Education Review, 29,* 86–97.

Slack, C. W. (1960). Introducing intensive office treatment for unreliable cases. *Mental Hygiene, 44,* 238–256.

Smith, R. R., Milan, M. A., Wood, L. F., and McKee, J. M. (1976). The correctional officer as a behavioral technician. *Criminal Justice and Behavior, 3,* 345–360.

Solzhenitsyn, A. (1974). *The gulag archipelago.* New York: Harper and Row.

Steffy, R., Hart, J., Draw, M., Torney, D., and Marlett, N. (1969). Operant behavior modification techniques applied to a ward of severely regressed and aggressive patients. *Canadian Psychiatric Association Journal, 14,* 59–67.

Stuart, R. B. (1970). *Trick or treatment: How and when psychotherapy fails.* Champaign, Ill.: Research Press.

Stuart, R. B. (1971). Behavioral contracting within the families of delinquents. *Journal of Behavior Therapy and Experimental Psychiatry, 2,* 1–11.

Sullivan, C., Grant, M., and Grant, J. D. (1957). The development of interpersonal maturity: Applications to delinquency. *Psychiatry, 20,* 373–386.

Szasz, T. S. (1961). The uses of naming and the origin of the myth of mental illness. *American Psychologist, 16,* 59–65.

Szasz, T. S. (1966). Psychotherapy: A sociocultural perspective. *Comprehensive Psychiatry, 7,* 217–223.

Szasz, T. (1970). Justice in the therapeutic state. *Comprehensive Psychiatry, 11,* 433–444.

Tannenbaum, F. (1933). *Osborne of Sing Sing.* Chapel Hill, N.C.: University of North Carolina.

Teuber, H. and Powers, E. (1953). The effects of treatment of delinquents. *Proceedings of the Association for Research into Nervous and Mental Disease, 31,* 138–147.

Tharp, R. and Wetzel, R. J. (1969). *Behavior modification in the natural environment.* New York: Academic.

Thoresen C. E. and Mahoney, M. J. (1974). *Behavioral self-control.* New York: Holt, Rinehart, and Winston.

Thorne, G. H., Tharpe, R. G., and Wetzel, R. J. (1967). Behavior modification techniques: New tools for probation officers. *Federal Probation, 31,* 21–27.

Toch, H. (1970). Care and feeding of typologies and labels. *Federal Probation, 34*(3), 15–19.

Truax, C. B. (1966). Reinforcement and nonreinforcement in Rogerian psychotherapy. *Journal of Abnormal Psychology, 71,* 1–9.

Tyler, V. O. and Brown, G. D. (1968). Token reinforcement of academic performance with institutionalized delinquents. *Journal of Educational Psychology, 59,* 164–168.

Ullmann, L. P. and Krasner, L. (1969). *A psychological approach to abnormal behavior.* Englewood Cliffs, N.J.: Prentice-Hall.

U. S. Department of Commerce, (1977). *Statistical Abstract of the United States.* Washington, D.C.: U. S. Government Printing Office.

U. S. Department of Justice, (1977). *Uniform crime reports for the United States.* Washington, D.C.: U. S. Government Printing Office.

Walker, R. G. and Kelly, F. E. (1960). Predicting the outcome of a schizophrenic episode. *Archives of General Psychiatry, 2,* 492–503.

Warren, M. Q. (1967). The community treatment project: History and perspective. *Law Enforcement Science and Technology, 1,* 191–200.

Warren, M. Q. (1967). The community treatment project after five years. *California Department of Corrections,* (mimeo).

Warren, M. Q. (1969). The care for differential treatment of delinquents. *Annals of the American Academy of Political and Social Science, 381,* 47–60.

Warren, M. Q. (1970). The community treatment project. In N. Johnson, L. Savitz and M. E. Wolfgang (Eds.), *The sociology of punishment and correction.* New York: Wiley, pp. 671–683.

Warren, M. Q. (1971). Classification of offenders as an aid to efficient management and effective treatment. *Journal of Criminal Law, Criminology, and Police Science, 62,* 239–258.

Whaley, D. L. and Malott, R. W. (1971). *Elementary principles of behavior.* New York: Appleton-Century-Crofts.

Winer, J. B. (1962). *Statistical principles in experimental design.* New York: McGraw-Hill.

Witherspoon, A. D. (1971). *A behavioral observation index (BOI) designed to evaluate training of correctional officers in a prison setting.* Elmore, Alabama: Rehabilitation Research Foundation.

Wittenborn, J. R., Holzberg, J. D., and Simon, B. (1953). Symptom correlates for description diagnosis. *Genetic Psychology Monographs, 47,* 237–302.

Wolf, B. D. (1971). The government of Doctor Caligari. *National Review, 23,* 1461–1462.

Wolpe, J. (1976). *Theme and variations: A behavior therapy casebook.* New York: Pergamon.

World Health Organization. (1967). *Manual of the international statistical classification of diseases, injuries, and causes of death.* Based on the *Recommendations of the Eighth Revision Conference,* 1965, and adopted by the Nineteenth World Health Assembly, Volume I. Geneva, Switzerland.

Yates, A. J. (1970). *Behavior Therapy.* New York: Wiley.

Yochelson, S. and Samenow, S. E. (1976). *The criminal personality.* New York: J. Aronson.

Zigler, E. and Phillips, L. (1961). Social competence and outcome in psychiatric disorder. *Journal of Abnormal and Social Psychology, 63,* 264–271.

Zubin, J. (1967). Classification of the behavior disorders. *Annual Review of Psychology, 18,* 373–400.

AUTHOR INDEX

COUNSELING AND PSYCHOTHERAPY
A Behavioral Approach
By E. Lakin Phillips

Phillips advocates a "soft" behaviorism treatment—an adaptation and use of behavioral therapy techniques in outpatient counseling and psychotherapy. Within a behavioral framework he defines behavior, discusses how to analyze a patient's problems, and how to conduct, conclude and evaluate the treatment. Among the techniques suggested are those which help patients expand their understanding of and contributions to the status of their problems. Phillips also explores cybernetics and covers the diagnostic, conceptual and therapeutic considerations of the clinical situation.

1977   289 pp.

HUMAN RESOURCES FOR TROUBLED CHILDREN
By Werner I. Halpern and Stanley Kissel

Everyone who is concerned about children will find this a veritable encyclopedia on the many ways troubled or troubling children and their families can be helped. The wide range of clinical treatment options and resources currently available is presented systematically and comprehensively, with case illustrations linking theory to practice. Opening with an examination of the history of child treatment, the book goes on to explore public mental health facilities, community and school services, parent education and counseling, child guidance, family therapies, group treatment, behavior modification, and pharmacology. It also takes an in-depth look at options such as foster care, group homes, and day programs.

1976   263 pp.

HEROIN ADDICTION
Theory, Research, and Treatment
By Jerome J. Platt and Christina Labate

Drawing on over 2,000 published references, this definitive one-volume survey of heroin abuse covers the entire subject in documented detail. Beginning with the historic-legal background of addiction in the United States, federal anti-narcotic policies in this century and anti-narcotic legislation, the book then discusses heroin addiction from a medical and biological viewpoint. Explanations of heroin abuse are drawn from sociological, psychological, and psychoanalytical theories. The whole range of treatment methods are examined, along with such related topics as personality and social characteristics of the addict.

1976   417 pp.

WILEY-INTERSCIENCE
a division of JOHN WILEY & SONS
605 Third Avenue, New York, N.Y. 10016
New York • Chichester • Brisbane • Toronto   ISBN 0 471 03843-1

SUBJECT INDEX

difficulties of, 231-233
Credit card system, in MORE project, 156-157, 159-164
Crime, causes of, 5
"cleared," 4

Delay of gratification, fostering of, 194-197
Duration measure, 105

Education, in prison, 165-197
English, 177-179, 184-191, 194-197
Mathematics, 184-191, 194-197
release, 11
EMLC, see Experimental Manpower Laboratory for Corrections
Employability skills, teaching of, 207-226
Encounter groups, 11, 12
Ethical programs, criteria, 123-126
guidelines, 120-126
Evaluation, behavioral approach, 95-107
comparative studies, 117
long term objectives, 115-117
procedures, 98-114
short term objectives, 115-117
Expenditures, daily, 5
Experimental Manpower Laboratory for Corrections (EMLC), 139-142, 143, 144, 145-156
officer training project, 214
prison routine, 148-149
prison settings, 143-144
social characteristics of participants, 145-147
token economy procedures, 150-156

Fading, 260
Family visits, 10
Freedom and dignity, 129, 130
guidelines, 130-133
Frequency counting, 101, 102

General Education Diploma test (GED), 168, 172
Generalized conditioned reinforcer, 88
Good time, 131, 133, 134
Group homes, 11

Halfway houses, 92, 93
Halfway programs, 11, 12

I level classification system, 35, 37, 40, 41
Individualized behavioral procedures, applied to psychotic disorders, 64, 65
Individually Prescribed Instruction system (IPI), 166-168
Informed consent, 131
Inmate counterculture, 84, 85, 86
Interval recording, 102, 103
Intervention plans, individualized, 97
Involuntary civil commitment, 26

Jessness behavioral checklist, 35, 37, 38
Juvenile offender, 67
effectiveness of treatment, 42, 43

Latency, 104, 105

Manpower Development and Training Administration (MDTA), 139-141, 145, 146, 153
Mental illness model, 17
defined, 14
diagnosis, 19
criticism of, 19
reliability, 20, 21
validity of, 23, 24, 25, 26
diagnostic categories, consistency within, 21
exclusivity of, 22
prescribing treatment, 23
prognostic utility, 22
endurance of, 25
therapeutic approaches, experimental investigation of, 27
assessment, 28
criteria for acceptability, 29
outcome measures, 28
problems with, 31, 32
therapy success rates, 30
utility of, 26
Mental institutions, statistics of, 5
Midcity delinquency control project, 49, 50
Minnesota Multiphasic Personality Inventory (MMPI), 36
Modeling, 86, 87
MORE, see Motivating Offender Rehabilitation Environment